P9-DTA-294

Sunsational
Jani Bassett

The "Sunsational" Committee

Chairmen:
Susan Gluyas
Shannon Gridley

Testing - Tasting
Chairmen - Connie Cox & Ann Bostwick

Amy Armstrong
Sheila Brennan
Joie Cadle
Linda Coughlin
Patsy Farmer
Beverly Greear
Sheran Howle
Debbie Lawton
M.L. McEwan
Sydney Prevost
Barbara Price
Ellen Roddy

Layout and Design
Chairman - Judie Lay
Julia Daze
Carol Hansen
Pam Lichty
Mary Ann Villarroel

Marketing
Chairman - Mary Jo Anderson
Texann Buck
Terry King
Jill Tucker

Business Manager:
Mary Lu Greear

Special Assistance:
Collyn Slavens
Melinda O'Neill
Janice Nabbe
Joan Milligan
Nancy Warlow

Sunsational
Junior League of Orlando-Winter Park, Florida, Inc.

a cookbook

The purpose of the Junior League is exclusively educational and charitable and is to promote voluntarism; to develop the potential of its members for voluntary participation in community affairs; and to demonstrate the effectiveness of trained volunteers.

Money raised in the community furthers The Junior League's purpose and programs.

Cover design and Illustrations
by Jeni Bassett

First Edition

First Printing	October 1982	20,000 copies
Second Printing	October 1983	20,000 copies

Additional copies may be obtained by addressing:

Sunsational

Junior League of Orlando-Winter Park, Florida, Inc.
125 N. Lucerne Circle, East
Orlando, Florida 32801

For your convenience, order blanks are included in the back of the book.

Library of Congress Catalog Card Number: 82-83106
ISBN-0-9609426-0-2

Printed in the United States of America
by
Moran Printing Company
Orlando, Florida

Table of Contents

— indicates Microwave

May we suggest our divider and double divider pages, seasoned with spot art, to stimulate your visual appetite.

Recipe for Central Florida

To a trace of Seminole Indians, blend a box of Florida Crackers. Add New England settlers who founded Rollins College. Allow to mellow half a century. Add liberal tablespoons of orange and grapefruit flavorings to taste. Stir in measures of industry and allow to rise rapidly. Blend to an academic consistency and add Valencia and Seminole Community Colleges and the University of Central Florida. Stiffen with the Naval Training Center. Moisten with soft rains and cool lake breezes. Now fill with equal cups of fun and fantasy (begun with a little mouse who built a big house). Season with dashes of culture and entertainment. Flavor with an international airport and bake slowly in the warmth of a citrus sun.

The result? A **Sunsational**-ly delicious, taste-filled place to live -- Central Florida!

Enjoy liberal portions of unlimited servings garnished with fun and sun. Serves all.

Appetizers

Beverages
Jeni

Jeni

Appetizer Deluxe

1 large can artichoke hearts, drained and chopped
4 ounces cream cheese
1 tablespoon mayonnaise
1 tablespoon sour cream
2 tablespoons onion, minced
Small jar caviar
Saltines

Mix cream cheese, mayonnaise, onion and sour cream. Place artichokes on plate, then top with cream mixture. Cover with caviar and chill. Serve cold with saltines. 6 to 8 servings.

Asparagus Roll-Ups

14½ ounces asparagus spears, well drained
20 slices very soft white bread, crusts removed
8 ounces cream cheese, softened
4 ounces bleu cheese, crumbled
1 egg
Dash of Tabasco sauce
Dash of Worcestershire sauce
½ cup butter or margarine, melted

Flatten bread by rolling each slice with a rolling pin. In bowl, combine cheeses, egg, Tabasco sauce and Worcestershire sauce. Spread mixture evenly on each slice of bread. Place an asparagus spear on each slice of bread and roll up. (If the spears are longer than the bread, cut off the overhang and use 3 or 4 pieces of "extra" to fill one slice of bread.) Dip each roll-up in melted butter, then slice in thirds. (May be frozen at this point if not using right away.) Place slices on ungreased cookie sheet and bake at 425 degrees for 15 minutes. Makes 5 dozen.

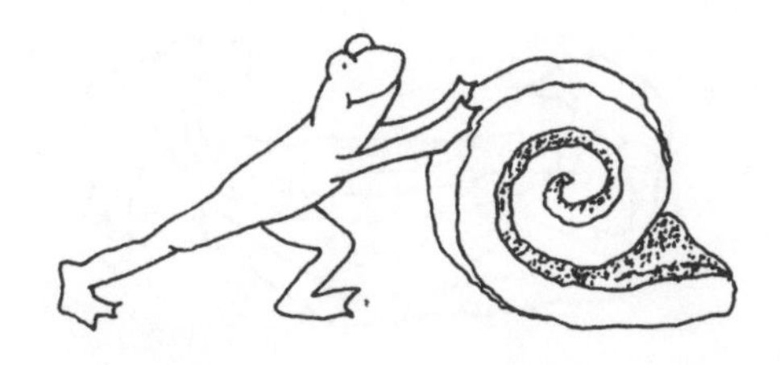

Appetizers

Cheese Asparagus Crisp

4 ounces cream cheese
1 can whole green
  asparagus spears
½ tablespoon mayonnaise
½ green pepper, chopped
1 teaspoon horseradish
1 egg, beaten
1 loaf thin sliced bread
1 stick butter, melted
3 ounces Parmesan cheese

Blend cheese, mayonnaise, pepper, horseradish and egg. Remove crusts and roll out flat. Spread cheese mixture on bread and roll around an asparagus spear. Dip in butter and sprinkle with Parmesan cheese. Refrigerate several hours. Cut into smaller pieces and bake at 350 degrees for 15 to 20 minutes. Serves 15 to 20.

Bacon Swiss Squares

5 slices bacon, crisply fried
  and crumbled, reserving
  drippings
5 slices processed Swiss cheese
5 slices white bread, remove
  crusts and toast
2 hard boiled eggs, thinly sliced
¼ cup green onion, sliced
Paprika

Brush toast with bacon drippings. Cut each slice of toast into quarters. Sprinkle with bacon. Layer each square with egg slice. Sprinkle onion over each square. Cut each slice of cheese into squares. Place one square of cheese onto each appetizer. Broil appetizers 3 inches from heat until the cheese melts (1-2 minutes). Sprinkle appetizers with paprika. Makes 20 pieces.

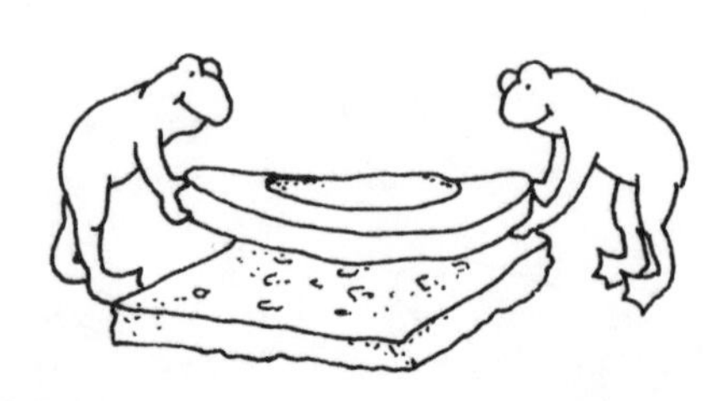

Caviar Pie

8 ounces cream cheese, softened to whipped consistency with cream
1 to 2 large white onions, chopped
6 hard boiled egg yolks, chopped
6 hard boiled egg whites, chopped
4 ounce jar black caviar

Layer in smallest glass Corning souffle' dish in the above order (ending with the caviar on top). Serve with Melba toast.

Note: May be prepared early in the day to be served.

Hot Clam and Cheese Spread

10½ ounces minced clams, drained
¼ pound processed cheese, cut in small pieces
3 tablespoons butter
1 small onion, finely chopped
½ green or red pepper, chopped
4 tablespoons catsup
1 tablespoon Worcestershire sauce
1 tablespoon sherry or milk
¼ teaspoon cayenne pepper
Garlic dill pickles, sliced

Melt butter in top of double boiler. Add onion and pepper to butter and saute' over direct heat 3 minutes. Add clams, cheese, catsup, Worcestershire sauce, sherry and cayenne pepper. Cook in double boiler until cheese melts. Stir often. May be made the day before. Serve in chafing dish with Melba toast, pumpernickel or rye with thin slices of garlic dill pickle. May be doubled for a large party.

Appetizers

Sesame Cheese Sticks

½ pound butter or margarine
1 cup Parmesan cheese
1 cup sesame seeds
1 loaf very thin Pepperidge Farm bread

Preheat oven to 250 degrees. Cream butter, cheese and sesame seeds. Remove crusts from bread and freeze slices. Spread frozen slices with butter mixture. Cut each slice into six strips and place on a cookie sheet. Bake 15 to 30 minutes. Cook until lightly browned and crisp. Makes 12 dozen.

Egg Caviar Mousse

12 hard boiled eggs
7 ounces lump fish caviar
2 envelopes unflavored gelatin
4 tablespoons water
3 tablespoons lemon juice
2 cups mayonnaise
½ teaspoon salt
½ teaspoon onion salt
¼ teaspoon pepper
2 teaspoons Worcestershire sauce
1 small onion, grated
Optional garnish: Ripe olives, pimiento strips

Dissolve gelatin with water and lemon juice in double boiler. Put eggs through food mill. Add rest of ingredients to gelatin, then mix in eggs and fold in caviar. Put in 6½ cup oiled ring mold. (Use 5 cup mold for ½ recipe.) Chill at least 3 hours — **do not** make the day before. Place a small bowl of ripe olives in center of ring. Cut strips of pimiento as garnish. Serves 25.

Garlic Cheese Ball

1 pound New York or aged Cheddar cheese, grated
6 ounces cream cheese, softened
½ teaspoon salt, or more to taste
1 clove garlic, mashed to a paste with the salt
3 dashes Tabasco sauce
1 tablespoon Worcestershire sauce
1 tablespoon mayonnaise
¼ teaspoon dry mustard
½ can chili powder
½ can paprika

Blend grated Cheddar cheese with cream cheese. Mix all ingredients except chili powder and paprika. Mix until a smooth paste consistency is formed. Shape into ball and roll in chili powder and paprika. Place in refrigerator 24 hours to ripen.

Cheese Clouds

½ cup sharp white Cheddar cheese, shredded (more cheese may be used)
4 ounce container whipped cream cheese
1 egg
1 teaspoon lemon juice
1 teaspoon chives
Dash of pepper
4 slices bacon, cooked, drained and crumbled
4 frozen patty shells, thawed

Preheat oven to 450 degrees. Combine and beat well the cream cheese, egg, lemon juice, chives and a dash of pepper. Stir in cheese and bacon. Chill. Roll one patty shell to 4 X 8 inch rectangle. Cut into 2 inch squares. Top each with a teaspoon of filling. Fold and seal. Place on ungreased baking sheet. Repeat with remaining shells. Chill or freeze until ready to bake. Lower oven to 400 degrees and bake for 12 to 15 minutes. Makes 32.

Pineapple Cheese Ball

16 ounces cream cheese, softened
¼ cup green pepper, finely chopped
8¼ ounces crushed pineapple, drained
½ teaspoon salt
2 tablespoons green onions, chopped
½ cup pecans, chopped

Combine cream cheese, green pepper, pineapple, onion and salt. Mix well and form into a rounded shape. Coat with pecans. Chill well. Serve with crackers. (Wheat Thins recommended.)

Note: This is a refreshing change from Cheddar-y cheese balls. It's really a crowd pleaser! A nice added touch is a coating of parsley.

Parsley Flat Bread Appetizers

1 small package Norwegian Flat Bread
1 stick butter or margarine
1¼ teaspoons Beau Monde seasoning (Spice Island)
3 tablespoons dried parsley flakes
½ cup grated Parmesan cheese

Preheat oven to 325 degrees. Cut bread slices in thirds. Let butter soften. Cream together butter, seasoning, parsley and cheese. Spread on flat bread. Bake 5 minutes. Watch closely as it is easy to burn. Cool. Keep in tight tin or Tupperware a week or freeze. Good as hors d'oeuvre or with a salad. Makes 5 dozen.

Note: Norwegian Flat Bread may be found in grocery gourmet section or cheese shops.

Roquefort Log

6 ounces cream cheese, softened
2 ounces Roquefort cheese, crumbled
2 tablespoons celery, finely chopped
1 tablespoon onion, minced
3 to 4 drops Tabasco sauce
Dash cayenne pepper
¾ cup pecans, chopped

Combine cheeses well. Blend in celery, onion, Tabasco sauce and pepper. Shape into a roll 1½ inches in diameter. Coat with pecans. Wrap in wax paper. Refrigerate until firm. Serve with crackers. Makes about 1 cup of cheese spread.

Hot Cheese Squares

1½ pounds sharp Cheddar cheese, grated
9 eggs
Large can El Paso Roasted Green Chilies

Preheat oven to 325 degrees. Butter a 9 X 13 inch pan. Drain, wash and chop peppers and place in bottom of pan. Top with cheese. Beat eggs one at a time until fluffy. Pour on top of cheese. Bake for 30 minutes or until firm. Makes 32 bite size squares. Can be prepared ahead and frozen. After frozen, thaw in refrigerator, then warm for 10 minutes at 200 degrees.

Family Secret Cheese Spread

16 ounces cream cheese
1 stick butter
1½ tablespoons shallots or green onions, finely chopped
1½ tablespoons capers, finely chopped
1 teaspoon anchovy paste
1 teaspoon paprika
Dash of cayenne pepper

Mix all ingredients well. The last 4 ingredients may be increased to taste. Chill and serve on Melba toast. This will keep in the refrigerator for 2 to 3 weeks. This can also be frozen. Before serving, thaw, and blend until smooth in mixer.

Chutney Cheese Spread

16 ounces cream cheese
½ cup chopped chutney, drained
½ teaspoon dry mustard
2 teaspoons curry powder
Slivered almonds, toasted
Melba rounds

Combine all ingredients except the almonds and form into a ball. Decorate with slivered, toasted almonds to cover ball. Chill and serve with Melba rounds. Serves 10 to 12.

Options: Chopped green onions can be sprinkled over top and served in a small dish. Recipe can be doubled and served in a hollowed pineapple half.

Chicken Liver Spread

1 pound chicken livers
6 slices bacon, fried well done
1 onion, finely chopped
1 large stalk celery, finely chopped
2 hard-boiled eggs, chopped
Salt and pepper to taste
Mayonnaise

When the bacon is cold, crumble it. Fry the chicken livers until done. When they have cooled, finely chop them. Add the other ingredients. Add enough mayonnaise to make the mixture spreadable. Serve on crackers or rye bread.

Conch Fritters

1 cup raw conch, finely chopped
1 medium onion, finely chopped
1 medium celery stalk, finely chopped
1 to 2 heaping tablespoons tomato paste
3 tablespoons Lea & Perrins sauce
1 tablespoon hot sauce
1 cup flour
1 heaping teaspoon baking powder
1 egg
Water
Salt, to taste
Optional: 1 clove garlic, dash lemon juice

Combine all ingredients except water. With a spoon add water until batter is semi-stiff. Heat oil over medium heat. Roll batter into small balls or drop by teaspoonfuls into hot deep fryer. Allow fritters to brown properly but not too dark.

Appetizers

Cheese Puffs

¼ pound sharp cheese
3 ounces cream cheese
1 stick butter or margarine
2 egg whites, beaten
1 loaf of unsliced bread, cut into 1¼ inch slices; remove crusts, cut each into 9 cubes

Melt the cheese and butter in the top of a large double boiler. Heat until blended. Remove from the heat. Add the beaten egg whites. Dip the bread cubes into the cheese mixture. Place on a well greased cookie sheet. Refrigerate 24 hours. Can be frozen. When ready to serve, bake 10 minutes at 375 degrees. Serve hot.

Chicken Liver Terrine

2 cups onion, minced
¾ cup butter, divided
1½ pounds chicken livers, trimmed
¼ cup gin
¼ cup port
¼ cup parsley, minced
3 eggs, hard-boiled
1 tablespoon juniper berries, crushed
1 teaspoon salt
¾ teaspoon allspice
¾ teaspoon thyme
Salt and pepper to taste

Saute' onion in ½ cup butter until soft. Transfer with slotted spoon to a bowl. To the fat left in the pan, add chicken livers and cook over moderately high heat for 3 minutes or until livers are brown on the outside but slightly pink on the inside. Transfer to the bowl with a slotted spoon. Deglaze the pan with gin and port, scraping the sides and bottom of the pan to get brown bits. Add the mixture to the bowl. Add the remaining butter, parsley, eggs, berries, salt, allspice and thyme to the other ingredients. In a food processor fitted with a steel blade, purée the mixture. Add salt and pepper to taste. Transfer the mixture to the terrine and chill it, covered with plastic wrap directly on the surface for at least six hours. Let the terrine come to room temperature before serving. (Plastic wrap should be placed directly on the terrine or it will turn slightly greenish in color due to parsley. It is not spoiled!) Good served with Melba toasts.

Crab Meat Hors d'oeuvre

1 cup crab meat
8 tablespoons butter, divided
4 tablespoons flour
1¼ teaspoons salt
1 cup milk
1 tablespoon onion, chopped
2 tablespoons parsley, chopped
2 tablespoons bread crumbs
18 slices bacon

Use 4 tablespoons butter, flour, salt and milk to make thick white sauce. Saute' onion in rest of butter. Add parsley, crab meat and bread crumbs. Saute' one minute. Combine crab mixture and white sauce and cool. Quarter bacon slices (once lengthwise and once crosswise). Place ¼ to ½ teaspoon of crab mixture on bacon slice, roll and spear with toothpick. Place on broiling pan and bake at 375 degrees until bacon is done. Serve hot. Can fix day ahead and bake at last minute. Serves 8 to 12.

Hot Crab Fondue

7½ ounces canned Alaskan King crab, drained and flaked
5 ounce jar processed sharp American cheese spread
8 ounces cream cheese
¼ cup light cream
½ teaspoon Worcestershire sauce
¼ teaspoon garlic salt
½ teaspoon cayenne pepper
French bread, Melba rounds or toast points

In top of double boiler and over boiling water, combine cheese spread and cream cheese. Stir constantly until blended and smooth. Add remaining ingredients and heat until well blended, stirring occasionally. Serve hot in fondue pot or chafing dish with chunks of bread, Melba rounds or toast points. Hint: Add extra cream if fondue gets too thick. Makes 2½ cups.

Appetizers

Texas Crab Grass

10 ounces frozen spinach, cooked and drained
8 ounces fresh crab meat
1 onion, chopped and sautéed
1 cup Parmesan cheese
½ stick butter

Mix all ingredients and heat. Serve on crackers.

Note: 1 can claw crab meat may be substituted for the fresh crab meat.

Crab Pate'

6 ounces frozen crab meat
3 eggs, hard-boiled
½ cup butter
½ cup mayonnaise
2 tablespoons lemon juice
1/3 cup Parmesan cheese
1½ teaspoons horseradish
¼ teaspoon salt
½ teaspoon garlic powder
¼ teaspoon pepper

Whip butter, mayonnaise and lemon juice until fluffy. Add remaining ingredients and fold in chopped hard-boiled eggs and shredded crab, reserving a garnish piece. Place in attractive serving mold; chill overnight. Garnish with piece of crab and sprinkle of parsley. Serve with crackers. Can not be frozen. Serves 12.

Crab Muffins

7 ounces canned crab, drained (frozen crab can be used)
¾ stick of margarine
5 ounce jar Kraft Old English Cheese Spread
1½ teaspoons mayonnaise
⅛ teaspoon garlic salt
6 English muffins, split

Let margarine and cheese soften and mix together. Add mayonnaise, garlic salt and crab. Mix well. Spread mixture on split English muffins. Broil for 5 minutes until mixture is hot and melted. Cut into small wedges for appetizers or can also be used as a meal with salad and vegetable.

Bacon-Horseradish Dip

½ cup bacon, cooked and crumbled
1 tablespoon horseradish, drained of excess water
1 cup sour cream
¼ cup mayonnaise
1 slice of medium onion, minced
1 tablespoon parsley

Mix well and chill for 1 hour before serving.

Spinach Dip

20 ounces frozen spinach, thawed and drained
½ cup fresh parsley or ¼ cup dried
1 bunch green onions, chopped (tops also)
1 cup mayonnaise
1 teaspoon dill
2 teaspoons Season All (jar) salad seasoning
Dash garlic powder
½ teaspoon lemon juice
Dash cayenne pepper

Mix above ingredients and chill for 3 hours. Serve on crackers.

Broccoli Dip

2 packages frozen chopped broccoli, cooked and drained
1½ 6-ounce packages Kraft Squeeze-a-Snack garlic flavored cheese spread
1 cup mushroom pieces, sautéed in butter
1 onion, finely chopped, simmered in butter
2 cans mushroom soup, undiluted
1½ cups slivered almonds

Simmer cheese to melt. Stir in mushrooms. Add the remaining ingredients. Serve with Fritos or crackers.

Crab Meat Dip

12 ounces fresh crab meat
16 ounces cream cheese
¼ cup Hellman's mayonnaise
1 clove garlic, crushed
⅛ cup white wine
1 teaspoon Dijon mustard
2 teaspoons powdered sugar
Salt, freshly gound pepper, Tabasco sauce, Worcestershire sauce, lemon juice to taste
1/3 cup slivered almonds, toasted
¼ cup fresh parsley, minced
Horseradish, optional

Combine cream cheese, mayonnaise, garlic, wine, mustard, sugar and seasonings. Fold in crab meat and heat. Serve in a warm chafing dish and sprinkle with almonds and parsley. Serve hot with Melba rounds or cold with raw vegetables. Serves 12 to 14.

Hot Crab Meat Dip

2 cups crab meat
½ cup butter
1 small bunch green onions, chopped
½ cup parsley, chopped
2 heaping tablespoons flour
2 cups light cream
½ pound Swiss cheese, grated
Red pepper sauce to taste
1 tablespoon sherry
Salt to taste

Melt butter in heavy pot. Saute' onions and parsley. Blend in flour, cream and cheese until cheese melts. Add other ingredients and gently fold in crab. Serve with Old London rounds or other crackers. Makes 6 cups.

Sombrero Dip

1½ pounds ground beef
½ cup green pepper, diced
½ cup onion, chopped
3 tablespoons chili powder
Dash of salt and pepper
1 small bottle Heinz hot ketchup
1 16-ounce can red kidney beans, semi-mashed
Garnish: 12 ounces sharp Cheddar cheese, grated
Sliced Spanish olives
Onions, chopped
Doritos or Nacho chips

Brown ground beef with green pepper and onion. Add chili powder, salt and pepper and ketchup. Add kidney beans and let cook 30 minutes in skillet. Pour into a round casserole dish and garnish with grated Cheddar cheese, olives, and onion. Serve while hot with Doritos or Nacho chips.

Spicy Bean Dip

16 ounces refried beans
Tabasco sauce, approximately 1 teaspoon
12 ounces Marie's avocado salad dressing
1 cup lettuce, shredded
4 ounces sharp Cheddar cheese shredded
Doritos or Fritos

Preheat oven to 325 degrees. Spread refried beans in bottom of glass pie dish. Sprinkle Tabasco sauce evenly over beans. Spread 8 ounces of the avocado dressing over mixture. Then drop shredded lettuce evenly over dressing. Sprinkle shredded Cheddar cheese evenly over all. Bake at 325 degrees for 20 minutes or until cheese in melted and slightly bubbly. Use Doritos or Fritos for dipping.

Appetizers

Dill Dip

8 ounces sour cream
8 ounces mayonnaise
1 tablespoon parsley
1 tablespoon onion, minced
1 tablespoon dill weed

Combine above ingredients and serve with chips or fresh vegetables.

Smoked Fish Log

2 smoked mullet or other smoked fish (oily fish is best)
8 ounces cream cheese
Juice from 1 lemon
1 medium onion, chopped
1 tablespoon horseradish
¼ teaspoon salt
½ cup pecans, chopped
3 tablespoons parsley, chopped
Assorted crackers

Flake fish. Combine with cream cheese, lemon juice, onion, horseradish and salt. Mix thoroughly and chill for several hours. Shape fish mixture into log. Mix parsley and pecans together. Roll log in mixture. Serve with crackers.

Note: Can be made ahead. Freezes well.

Pimento Cheese Ball

8 ounces cream cheese
8 ounces New York State or any extra sharp Cheddar cheese, grated
8 ounces pimento cheese
½ teaspoon red pepper
1 clove garlic, pressed
Pecans, chopped

Mix all ingredients together except pecans. Shape into a ball and roll in chopped pecans.

Lemon Meatballs

1 pound ground beef
¼ pound sharp Cheddar cheese
½ green pepper
12 pimiento stuffed green olives
1 cup fine bread crumbs
1 egg
½ cup milk
3 tablespoons lemon juice
1 teaspoon salt
6 slices bacon, cut into halves

Preheat oven to 400 degrees. Grind cheese, green pepper and olives together in food processor. Combine with ground beef and add bread crumbs, egg, milk, lemon juice and salt. Mix thoroughly. Roll ingredients into 12 balls. Wrap in ½ slice bacon each. Secure with toothpicks. Bake at 400 degrees for 30 minutes. Makes 1 dozen.

Note: This is also good as a meat loaf.

Manhattan Meatballs

1 pound ground pork
1 pound ground veal
2 cups bread crumbs
2 eggs
½ cup onion, chopped
2 tablespoons parsley
2 teaspoons salt
2 tablespoons margarine
2 cups apricot preserves
¾ cup barbecue sauce
Note: if you prefer, ground beef can be substituted for veal and/or pork

Preheat oven to 350 degrees. Combine meat, bread crumbs, eggs, onion and seasonings; mix lightly. Shape into small meatballs; brown in the margarine. Drain and place in a 9 X 13 inch pan. Combine preserves and barbecue sauce; pour over meat. Bake 30 minutes.

Note: If you desire more sauce, add an 8 ounce jar of preserves with ¼ more barbecue sauce. Makes about 7 dozen. Can freeze after cooking.

Appetizers

Chipped Beef Ball

3 ounces chipped beef
1/3 cup scallions, green tops only
8 ounces cream cheese
1 teaspoon Accent
1 teaspoon Worcestershire sauce

Finely chop chipped beef and scallions. Set aside half of beef. Mix well all remaining ingredients. Shape into ball. Roll ball in rest of beef. Serve with crackers.

Starter

12 ounces cream cheese
21 ounces beef consomme', divided
Salt and pepper to taste
8 drops Tabasco sauce
2 teaspoons Worcestershire sauce
1 teaspoon curry powder
Chopped chives or parsley for garnish

Blend cheese, 2 tablespoons consomme' and all seasonings in blender until smooth. Add remaining consomme' except for ½ can which is reserved. Blend 2 seconds only, pour into serving cups, demitasse or cream soup, and refrigerate until firm. Use ½ can reserved consomme' and pour thin layer over each and garnish with chives or parsley. Refrigerate.

Mock Boursin

8 ounces cream cheese
½ stick butter, softened
1 medium clove garlic
¼ teaspoon seasoned salt
2 tablespoons parsley
2 tablespoons chives
4 peppercorns
Tabasco sauce to taste

Drop garlic into food processor, while running, using steel blade. Add other ingredients and process until smooth. Best if made a few hours ahead so flavors blend. Serve with crackers.

Note: Can be frozen but is not as creamy.

Walnut Smokey Cheese Spread

16 ounces Cheese Whiz
½ cup mayonnaise
3 teaspoons liquid smoke
1 teaspoon Worcestershire sauce
2/3 cup walnuts, chopped

Mix all ingredients together and serve as a spread for an open face party sandwich or as a dip with crackers or chips.

Mushroom Rolls

1 pound mushrooms, minced
2 tablespoons butter
2 green onions, chopped including tops
1 tablespoon parsley
1 teaspoon seasoned salt
¼ teaspoon tarragon
2 tablespoons flour
½ cup light cream
2 packages crescent rolls

Preheat oven to 375 degrees. Melt butter and add mushrooms, onion and seasonings. Saute' until liquid is absorbed. Turn heat to medium and stir in flour until well blended. Stir in cream and mix until thick. Remove from heat and cool. When mushroom mixture has cooled, spread on individual crescent rolls and roll up. Place on greased baking pan and bake until brown, approximately 10 minutes. Cut into thirds. Serve hot. Makes 2 dozen.

Party Mushrooms

1 pound fresh mushrooms
1/3 cup red wine vinegar
1/3 cup oil
1 small onion, cut into rings
1 teaspoon salt
2 teaspoons parsley
1 teaspoon mustard
2 tablespoons brown sugar

Mix together all ingredients. Add mushrooms. Simmer 30 minutes. Serve warm or cold. When serving warm, it is nice to serve on thin buttered slices of French bread.

Mushroom-Sausage Strudel

2 pounds sweet Italian sausage
2 pounds mushrooms, minced and squeezed dry
¼ cup shallots or green onions, minced
8 sheets strudel dough, 16 X 22 inches
2 tablespoons oil
6 tablespoons butter
Salt and pepper to taste
6 ounces cream cheese
Melted butter (about ¾ cup)
Bread crumbs

Preheat oven to 400 degrees. Remove sausage meat from casing. Bake until no longer pink. Crumble into small pieces. Saute' mushrooms with shallots in butter and oil. Cook until pieces separate and liquid has evaporated. Season to taste with salt and pepper. Combine with sausage and blend in cream cheese. Spread a sheet of strudel dough on a damp towel, narrow end towards you. Brush with melted butter and sprinkle on bread crumbs. Repeat with second and third sheets, and then butter but do not crumb fourth sheet. Put half the sausage-mushroom mixture on narrower edge of strudel dough, leaving a 2 inch border at the sides. Fold sides inward, then using edge of towel, roll. Put strudel on buttered baking sheet, brush with melted butter. Repeat for second studel. Bake at 400 degrees until brown, about 20 minutes. Serves 8.

Note: Lovely as a brunch first course. Can make and bake ahead, store overnight in refrigerator. Can be frozen.

Stuffed Mushrooms

1 pound large mushroom caps
½ pound Cheddar cheese, grated or 8 ounces cream cheese and chives, whipped
½ pound bacon, fried crisp

Preheat oven to 350 degrees. Wash and clean the mushroom caps. Mix the cheese with the bacon that has been crumbled. Stuff the caps and bake 10 minutes. Makes 2 dozen plus.

Pecan Spread

8 ounces cream cheese
2 tablespoons milk
3 ounces smoked beef, finely chopped
¼ green pepper, finely chopped
2 tablespoons dehydrated onion
½ teaspoon garlic salt
¼ teaspoon pepper
½ cup sour cream

Preheat oven to 350 degrees. Mix above ingredients together. Spread into baking dish.

Topping:
¼ cup pecans, finely chopped
2 tablespoons butter

Saute' nuts in butter until well coated. Spread over top of cream cheese mixture. Bake in preheated oven for 20 minutes. Serve hot with Triscuits.

Phillipino Pizza

¾ cup mayonnaise
½ cup Parmesan cheese
1/3 cup green onions, chopped
6 strips bacon, cooked and crumbled
2 dashes Worcestershire sauce
Party rye bread

Combine all ingredients except bread. Place in air tight container in refrigerator until ready to use. (Can be stored for one month). Spread on bread and broil for only a few minutes. Makes 2 dozen plus.

Onion Puffs

8 ounces cream cheese
1 tablespoon milk
¾ cup mayonnaise
1 tablespoon onion, grated
Salt to taste
Tabasco sauce to taste
Party rye or party pumpernickle bread slices
Paprika

Preheat oven to 350 degrees. Cream together the cream cheese, milk, mayonnaise, grated onion, salt and Tabasco sauce. Spread the mixture on the bread slices and sprinkle with paprika. Bake on a cookie sheet for 10 minutes, or until tops are lightly browned. You may freeze on the cookie sheet before baking. Thaw before baking. Serve warm. Makes 32 pieces.

Oysters Rockefeller

1 package chopped spinach, cooked
6 small onions, grated
4 stalks celery, chopped
1/3 bunch parsley
1 stick butter, melted
¼ cup bread crumbs
2 tablespoons anchovy paste
2 tablespoons Worcestershire sauce
5 dashes Tabasco sauce
½ teaspoon salt
½ lemon, squeezed
1 tablespoon licorice flavored liquor (substitute for absinthe)
5 dozen big oysters

Preheat oven to 350 degrees. Put all ingredients except oysters into the blender and blend until it is "saucy". Place oysters (opened and in half shells) in rock salt in large baking pan. Put mixture on top of each oyster, enough to cover, sprinkle with bread crumbs and Parmesan cheese. Bake 25 minutes or until brown.

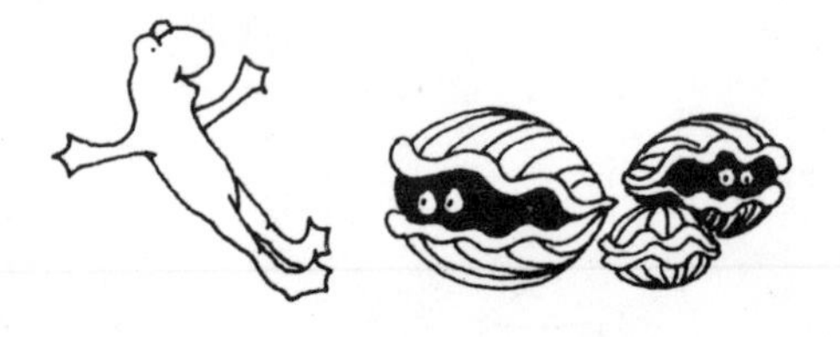

Chicken Quiche Almondine

½ cup chicken, diced
3 tablespoons almonds, slivered
9 inch pie crust, unbaked
1½ cups Swiss cheese, shredded
3 eggs
1½ cups milk
½ teaspoon salt
⅛ teaspoon pepper
¼ teaspoon mace
4 tablespoons Parmesan cheese

Preheat oven to 350 degrees. Place chicken and almonds in pie crust. Then add Swiss cheese. Beat eggs lightly in a medium bowl. Blend in milk, salt, mace and pepper. Pour over cheese. Sprinkle on Parmesan cheese. Bake for 30 to 35 minutes or until a knife inserted near center comes out clean. Allow to stand 10 minutes before serving. Serves 6 for dinner or 18 for appetizers.

Judy's Sandwich

16 slices bread
16 slices bacon
1 can cream of mushroom soup

Preheat oven to 200 degrees. Remove crusts from bread, roll lightly with rolling pin. Spread soup on bread and roll jelly-roll style. Cut bacon into thirds as well as bread. Wrap bacon around bread pieces. Place on ungreased baking sheets and bake for 3 hours. Makes 48. May be frozen and reheated as needed.

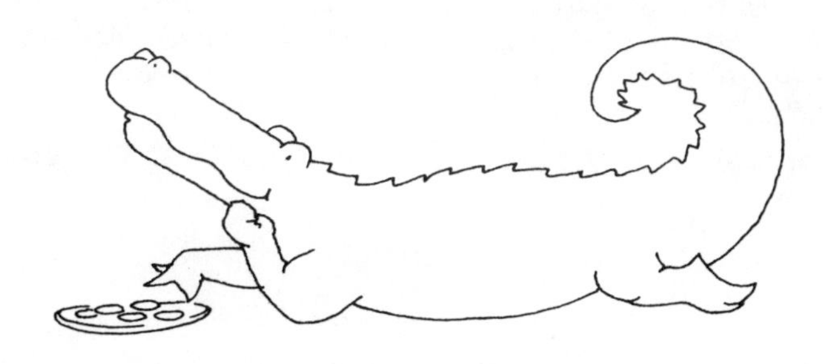

Appetizers

Pineapple Surprise

5 ounces water chestnuts
¾ cup pineapple chunks, drained
12 lean bacon slices, halved
Lemon juice
¼ cup soy sauce
Wooden toothpicks

Quarter each water chestnut. Place each water chestnut piece on a chunk of pineapple; roll in half bacon slice. Dip in lemon juice. Fasten with a toothpick. Place on a baking sheet. Sprinkle with soy sauce. Broil 7 to 8 inches from heat until brown and crisp.

Mini-Quiche Rockefeller

Pastry:
1 cup butter
6 ounces cream cheese
2½ cups flour, unsifted
¼ teaspoon salt

Soften butter and cheese. Gradually add flour and salt. Shape into two rolls; wrap and chill overnight. Next day remove from refrigerator and preheat oven to 400 degrees. Slice pastry approximately 1 inch thick and press into small muffin tins. Do not make rims. Bake 8 minutes in preheated oven.

Filling:
1 pound sausage
½ cup onion, chopped
3 eggs, beaten
¼ cup milk
6 ounces spinach, chopped
½ cup mushrooms, chopped
1½ cups Monterey Jack cheese, shredded
¼ teaspoon oregano
Parmesan cheese

Preheat oven to 350 degrees. Brown sausage and onions. Combine next 6 ingredients and mix with sausage and onion. Pour into pastries and sprinkle with Parmesan cheese. Bake 20 to 25 minutes. Makes 48 mini pastries or a 9 inch quiche.

Note: For a pie extend cooking time to 40 minutes. Can do ahead and freeze.

Cold Shrimp Roquefort

8 large shrimp
2 ounces Roquefort cheese
1½ ounces cream cheese
½ teaspoon scallions, finely chopped
1 teaspoon Cognac or Brandy
Parsley, chopped

Steam shrimp until just pink; then shell and devein. Cut a deep slit down the back to make a pocket to hold the Roquefort mixture. Mix well the Roquefort, cream cheese, scallions and Cognac or Brandy (a food processor does this easily). Stuff shrimp. Roll the stuffed portion in chopped parsley. Chill. Can be prepared ahead. Will keep overnight in refrigerator. Makes 8 large stuffed shrimp.

Spiced Shrimp

2 pounds medium shrimp, cooked and cleaned
1 pound fresh mushrooms, quartered
1 cup water
1/3 cup olive oil
2/3 cup vinegar
2 tablespoons fresh lemon juice
2 cloves garlic, halved
1¼ teaspoons salt
½ teaspoon thyme
½ teaspoon peppercorns
⅛ teaspoon nutmeg
7 or 8 scallions, sliced, including tops
2 bay leaves
¾ cup small pimiento-stuffed olives

Combine mushrooms, water, oil, vinegar, lemon juice, seasonings and scallions in saucepan. Bring to a boil and cook. Cover for 5 minutes. Pour into a bowl. Add olives and shrimp and cool. Cover and chill 6 to 8 hours (or overnight) before serving.

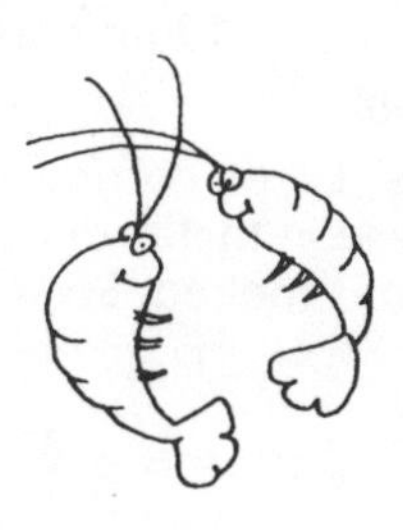

Appetizers

Marinated Party Shrimp

3 pounds shrimp, cooked
4 tablespoons vinegar
2/3 cup olive oil
4 tablespoons prepared mustard
Salt and pepper to taste
2 heaping teaspoons paprika
2 whole onions, sliced into thin rings
1 jar capers, divided
2 teaspoons celery seed

Mix above ingredients together, except shrimp, using half the jar of capers. Add shrimp; chill overnight. Turn shrimp several times while they are chilling. Just before serving, add rest of capers. Cover a platter with large lettuce leaves. Center with shrimp mixture.

Jimmy Dean Sausage Rounds

1 pound Jimmy Dean sausage (hot)
1 pound Velveeta cheese
One loaf of party rye bread

Preheat oven to 300 degrees. Brown sausage and then drain all grease left in pan. Add cheese until it is melted and mixed well with the sausage. Spread on small rounds of rye bread and heat for 20 minutes in a 300 degree oven. Serve warm. Makes 3 dozen plus.

Note: Can do one day ahead, but if not freezing, spread on bread when ready to bake.

Debe's Lil' Rubens

12 ounces canned corned beef
16 ounces sauerkraut
1 cup Thousand Island dressing
½ pound Swiss cheese, shredded
1 loaf party rye bread

Preheat oven to 350 degrees. Layer corned beef, sauerkraut, Thousand Island dressing and Swiss cheese in that order on individual party rye. Bake for 10 minutes or until cheese is melted. Serve hot. Makes 3 dozen plus.

Orange Champagne Cooler

Orange juice
Champagne

Mix orange juice and champagne in equal amounts. Serve in tall glasses over ice. Make orange juice first and then add the Champagne when serving.

Hot Spiced Cider

2¼ cups sugar
1 quart water
2 sticks cinnamon
8 whole allspice
10 whole cloves
1 piece ginger root (quarter size)
1 quart orange juice
½ pint lemon juice (less if desired)
2 quarts apple cider

Combine sugar and water. Boil 5 minutes. Add spices. Let stand covered for 1 hour. Strain. Before serving, combine syrup, fruit juices and cider. Bring to boil. Serve hot. Delicious beverage for cool weather. May also add sliced oranges and lemons. Serves 12.

Frozen Strawberry-Banana Slush

2 small packages strawberry Kool-ade
2 quarts water
2 bananas, mashed
2 cups sugar
Juice of 2 lemons
46 ounces pineapple juice

Mix all ingredients well and freeze. Remove from freezer 1½ hours before serving. Spoon into cups or glasses. Serve as a slush. Very refreshing. Serves 32. Makes 1 gallon.

Beverages

Strawberry-Banana Daiquiris

6 ounces limeade concentrate
10 ounces frozen strawberries
  in syrup
¾ to 1 cup light rum
1 banana
Crushed ice

Combine half of first four ingredients in container of electric blender. Blend well, adding enough crushed ice to make mixture slushy. Empty blender container and repeat procedure with remaining ingredients. First four ingredients may be blended and frozen for one to two weeks. When ready to use, thaw slightly. Place in blender and add crushed ice to make mixture slushy. Serves 8. Can freeze, but use in two to three days.

Kahlua

2 ounces instant coffee
4 cups sugar
2 cups distilled water
1 pint 100-proof vodka
1 vanilla bean, split

Heat water almost to boiling. Add coffee and sugar. Stir until dissolved and syrupy. Then bring to a boil. Cool. Add vodka. Spoon off film. Split vanilla bean lengthwise and add to mixture. Pour liquid into ½ gallon dark glass container. (The kind apple juice comes in). Age for 3 weeks. Strain and bottle. Yummy over ice cream. Makes 5 cups.

Piña Colada

Crushed ice
3 heaping teaspoons crushed
  pineapple
2 ounces coconut milk or
  1 teaspoon coconut extract
  and 1 ounce milk
3 or more strawberries
1 tablespoon vanilla ice cream
4 or more ounces rum
Lemon juice to taste, optional
Powdered sugar to taste, optional

Fill blender ¾ full with crushed ice. Add remaining ingredients, cover and process on high for 5 to 10 seconds. Serves 6 to 8.

Mocha Punch

2/3 cup instant coffee
2/3 cup sugar
2/3 cup water
1/3 cup Nestle's instant chocolate
1 pint vanilla ice cream
(sometimes use 1 quart)
2 quarts cold milk
1 quart chocolate ice cream

Combine coffee, sugar, water and instant chocolate and mix well. Beat in vanilla ice cream. Blend in milk. Pour into punch bowl and spoon chocolate ice cream over. This is excellent for a morning get-togther with the ladies. Sometimes add creme de cacao or Kahlua to taste.

Sunshine Punch

46 ounces pineapple juice
2-liter bottle 7-Up
12 ounces orange concentrate
½ teaspoon peppermint extract
12 ounces apricot nectar
2 trays of 7-Up ice cubes with cherries

Chill the fruit juices and 7-Up. Just before serving, mix all the juices together in a large punch bowl. Makes 30 cups.

Note: For a more spirited punch, add vodka.

Daiquiri Punch

2 quarts lemon juice
4 quarts orange juice
4 quarts lime juice
1 pound powdered sugar
4 quarts club soda
2½ fifths light rum

Mix juices and powdered sugar together. Chill several hours or overnight. When ready to serve, add club soda and the rum.

Beverages

Strawberry Tea Punch

1½ quarts boiling water
3 family-size tea bags
½ cup sugar
6 ounces lemonade concentrate
10 ounces frozen strawberries, thawed

In ceramic or metal pitcher, pour water over tea bags, brew 4 minutes. Remove tea bags and stir in sugar, lemonade and strawberries. Serve over ice. Serves 8 to 10.

Orange Juice Punch

36 ounces orange juice concentrate
36 ounces lemonade concentrate
36 ounces water
6 bottles gingerale (32 ounce size)

Thaw orange juice and lemonade. Add water and mix. Add gingerale just before serving. Serves 56.

Hot Cranberry Punch

3 cups apple juice
2½ cups pineapple juice
2 cups cranberry juice
½ cup light brown sugar, packed
¼ teaspoon salt
2 sticks cinnamon
1 teaspoon whole cloves
½ teaspoon whole allspice

In coffee percolator mix juices, brown sugar and salt. In basket place cinnamon, cloves and allspice. Plug in coffee pot and run through cycle. Serves 10.

St. Paddy's Day Punch

½ gallon vanilla ice cream
½ pint whole milk
24 ounces gingerale
Peppermint or cream de menthe flavoring
Green food coloring

Soften ice cream in punch bowl with milk. Add peppermint flavoring to taste. At last minute add gingerale and green food coloring. 36 servings.

Luncheon Iced Tea

1 quart strong tea
1 quart gingerale
12 ounces lemonade concentrate
Sugar to taste
Sprigs of mint

Mix first four ingredients together and serve over ice. Garnish with sprigs of mint. Serves 8.

Note: For a lower calorie drink, use diet gingerale and omit sugar.

Dutchie's Iced Tea

4 family-size tea bags
¾ cup sugar
1 small can lemonade concentrate
1 small can limeade concentrate
Mint leaves, if available

Boil 2 quarts of water; pour over tea bags and steep. Remove tea bags and stir in sugar, lemonade and limeade. Mix and add cold water to make one gallon. It's good with mint leaves added.

Beverages

Holiday Spiced Tea

3 teaspoons tea steeped in
  2 cups boiling water
6 (3inch) cinnamon sticks
2 teaspoons whole cloves
½ teaspoon whole allspice
1 lemon, sliced thin
10 cups cranberry juice
10 cups apple cider
2 cups water
½ cup brown sugar

Combine the ingredients. Bring to a rapid boil. Reduce the heat. Simmer 15 to 20 minutes. Remove the lemon slices. Serve hot!

Hot Buttered Rum

1 quart vanilla ice cream,
  softened at room temperature
1 pound butter, melted
1 pound brown sugar
1 pound confectioners' sugar
2 teaspoons ground cloves
2 teaspoons cinnamon
2 teaspoons ground nutmeg
Rum

Combine the ice cream, butter, brown sugar, confectioners' sugar and spices. Keep the mixture frozen. Mix 2 to 3 tablespoons of the mixture with 1 jigger of rum in a mug. Fill the mug with hot water. Stir and serve.

Sangria

12 ounces orange juice concentrate
12 ounces lemonade concentrate
12 ounces limeade concentrate
2 quarts gingerale
1.5 liters of Burgundy
Ice
Sliced apples, oranges, etc.

Combine ingredients in punch bowl. Mix well and serve.

Breads

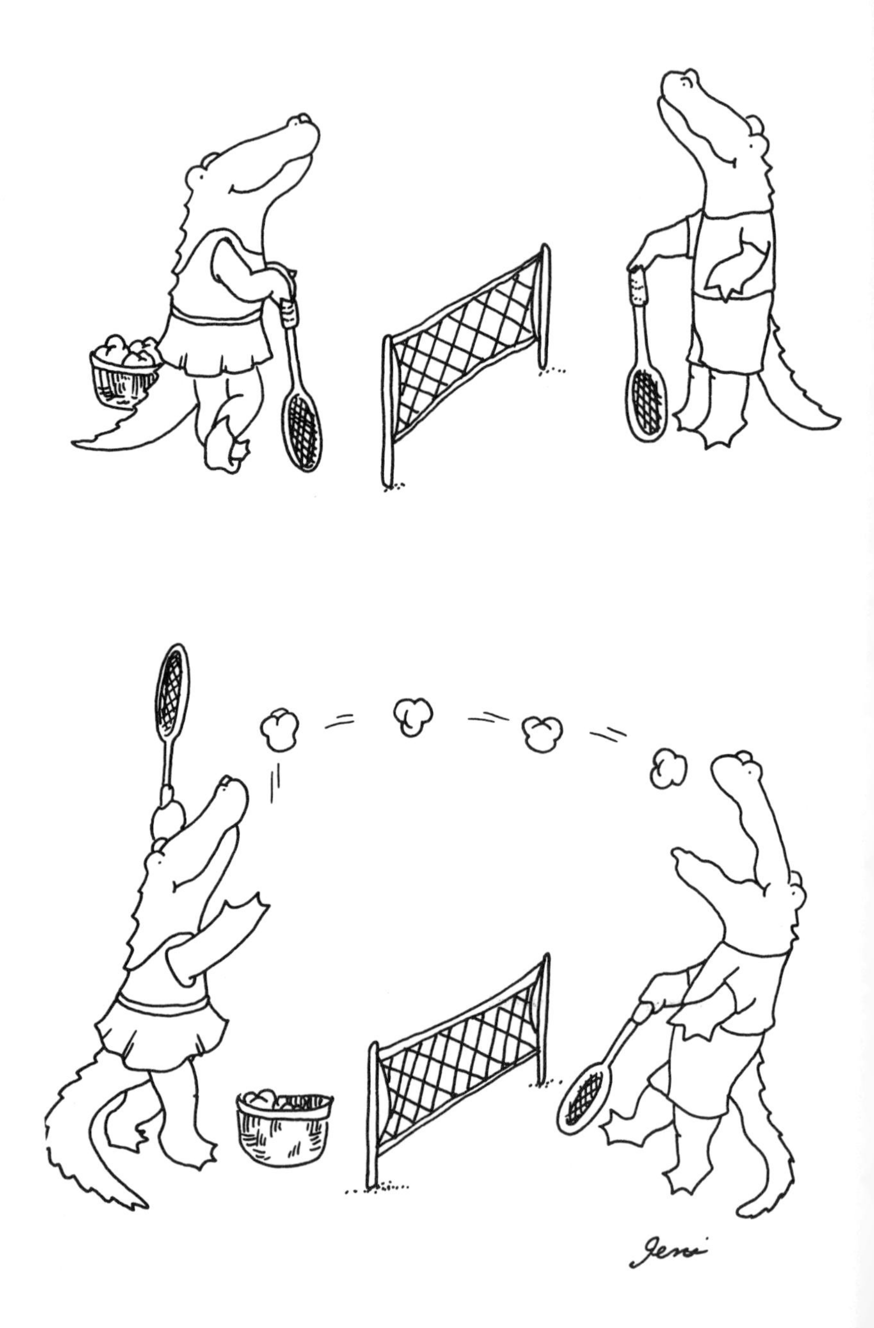

Old Fashion Honey Wheat Bread

1½ cups water
1 cup cream style cottage cheese
½ cup honey
¼ cup butter
1 egg
5½ to 6 cups flour
1 cup whole wheat flour
2 tablespoons sugar
3 teaspoons salt
2 packages active dry yeast

Heat first four ingredients in medium saucepan until warm (120 to 130 degrees). Combine warm liquid and 2 cups all purpose flour and the remaining ingredients in a large bowl. Beat 2 minutes at medium speed. By hand, stir in remaining 3½ to 4 cups of all purpose flour and the 1 cup of whole wheat flour to make a stiff dough. Knead dough on floured surface until smooth and elastic (about 2 minutes). Place in greased bowl. Cover and let rise in warm place until doubled in size (about 45 to 60 minutes). Grease two 5 X 9 inch or 4 X 8 inch loaf pans. Punch down dough. Divide and shape into 2 loaves. Place in greased pans. Cover and let rise in warm place until light and doubled in size (45 to 60 minutes). Heat oven to 350 degrees. Bake 40 to 50 minutes until golden brown or sounds hollow when tapped. Immediately remove from pans and brush warm loaves with melted butter. Makes 2 loaves. Can freeze.

Persimmon Bread

2½ cups sugar
1½ cups shortening
½ teaspoon salt
2 teaspoons allspice
2 teaspoons soda
3 eggs
2 teaspoons cinnamon
1 teaspoon nutmeg
2½ cups flour
2 cups ripe persimmons, mashed
2 cups nuts, chopped
2 cups raisins

Preheat oven to 350 degrees. Cream shortening and sugar well. Add salt, allspice, soda and eggs, beating well after each addition. Mix cinnamon, nutmeg and flour; add to batter alternately with persimmons, saving ½ cup of flour to dredge nuts and raisins. Fold in nut and raisin mixture and bake 1 hour in greased loaf pans. Makes 2 large or 3 small loaves.

Note: Persimmons should be soft to touch and a deep orange color. Underripe persimmons are very tart.

Breads

Milk and Honey Bread

1 cup milk
2/3 cup honey
¼ cup butter
2 eggs
1½ cups flour
1 cup whole wheat flour
1 tablespoon baking powder
1 teaspoon salt
½ cup wheat germ, toasted
1 cup walnut halves or chunks

Preheat oven to 325 degrees. Heat the milk and honey together until the honey is dissolved. Then stir in the butter. When the milk and honey mixture is somewhat cooled, beat in the eggs. Sift together the flours, baking powder and salt. Add the wheat germ and gradually stir the dry mixture into the liquid. Stir in the walnuts, mix well and turn into a greased loaf pan. Bake for 1 hour.

Cranberry Bread

2 cups fresh cranberries
2 cups flour
1 cup sugar
Salt to taste
1½ teaspoons baking powder
½ teaspoon baking soda
½ cup Crisco
¾ cup orange juice
1 egg, well beaten
½ cup nuts, chopped

Wash cranberries, drain and chop. Sift flour, sugar, salt, baking powder and soda. Cut in shortening until coarse. Mix orange juice with egg and add to dough mixture, using mixer on low speed. Add nuts. Fold in cranberries. Pour in greased and floured loaf pan. Bake at 350 degrees for 1 hour.

Lemon Bread

½ cup vegetable oil
1 cup sugar
2 eggs
½ cup milk
1 teaspoon vanilla

Rind of 1 lemon, grated
1½ cups flour
1 teaspoon baking powder
½ teaspoon salt

Icing:
½ cup sugar
Juice of 1 lemon

Preheat oven to 350 degrees. Beat together oil, sugar and eggs. Add milk, vanilla and lemon rind. Beat well. Sift together flour, baking powder and salt, then add to egg mixture. Pour into greased loaf pan and bake 50 minutes. Remove from pan at once, wrap sides and bottom in foil. Top with icing of combined sugar and lemon. Wrap entire loaf in foil. Cool. Best if served the next day.

Orange - Date Nut Bread

1 orange
½ cup boiling water
1 cup dates, chopped
1 cup sugar
2 tablespoons butter or margarine, melted
1 egg, beaten

2 cups all-purpose flour, measured before sifting
1 teaspoon baking powder
¼ teaspoon salt
1 teaspoon baking soda
2/3 cup pecans or walnuts, chopped

Preheat oven to 350 degrees. Wash and squeeze orange and add to the juice enough boiling water to yield 1 cup. Remove pulp from orange and put peeling through food grinder. Combine dates, orange liquid, sugar, butter and egg. Sift dry ingredients together three times and add. Mix well and stir in nuts. Turn into greased loaf pan and bake (325 degrees for glass pan) about 50 minutes or until bread tests done. Cool in pan. Makes 1 loaf. Freezes beautifully.

Breads

Seasoned Bread

1 stick butter, softened
1 teaspoon parsley flakes
¼ teaspoon oregano
¼ teaspoon dill weed
1 clove garlic, minced
French bread or English muffins
Parmesan cheese

Preheat oven to 400 degrees. Mix butter, parsley, oregano, dill weed and garlic and spread on bread. Sprinkle with Parmesan cheese. Bake for 10 minutes. Makes 6 to 8.

Note: Very simple, but looks and tastes like you've gone to a lot of trouble.

Herb Bread

1 loaf Italian bread
8 tablespoons butter, softened
½ teaspoon thyme
½ teaspoon summer savory
¼ teaspoon salt
¼ teaspoon paprika
Dash cayenne pepper

Preheat oven to 375 degrees. Cut crust from the Italian bread. Score once lengthwise and crosswise at 1 to 1½ inch intervals. Mix other ingredients for herb butter. Put herb butter in all crevices and on top and sides. Bake for 15 minutes. Serves 6 to 8.

Cheese Bread

2 pound loaf unsliced bread
2 cups Cheddar cheese, grated
2 sticks butter, softened
½ teaspoon garlic powder

Preheat oven to 400 degrees. Cut bread into one inch slices, do not cut through the bottom. Slice in half lengthwise (top to bottom) not cutting through the bottom. Place on baking sheet. Combine cheese, butter and garlic powder. Spread between, on sides and top of each section. Press loaf together. Wrap in foil. Bake for 15 minutes.

Sour Cream Onion Bread

2 cups all-purpose flour
1 package active dry yeast
½ cup green onions with tops, sliced
2 tablespoons butter
½ cup sour cream
1/3 cup milk
2 tablespoons sugar
1 teaspoon salt
1 egg

In mixer bowl stir together 1 cup flour and yeast. In a saucepan cook onion in butter until tender. Stir in sour cream, milk, sugar and salt; beat slowly to lukewarm (110 to 115 degrees F.). Add to dry ingredients in mixer bowl along with the egg. Beat at low speed of electric mixer for ½ minute and beat for 3 minutes at high speed. By hand, stir in remaining flour and spoon batter into greased round 1 quart casserole. Cover and let rise in warm place for 1 hour or until double. Bake in 375 degree oven for 35 to 40 minutes. Cover with foil the last 10 minutes to prevent over browning. Cool 10 minutes in casserole, remove from dish and cool on rack.

Dill Bread

2 packages yeast
1 tablespoon sugar
1 cup warm water
2 cups cottage cheese
2 tablespoons soft butter
2 eggs, slightly beaten
3 tablespoons sugar
2 tablespoons dried onion flakes or 4 tablespoons fresh onion, chopped
4 tablespoons dill seeds
2 teaspoons salt
½ teaspoon baking soda
4 to 5 cups flour

Preheat oven to 350 degrees. In a small bowl put yeast and 1 tablespoon sugar in warm water. Set aside. Heat cottage cheese to lukewarm (may add butter to melt) in a small saucepan. Beat eggs in a large bowl. Add remaining sugar, onions, dill seeds, salt and baking soda. Pour in yeast mixture. Then add cottage cheese and butter. Mix. Add flour slowly until batter is stiff. Let rise until doubled (45 minutes). Punch down. Put into two greased loaf pans and let rise again for 45 minutes. Bake for 30 to 50 minutes. Makes 2 loaves. May freeze.

Breads

Carrot Quick Bread

¾ cup sugar
¼ cup unsulphured molasses
2/3 cup salad oil
2 eggs
1½ cups all-purpose flour,
  unsifted
1 teaspoon baking soda
½ teaspoon baking powder
½ teaspoon salt
1 teaspoon cinnamon
1 cup raw carrots, grated
½ cup nuts, chopped

Preheat oven to 375 degrees. In large mixing bowl beat together sugar, molasses, oil and eggs. Blend in dry ingredients which have been sifted together. Stir in carrots and nuts. Pour into well greased 5 X 9 inch loaf pan. Bake for 45 to 60 minutes or until it tests done. If top darkens too much before bread is finished baking, place a piece of foil loosely over top of pan. Cool in pan on rack for 5 minutes, then turn onto rack to finish cooling.

Middle East Bread

1 package Middle East bread (Pita)
1 stick butter, melted
1½ teaspoons curry powder or to taste
Parmesan cheese

Preheat oven to 250 degrees. Cut around the crust and separate each loaf or slice of bread. Cut into bite size pieces. Combine the curry powder with the melted butter and brush over each piece of bread with a pastry brush. Sprinkle with Parmesan cheese and bake for 20 to 30 minutes on a cookie sheet.

Note: For different taste, try dill weed, onion salt or garlic powder. This is good as an appetizer with drinks or with a salad or soup.

Bread stays fresher longer at room temperature or frozen. Do not refrigerate.

Zucchini Bread

3 eggs
1 cup oil
2 cups sugar
2 cups zucchini, peeled and grated
1 teaspoon vanilla
3 cups flour
1 teaspoon soda
½ teaspoon baking powder
1 teaspoon salt
2 to 3 teaspoons cinnamon
½ cup nuts, chopped

Preheat oven to 325 degrees. Beat eggs until light and fluffly. Add oil, sugar, zucchini and vanilla. Mix flour, soda, baking powder, salt and cinnamon in a bowl. Add flour mixture and blend. Add nuts. Bake in 2 greased 5 X 9 inch loaf pans for 1 hour. Remove from pans at once and cool on rack.

Sweet Potato Nut Bread

½ cup butter
½ cup shortening
2 2/3 cups sugar
4 eggs
2 cups sweet potatoes, mashed
3½ cups flour
1 teaspoon salt
1 teaspoon cinnamon
1½ teaspoons nutmeg
2 teaspoons baking soda
1 cup walnuts, chopped
2/3 cup cold, strong black coffee

Preheat oven to 375 degrees. Cream butter, shortening and sugar. Add eggs, one at a time, mixing well after each. Blend in sweet potatoes. Sift together dry ingredients; add nuts. Stir into creamed mixture alternately with cold coffee. Pour into 2 greased loaf pans and 8 muffin cups. Bake 1 hour for loaves and 25 minutes for muffins.

Dilly Cheese Bread

3 1/3 cups Bisquick mix
8 ounces (or more) sharp Cheddar cheese, shredded
1¼ cups milk
2 eggs, slightly beaten
¼ teaspoon dill weed

Preheat oven to 350 degrees. Combine Bisquick and cheese. Add milk and eggs, then dill weed. Mix until moistened. Pour into greased and floured 5 X 9 inch loaf pan. Bake for 55 minutes. Serve in thin slices toasted. Makes 20 slices. Can be prepared ahead and frozen.

Green Chile Cornbread

2 eggs
1¼ cups oil
1 to 4 green chilies
9 ounces cream style corn
½ cup sour cream or plain yogurt
1 cup yellow cornmeal
½ teaspoon salt
2 tablespoons baking powder
2 cups Cheddar cheese, grated

Preheat oven to 350 degrees. Beat eggs, oil and chilies. Add corn, yogurt (or sour cream), cornmeal, salt, baking powder and 1½ cups cheese. Blend. Pour into 9 inch square pan and sprinkle remaining cheese on top. Bake for 1 hour. Serves 6 to 8.

Cornbread for a Crowd

1½ cups oil
3 cups self-rising cornmeal
4 eggs, beaten
15 ounces canned cream corn
1 pint sour cream

Preheat oven to 425 degrees. Combine oil, cornmeal, eggs, corn and sour cream and pour into greased 11 X 13 inch pan. Bake for 15 minutes at 425 degrees, then lower temperature to 375 degrees and cook for another 30 minutes. Serves 12.

Note: Best if cooked in hot cast iron skillet. May drizzle honey over hot bread.

Butter Sticks

1 loaf Italian bread
1 cup butter, softened
1 teaspoon chervil
1 teaspoon basil leaves
½ teaspoon garlic powder
½ teaspoon onion powder

Preheat oven to 425 degrees. Cut the bread in half lengthwise. Also cut the loaf in half crosswise. Cut each of the 4 pieces lengthwise to make 3 wedges. (A total of 12 wedges). In a small bowl combine the remaining ingredients. Blend well. Spread the butter mixture on the cut surface of the bread wedges. Bake on an ungreased 10 X 15 inch baking sheet for 7 to 9 minutes or until golden brown. Makes 12 (10-inch) sticks.

Good 'n Easy Biscuits

1 cup self-rising flour
½ cup milk
3 tablespoons mayonnaise

Preheat oven to 400 degrees. Mix all ingredients well. Spoon into greased muffin tins. Bake for 15 minutes. Makes 8. Super easy!

Variations: Use 3 tablespoons sour cream instead of mayonnaise.

Breads

Tiny Flat Biscuits

2 cups flour
3 teaspoons baking powder
1 teaspoon salt
2 teaspoons sugar
5 tablespoons Crisco
¾ cup milk

Blend first five ingredients with pastry blender. Work with fingers until crumbly. Gradually add ¾ cup milk and blend thoroughly. Roll on floured board. Cut with 2 inch cookie cutter. Place on cookie sheet and brown on bottom at 500 degrees for 3 to 5 minutes. Broil to brown on top for 3 to 5 minutes. Serves 8.

Note: Can make biscuits ahead and freeze. Thaw and bake at last minute.

Tiny Marmalade Biscuits

½ cup orange marmalade
2 tablespoons soft butter
2 cups Bisquick baking mix
½ cup cold water

Mix the marmalade and butter. Spread in 8 X 8 X 2 inch pan. Preheat oven to 425 degrees. Stir the Bisquick and water to form a soft ball. On a floured board, knead 5 times. Roll into 8 inch square. Place over the marmalade mixture, making sure the corners are covered. Cut into 36 squares. Bake for 15 to 20 minutes. Invert pan over a serving plate. Biscuits will break into tiny squares, bite size. Serve warm. Makes 36.

Popovers for Two

½ cup all-purpose flour, sifted
½ cup milk
1 egg
¼ teaspoon salt

Preheat oven to 425 degrees. Grease four custard cups or use Teflon muffin tin. Beat all ingredients together until batter is smooth. Bake 35 to 40 minutes or until golden brown. Serve hot with butter. Prick before removing from oven to allow steam to escape. 4 popovers.

Hush Puppies

2 cups cornmeal
1 cup all-purpose flour
1 cup onions, finely chopped
¼ cup sugar
Salt to taste
1 tablespoon baking powder
1 to 1¼ cups buttermilk

Mix ingredients in order listed, mixing well after each ingredient. Deep fry in a hot pot of oil (450 degrees) until golden brown. Makes 12 to 24 hush puppies depending on the size of the spoon used.

Note: Drop by teaspoon or tablespoonful into oil. Dip spoon in hot oil so mixture will not stick to spoon. They do expand when cooking.

French Jam Roll-Ups

12 slices day-old bread, rolled flat
½ cup your favorite jam
1/3 cup milk
2 eggs
1 teaspoon sugar
¼ teaspoon ground nutmeg
Butter
Confectioners' sugar

If desired, remove crusts from bread. Spread each bread slice with about 2 teaspoons jam. Roll up. In small bowl beat milk, eggs, sugar and nutmeg. Dip each roll-up in egg mixture and grill in butter on all sides until hot and golden. Serve warm sprinkled with confectioners' sugar. Serve with additional jam if desired. Serves 4.

Skyline Apple Muffins

1½ cups brown sugar, firmly packed
2/3 cup oil
1 egg
1 cup sour milk or buttermilk
1 teaspoon soda
1 teaspoon salt
1 teaspoon vanilla
2½ cups flour
1½ cups raw apples, diced
½ cup pecans, chopped
1/3 cup sugar
1 tablespoon butter, melted

Preheat oven to 325 degrees. Combine brown sugar, oil and egg in a bowl. In another bowl combine buttermilk, soda, salt and vanilla. Add milk mixture to sugar mixture alternately with flour, beating well after each addition. Fold in apples and pecans. Pour into lined muffin tins, filling ½ full. Combine sugar with melted butter and sprinkle on top of each muffin. Bake for 45 minutes. Makes approximately 10 to 12 muffins.

Apple Muffins

1 egg
2/3 cup gingerale
¼ cup sugar
2 cups Bisquick
1 teaspoon cinnamon
¼ teaspoon nutmeg
⅛ teaspoon cloves
1 apple, chopped

Preheat oven to 400 degrees. Beat egg and add gingerale and sugar. Add Bisquick, cinnamon, nutmeg and cloves and mix well. Stir in apple. Spoon into greased muffin pan. Cook until brown, about 10 to 12 minutes.

Icing:
1 cup confectioners' sugar
2 tablespoons mayonnaise
1 teaspoon cinnamon
1 teaspoon vanilla

Mix the above ingredients until smooth. Spread on hot muffins. Makes 12 to 18 muffins.

Sticky Pineapple Muffins

¾ cup crushed pineapple, drained
½ cup margarine, softened
½ cup brown sugar
1 teaspoon cinnamon
2 cups Bisquick
2 tablespoons sugar
¾ cup cream or ½ cup milk plus ½ cup melted margarine

Preheat oven to 425 degrees. Mix the first four ingredients together and spoon into greased muffin tins. Mix the last three ingredients and spoon over pineapple mixture. Bake 15 to 20 minutes. Invert IMMEDIATELY when done so sticky part will be on top. 12 muffins.

Onion-Cheese Muffins

¾ cup French fried onions
1½ cups Bisquick baking mix
½ teaspoon onion salt
1/3 cup Cheddar cheese, shredded
1 egg
½ cup milk

Line 6 custard or coffee cups with paper liners. Crush onions with rolling pin; reserve ¼ cup. Stir together remaining crushed onions, the baking mix, onion salt, cheese, egg and milk; beat vigorously ½ minute. Divide half of the batter among cups; sprinkle with half of the reserved onions. Arrange custard cups about 1 inch apart in circle in microwave oven. Cook until no longer doughy, 1½ to 2 minutes. Repeat with remaining batter and crushed onions. Serve warm. 12 muffins.

Breads

Raisin-Bran-Walnut Muffins

15 ounce box Raisin Bran cereal
1 quart buttermilk
1 cup oil
2½ cups sugar
4 eggs
5 cups flour
2 teaspoons salt
4 teaspoons baking soda
1 cup walnuts, chopped

Preheat oven to 400 degrees. Mix cereal, buttermilk, oil, sugar and eggs (one at a time). Mix well. Add sifted flour, salt and soda all at one time and stir dry ingredients into cereal. Add chopped walnuts. Cover and refrigerate at least 6 hours before cooking. Place in greased muffin tins. Bake for 15 to 20 minutes. Mix will keep in the refrigerator for 4 to 5 weeks. Makes 4 to 5 dozen.

Oatmeal Refrigerator Rolls

½ cup shortening
3 tablespoons sugar
1 teaspoon salt
½ cup boiling water
1 cup rolled oats
1 package yeast
½ cup lukewarm water
1 egg, beaten
2½ cups sifted flour, separated
Melted butter

Measure the shortening, sugar and salt in a bowl. Add the boiling water and mix. Add the rolled oats and cool to lukewarm. Soften the yeast in the lukewarm water; add the egg and mix well. Add the yeast and egg to the oatmeal mixture. Stir in 1 cup of flour. Beat hard. Add the remaining flour. Mix well. Form into a ball. Grease the top of the dough slightly. Cover the bowl with a damp towel and plate. Store in the refrigerator until needed. About 2 hours before baking, roll into a circle ¼ to ½ inch thick. Cut into wedges, brush with melted butter. Roll toward point in the crescent shape. Let rise. Bake about 15 minutes at 400 degrees to 450 degrees.

Bread made with fruit or nuts should be tested with a straw or wire cake tester.

Ice Box Rolls

1 cup shortening
¾ cup sugar
2 teaspoons salt
1 cup boiling water
1 cup cold water
¼ cup lukewarm water
2 packages dry yeast
2 eggs, beaten
7 cups all-purpose flour, unsifted

Preheat oven to 425 degrees. Cream shortening, sugar and salt together. Pour boiling water over these ingredients. Add cold water, then yeast which has been dissolved in ¼ cup lukewarm water. Add beaten eggs and mix. Add flour a little at a time and mix well after each addition. Cover and place in refrigerator overnight. Roll and make up 2 hours before baking. Cut with a biscuit cutter and place on ungreased baking sheet or shape into cloverleaf rolls by rolling into small balls and placing 3 balls into each muffin cup. Brush with melted butter. Let rise 2 hours or until doubled in size. Bake for 15 minutes. 2 to 3 dozen.

Note: Can be done ahead. Dough keeps in refrigerator up to one week. Must allow time for rising (2 hours). Can be frozen. Variation: Pinch off dough and roll in balls. Cover and let rise (about 1½ hours). Drop in deep fat and fry as you would hush puppies.

Granny's Rolls

1 cup warm water
1 package yeast
¼ cup sugar
½ teaspoon salt
3¼ cups self-rising flour
1 egg
½ cup Crisco
Melted butter

Dissolve yeast in water. Add sugar, salt and ½ of flour. Beat with mixer. Add egg and Crisco. Beat by hand, adding remaining flour. Form ball in bowl and cover with damp cloth. Two hours before baking, remove cloth and roll out on floured wax paper until ½ inch thick. Cut with cutter, roll in melted butter. Place side by side on greased baking pan. Bake at 400 degrees for 12 to 15 minutes.

Note: Prepare 2 hours before serving.

Coffee Cake Supreme

1 cup butter
2 cups sugar
3 eggs
13 ounces evaporated milk
1 teaspoon vanilla extract
¼ teaspoon almond extract
3 cups flour
4 teaspoons baking powder
1 teaspoon salt

Cinnamon mixture:
1½ cups sugar
1 tablespoon cinnamon

For the cinnamon mixture, mix the sugar and cinnamon together well. Preheat the oven to 350 degrees. Cream the butter and the sugar. Add the eggs, one at a time. Add the milk, vanilla and almond extract. Add the flour, baking powder and salt. Beat well. Pour 1 cup of batter into each of 2 greased and floured 8 X 8 inch aluminum pans. Sprinkle ½ cup of cinnamon mixture over the batter. Pour another cup of batter over the cinnamon, then remaining cinnamon on top of that. Bake for 45 minutes.
Note: This freezes well. You can also use a 9 X 13 inch pan.

Peach Brandy Coffeecake

2 cups flour
½ teaspoon salt
2 teaspoons baking powder
2 cups sugar
3 eggs
1 cup salad oil
16 ounces canned peaches, mashed
3 teaspoons Brandy flavoring
1 cup chopped nuts
Confectioners' sugar

Preheat oven to 350 degrees. Grease 10 inch tube pan. Sift dry ingredients together. Beat eggs; stir in oil, peaches, brandy flavoring and nuts. Add dry ingredients and mix well. Pour into tube pan. Bake 1 hour and 10 minutes. Cool on rack 10 minutes; unmold and sprinkle with confectioners' sugar.

Lightly oil the cup or spoon used to measure honey or molasses.

Cheese & Eggs

GREATEST
on
THE
MAN
Jeni

Cheese Strata

10 slices white bread, crusts removed
1/3 cup butter, softened
3 cups sharp Cheddar cheese, grated
4 eggs, lightly beaten
3 cups milk
1½ teaspoons salt
1 teaspoon dry mustard
Pinch of cayenne pepper
Parsley, finely chopped
Paprika

Spread bread with butter. Cut each slice into 4 strips. In a buttered 2 quart casserole, make alternate layers of bread strips and cheese, ending with cheese. Beat eggs, add seasonings and milk. Pour over bread and cheese layers. Cover and refrigerate 24 hours or more. Take out one hour before baking. Bake at 350 degrees 50 to 60 minutes. Sprinkle with parsley and paprika. Serves 8.

Note: May also be made in a rectangular dish but you will need four or five more slices of bread.

Baked Cheese Grits

1 cup stone ground grits
1 quart milk
1 stick butter
½ teaspoon garlic salt
½ teaspoon salt
½ teaspoon pepper, freshly ground
1 cup sharp Cheddar cheese, grated

Bring milk to a boil and add butter. Stir until butter is melted. Gradually add grits, stirring constantly. Lower heat and cook grits until consistency of cream of wheat. Remove from heat; add garlic salt, salt and pepper. Beat with electric mixer for 5 minutes. This is an important step in order for grits to be light. Pour into lightly buttered 9 X 13 inch baking dish. Chill until firm. Cut into long strips and place them in a casserole so that they overlap slightly to give surface effect of ridges or shingles. Sprinkle 1 cup or more of cheese on top. Bake at 350 degrees for 30 minutes. This may be done a day or two ahead and heated before serving. Leftovers may be wrapped in foil and frozen. Serves 6 to 8.

Cheese & Eggs

Cheese Grits

1½ cups grits
1 teaspoon salt
6 cups water
1 pound sharp Cheddar cheese, grated
1½ sticks margarine or butter
3 eggs, beaten
2 teaspoons MSG seasoning salt
1 teaspoon Tabasco sauce
1 teaspoon paprika

Preheat oven to 300 degrees. Cook the grits in salted water until done. Add the grated cheese and butter to the cooked grits. Beat the eggs with the seasonings and add this to the grits. Pour into a large buttered casserole. Bake at 300 degrees for 1 hour.

Sausage-Cheese Pie

1¼ pounds of ground sausage, browned and crumbled
2 cups Monterey Jack cheese, cut in ½ inch cubes
2 cans crescent rolls
⅛ teaspoon salt
⅛ teaspoon pepper
1 tablespoon oregano
2 tablespoons Parmesan cheese
3 eggs, lightly beaten

Preheat oven to 325 degrees. Unroll crescent rolls and separate dough into 16 triangles. Place 8 or 9 triangles in a 9 inch pie pan pressing sides together to form crust. Combine remaining ingredients in a bowl. Mix and then pour into crust. Roll out remaining triangles so longest side is 8 inches long. Cut into ½ inch strips. Place 5 strips across the pie, seal and flute edge. Bake 60 to 70 minutes or until knife inserted 2 inches from edge comes out clean. Do NOT overcook. 6 servings.

Bacon and Sausage Strata

1 pound hot sausage
½ pound bacon
6 slices bread, cubed
8 ounces Cheddar cheese, grated
4 eggs
½ teaspoon salt
½ teaspoon dry mustard
2 drops Worcestershire sauce
2 cups milk

Fry sausage and bacon separately, drain and crumble together. Alternate layers of bread, meat and cheese (in that order) into a buttered 9 X 13 inch pan. (One layer each) Beat eggs and add salt, Worcestershire sauce, dry mustard and milk. Pour over casserole and cover with foil. Refrigerate overnight. Remove foil and bake 1 hour at 325 degrees. 6 to 8 servings.

Macaroni Mousse

1 cup macaroni
1½ cups milk, scalded
½ cup butter, melted
1½ cups Cheddar cheese, grated
1 small jar pimientos, drained and chopped
3 eggs, beaten
1 tablespoon parsley, chopped
1 tablespoon onion, chopped
Paprika

Preheat oven to 325 degrees. Cook and drain the macaroni. Heat the milk. Add the remaining ingredients. Pour over the macaroni, mixing well. Place in a buttered casserole. Sprinkle with paprika. Bake until set, about 45 minutes. Serves 6 to 8.

Cheese & Eggs

Layered Mexican Chili

8 tortillas fresh or frozen (thawed)
2 cans chili without beans
1 large onion, chopped
12 ounces sharp Cheddar cheese, grated

Preheat oven to 350 degrees. Tear tortillas in quarters. Line a 12 X 8 inch casserole with ½ of the tortillas. Heat 1 can chili and cover the tortillas with it. Sprinkle half the onion over the chili and sprinkle half the cheese over the onion. Repeat all four layers as prepared above: tortillas, chili, onion, cheese. Bake 30 minutes at 350 degrees. Drain and remove the oil. Serve with plain Doritos, tossed salad and fruit ice dessert. Serves 4 to 6.

Hot and Hearty Breakfast

8 strips of bacon
1 medium onion, finely chopped
½ medium green pepper, cut into 1 inch strips
½ jalapeño pepper, finely chopped (optional)
4 large baking potatoes, cooked and cubed, with skin
2/3 cup Cheddar cheese, grated
8 eggs, lightly beaten
Salt and pepper to taste
(If you don't like hot foods, you can substitute 1½ cups mushrooms for jalapeño pepper and add ¼ teaspoon tarragon for seasoning)

Fry bacon in 12 inch skillet over medium-low heat until crisp. Set bacon aside to drain. Retain 3 tablespoons of drippings in skillet. Add onion, green pepper and jalapeño pepper to skillet and cook until soft. Add potatoes and cook for 6 minutes, stirring occasionally. Spread cheese over the mixture until cheese melts. Pour eggs, seasoned with salt and pepper, over the mixture. Stir gently and cook until done. Sprinkle with bacon pieces and serve immediately. Serves 4.

To preserve egg yolks in refrigerator, slide into a bowl and cover with water.

Cheaper by the Dozen Egg Casserole

1 dozen hard-boiled eggs, cut in quarters
½ pound fresh mushrooms
4 tablespoons butter
10 ounces frozen peas, cooked
1 can water chestnuts, sliced
1 can cream of chicken soup
1 cup sour cream
1 teaspoon onion, minced
3 tablespoons pimiento
½ cup sherry
Salt and pepper
1 cup bread crumbs, buttered

Preheat oven to 375 degrees. Saute' mushrooms in butter. Put in bottom of casserole. Arrange in layers the eggs, peas and water chestnuts. Heat the cream of chicken soup, sour cream and onion. Add pimientos, salt, pepper and sherry. Pour over layered casserole. Top with buttered bread crumbs. Bake 20 minutes. Serves 8 to 10. Can freeze. Great for a brunch.

An In-eggs-pensive Brunch Idea

4 eggs
2 cups plain croutons
4 ounces Cheddar cheese, shredded
2 cups milk
½ teaspoon salt
½ teaspoon prepared mustard
Pepper to taste
4 slices bacon, cooked

Preheat oven to 325 degrees. In casserole layer croutons, then cheese. Mix eggs, milk, salt, pepper and mustard together and pour over the cheese. Crumble the bacon on top. Bake for 1 hour. Let stand a few minutes before serving. Serves 4.

Cheese & Eggs

Egg-ceptional Quiche

1 deep dish pie crust
½ pound bacon, fried and diced
1 tablespoon bacon drippings
¾ cup onion, chopped
½ pound mushrooms, sliced
4 eggs
½ cup milk
1 cup light cream
Dash of nutmeg
1¼ cups Swiss cheese, shredded
¼ cup Parmesan cheese, grated

Bake pie crust at 400 degrees for 5 minutes. Saute' onion and mushrooms in bacon drippings. Drain and set aside. Beat eggs and mix with milk, cream and nutmeg. Layer bacon, mushrooms, onion and cheese in pie crust. Pour egg/milk mixture over top. Sprinkle with Parmesan cheese. Bake at 375 degrees for 45 to 60 minutes. (Done when knife comes out clean). Remove from oven and let sit for 15 to 20 minutes before cutting. Serves 4 to 6 as a main course.

Giant Ham Quiche

Favorite pie crust recipe to fill
  12 inch spring form pan or
  quiche pan
3 cups Swiss cheese, grated
½ pound ham, slivered
½ pound bacon, fried and
  crumbled
7 eggs
1 pint whipping cream
½ teaspoon nutmeg
¼ teaspoon pepper
1 teaspoon salt
2 dashes Tabasco sauce

Preheat oven to 350 degrees. Line pan with pie crust (bottom and sides). Top pie crust with cheese, ham and bacon. In a large bowl beat eggs, whipping cream and spices together. Pour over ham and bacon. Bake at 350 degrees for 45 to 60 minutes or until inserted knife comes out clean. Serves 8.

Perfect hard-cooked eggs: Place eggs in a saucepan and cover with water; bring to boil, lower heat to simmer, and cook 14 minutes. Pour off hot water and add cold water. Shells will come off easily.

Sour Cream and Onion Quiche

1½ cups onion, sliced
4 tablespoons butter or margarine
¼ teaspoon pepper
1 pint sour cream
¼ teaspoon nutmeg
3 eggs
¼ teaspoon salt
Dash Tabasco sauce
9 inch pie crust, unbaked

Preheat oven to 350 degrees. Cook onion in butter until transparent. Beat remaining ingredients in separate bowl until eggs are thoroughly blended. Add onions. Mix, pour into pastry shell and bake at 350 degrees for 35 to 40 minutes. 6 servings.

Note: Good for lunch or brunch with mixed green salad. Also good cocktail buffet item.

Green Chile Quiche

9 inch pie crust, unbaked
2 small cans green chilies, chopped
4 to 5 slices bacon, cooked and crumbled
3 eggs
1 pint light cream
Dash of pepper
¼ teaspoon salt
4 ounces Swiss cheese, grated
4 ounces Cheddar cheese, grated

Preheat oven to 350 degrees. Make your favorite pie crust. Sprinkle bacon and chopped chilies on bottom. Whip all other ingredients until fluffy. Pour on top and bake for 45 minutes or until firmly set. Serves 6. Great for brunch.

Shred Cheddar or Swiss cheese and freeze; whenever you need some just measure.

Keep soft cheese - American, Swiss, etc. from sticking to a grater by first rubbing grater with a dab of butter with a paper towel.

Cheese & Eggs

Green Chile and Cheese Dip

2 tablespoons salad oil
2 medium onions, chopped
1 tablespoon flour
½ cup regular strength broth
½ cup sour cream
4 ounces green chiles, chopped
4 ounces pimientos, chopped
3 cups mild Cheddar cheese, shredded
Tortilla chips

In a chafing dish combine salad oil and onion. Cook stirring until soft. Blend in flour. Gradually add broth, then sour cream. Heat until boiling and slightly thickened. Add chiles (this dip can turn out moderate to hot, depending on the strength of the chopped green chiles) and pimientos to sauce; then gradually stir in shredded cheese until melted. To serve, keep warm and scoop onto tortilla chips. Makes 2½ cups or 12 servings.

Sausage-Egg Casserole

1 pound bulk sausage
6 eggs
2 cups milk
1 teaspoon salt
1 teaspoon mustard
2 or 3 slices bread, cubed
Cheddar cheese, grated

Brown the sausage; drain. Beat the eggs with the milk, salt and mustard. Place the bread in the bottom of a 9 X 13 inch buttered casserole. Crumble the sausage over the bread, then top with the cheese. Pour the egg mixture over all. Refrigerate overnight. Bake for 30 to 40 minutes at 350 degrees.

Christmas hint: Serve this to family members for brunch on Christmas morning. It is delicious with waffles or pancakes and coffee, spiced tea or orange juice. Also it is great because you make it the night before - lets you enjoy the Christmas morning fun!

Soups

gene

Corn Chowder

Sauce:
4 tablespoons butter
4 tablespoons flour
Pinch of salt
2½ quarts half and half
½ cup parsley, chopped
1 to 2 teaspoons honey
1 bay leaf
¼ teaspoon black pepper
Nutmeg to taste
Water
4 unpeeled potatoes, diced

In a heavy saucepan, melt butter. Add flour and salt. Cook over low heat for 10 minutes. This is the roux or thickener for the soup. Add the half and half to the roux. Cook, stirring constantly, for 15 minutes. Add the parsley, honey, bay leaf, pepper and nutmeg. Reserve. Parboil the potatoes in water to cover for 7 to 8 minutes. Drain and reserve.

Base:
12 tablespoons butter
1 large Spanish onion, minced
4 cloves garlic, minced
1 leek, white part only, sliced
3 scallions, chopped
¾ teaspoon dry mustard
⅛ teaspoon cayenne pepper
Salt to taste
6 stalks celery, diced
6 to 7 ears corn, shucked, and kernels cut off the cobs
3 Marga vegetable cubes
1½ teaspoons thyme

Melt butter. Saute' the onion, garlic, leek and scallions for 20 to 25 minutes. Season with the mustard, cayenne and salt to taste. Raise the heat and add the celery. Cook 3 to 4 minutes. Add the corn and the vegetable cubes and cook the mixture for 3 to 4 minutes.

Add the parboiled potatoes and the sauce to the base mixture. Season with thyme and taste to correct the salt seasoning. Serve piping hot accompanied by fresh corn bread and Cheddar cheese. Makes 6 quarts.

Note: Marga vegetable cubes are available at health food stores. Vegetable bouillon cubes can be substituted for Marga vegetable cubes.

Soups

Cheese and Vegetable Chowder

¾ cup sharp cheese, grated
1 cup potatoes, diced
1 cup carrots, sliced
1 cup green pepper, diced
½ cup onion, chopped
10 ounces frozen green peas
4 tablespoons margarine
5 tablespoons flour
21½ ounces chicken broth
½ teaspoon salt
Dash of pepper
2 cups milk
Optional: parsley

Cook potatoes, carrots, green pepper, onion, green peas and margarine together for 20 to 25 minutes. Sprinkle in flour and mix thoroughly. Then add broth and cheese, cooking until cheese is melted. Add the rest of the ingredients and heat until hot but not boiling. If desired, garnish with parsley.

Cheddar Cheese Soup

1 pound sharp Cheddar cheese, grated
½ cup bacon, diced
1 tablespoon butter
1 cup carrots, chopped
1 cup onions, chopped
1 cup celery, chopped
¾ cup green pepper, chopped
3 cups chicken stock
1½ cups beer
3½ cups milk
2/3 cup flour
½ cup heavy cream
Salt and pepper to taste
Garnish: parsley, chopped

Saute' bacon in butter until crisp and brown. Remove bacon with slotted spoon and drain. Reserve. Add vegetables to bacon drippings and cook, stirring occasionally, until onion is transparent. Add vegetables to soup pot with stock and beer. Heat to boiling and simmer until vegetables are tender. Scald milk over medium heat. Combine cheese and flour in plastic bag; toss to combine. When milk is hot, add cheese/flour mixture. Cook and stir until cheese melts and mixture thickens. Add to soup pot with cream. Season to taste with salt and pepper. Heat to serving temperature and garnish with bacon and parsley. Serves 6 to 8.

Creamy Avocado Soup

1 large ripe avocado
1 1/3 cup chicken broth
8 ounces sour cream
½ cup half and half
¼ teaspoon salt
¼ teaspoon garlic salt
8 shakes of Tabasco sauce
Garnish: chopped chives

Peel, seed and slice the avocado. Mix the avocado in the blender or processor. Add the remaining ingredients and blend until smooth. Chill and serve with chopped chives as a garnish. Serves 6.

Chicken Curry Soup

3 cups chicken broth
2 tablespoons margarine or butter
¼ cup flour
1 cup light cream
½ teaspoon curry powder
Salt and pepper to taste
Optional: 1 cup chicken, diced
Garnish: cut up chives or apples

Over direct heat, melt butter; stir in flour to make roux. Slowly stir in broth and cream until thickened. Add curry, salt and pepper. If desired, a cup of diced chicken may be added. Top with chives or apples. Serves 4.

Cold Tomato and Cucumber Soup

64 ounces tomato juice
1 medium cucumber, grated
1 teaspoon salt
½ teaspoon pepper
5 dashes Worcestershire sauce
1 ounce lemon juice
1 tablespoon horseradish
Tabasco sauce to taste

Mix tomato juice and grated cucumber; add remaining ingredients and mix well. Refrigerate. Serve cold.

Note: May also be used as a Bloody Mary mix.

Soups

French Onion Soup

1½ pounds yellow onion, thinly sliced
1 tablespoon oil
3 tablespoons butter
1 teaspoon brown sugar, firmly packed
1 teaspoon salt
Dash of white pepper
2 to 3 tablespoons all-purpose flour
3 cans beef broth
3 cups water
1 to 2 beef bouillon cubes
½ cup white wine
Toasted French bread
6 ounces Gruyère cheese (Swiss cheese may be substituted)

Cook onion in oil and butter in a covered pan about 30 minutes. Uncover and add brown sugar, salt and pepper. Stir well. Continue cooking 30 minutes more or until golden brown, stirring often. Sprinkle in the flour, blend well, and cook for a few minutes while you bring the beef broth, water and bouillon cubes to a boil in a separate saucepan. Remove onion mixture from heat and stir in boiling beef broth. Simmer 20 minutes or longer. Add white wine and cook 20 minutes more. Pour soup into oven-proof bowls. Place slice of toasted bread on each and sprinkle with cheese. Brown under preheated broiler. Serve immediately. Serves 6.

Cream of Broccoli Soup

1 cup broccoli, diced, or 10 ounces chopped frozen broccoli
3 tablespoons butter
½ cup white wine
1/3 cup leeks, diced
1/3 cup onion, diced
1/3 cup celery, diced
3 tablespoons flour
3 cups chicken broth
Dash of thyme
¼ teaspoon pepper
½ teaspoon salt
1 cup light cream
Sliced almonds, optional

Melt the butter over low heat. Add the wine and saute' the vegetables over low heat. Blend in the flour, then the chicken broth. Let boil. Add the seasonings and then simmer until the vegetables are tender. Add cream and serve. Top with sliced almonds, if desired.

Carolina She-Crab Soup

2 cups white crab meat
2 tablespoons butter
1 tablespoon onion, finely grated
⅛ teaspoon pepper
¼ teaspoon salt or to taste
½ teaspoon mace
2 cups heavy cream
1 cup milk
1 tablespoon Worcestershire sauce
1 tablespoon flour
2 tablespoons water
4 tablespoons dry sherry
Paprika or parsley, finely chopped

Place crab meat in double boiler; add butter, onion, pepper, salt and mace. Simmer 5 minutes; then add heavy cream and milk (warmed before adding). Stir and add Worcestershire sauce. Thicken with paste made of flour and water. Add sherry and cook over low heat for 30 minutes. When serving, additional warmed sherry may be added. Sprinkle with paprika or parsley to garnish. Serves 6 to 8.

Shrimp and Crab Gumbo

1 pound shrimp, boiled
1 pint crab meat (claw is best)
1 or 2 ham hocks
2 quarts water
6 slices bacon
1 medium onion, chopped
1 green pepper, chopped
Parsley, chopped
2½ pounds canned tomatoes
8 ounces canned tomato paste
2 bay leaves
20 ounces frozen okra
Salt and pepper to taste
2 teaspoons file' powder
Rice

Boil the hocks in water for 2 hours. Replace any water that boils out. Clean boiled shrimp and chop into ¼ inch pieces. Pick through crab meat and remove shells. Fry bacon lightly and set aside, saving the grease. Fry the chopped onion and pepper in the bacon fat until soft. Remove hocks and chop lean meat from hocks. Chop bacon. Return all to the liquid that the hocks were cooked in. Add parsley, tomatoes, tomato paste, bay leaves, okra and salt and pepper to taste. Place on low boil for 30 minutes. Add shrimp and crab and boil 15 additional minutes. Add file' and cook until slightly thickened. Serve over rice.

Note: This is better on the second day.

Soups

Vichysquash

6 medium yellow squash, sliced
1 medium onion, peeled and sliced
Butter or margarine
½ cup chicken broth
Salt and pepper to taste
1 cup milk or light cream
Chives, chopped

Saute' the onion in butter in a large pan. When it is wilted, add the squash and the broth. Cover and cook briskly until it is tender, about 15 minutes. Cool in the refrigerator if in a hurry. Pureé the squash with the cooking liquid in a blender. Season with salt and pepper. When soup is cold, add the milk. Serve very cold, garnished with chives.

Lentil Soup

1 pound lentils, washed
¼ cup salad oil
3 cups cooked ham, diced
½ pound Polish sausage, cut in 1 inch slices
2 large onions, chopped
1 clove garlic, minced
2 cups celery, chopped
1 large tomato, cut in quarters
1 teaspoon Tabasco sauce
3 quarts water
1½ teaspoons salt
10 ounces chopped spinach, thawed
Wine to taste (optional)

In large kettle, heat oil. Add ham, sausage, onion and garlic. Cook 5 minutes. Add celery, tomato, lentils, Tabasco sauce, water and salt. Cover and cook over low heat 2 hours. Add spinach for last 10 minutes. Should be thick when done.

Note: Red or white wine may be added for additional flavor. Serve with French bread and a salad for a delicious meal.

Village Strawberry Soup

10 ounces frozen strawberries with juice
10 ounces sour cream
3 ounces lime juice
2 teaspoons salt
6 ounces confectioners' sugar
3 ounces grenadine
4 ounces light cream
Garnish: Fresh strawberries

Mix all ingredients together on low speed in blender until all are thoroughly combined and sour cream is dissolved. Chill and serve garnished with fresh strawberries. If not tart enough, add lime juice to taste. Serves 4 to 6.

Sunny Day Soup

6 whole oranges
2 bananas
8½ ounces canned crushed pineapple
1 small bottle of cherries
½ cup sugar
2 ounces coconut

Peel, seed and section oranges. Put oranges in blender or food processor. Add bananas, pineapple with juice and cherries. Stir in sugar. Process. Top with coconut. Serve in chilled glasses. Serves 8 to 10.

Soups

Oyster Bisque

1 quart oysters with liquid
1 cup celery, minced
¼ cup shallots, minced
8 tablespoons butter
4 cups milk, divided
2 cups heavy cream
4 egg yolks
Salt and white pepper to taste
Paprika to taste

In a kettle cook celery with shallots in butter over moderately low heat, stirring for 10 minutes. Stir in 3 cups milk and heavy cream with the strained liquid from the oysters. Bring mixture to a simmer. In a bowl beat egg yolks lightly and add 1 cup of the milk mixture in a stream, whisking. Whisk the yolk mixture into the milk mixture, add the oysters and salt and pepper to taste. Simmer the bisque, stirring, until it is slightly thickened and the edges of the oysters have curled. Do not let the bisque boil. Transfer to a tureen and sprinkle with paprika. Serves 8.

Soupe au Corail

3 cucumbers
1 small onion or less, sliced
1 cup tomato juice
1 tablespoon tomato paste
1 cup strong chicken stock
1 quart dairy sour cream
4 tablespoons dry sherry
Salt to taste
Pepper, freshly ground to taste
Basil leaves for garnish

Peel and slice cucumbers, remove seeds and place slices in the container of an electric blender or food processor. Add sliced onions, tomato juice and tomato paste and process until puréed. Add the chicken stock, sour cream and sherry and blend until smooth. Season with salt and pepper and refrigerate for several hours. Ladle into individual bowls. Garnish each with a fresh basil leaf. Serves 4 to 6.

If soups, stews or other foods are too salty, add a teaspoon of vinegar and a teaspoon of sugar and reheat.

Vegetables

Linguine with Artichokes

1 large can artichoke hearts, sliced
12 ounces linguine
6 tablespoons olive oil, divided
9 tablespoons butter, divided
1 tablespoon flour
1 cup chicken broth
1 clove garlic, mashed
Salt and pepper to taste
2 teaspoons lemon juice
1 teaspoon parsley
4 ounces canned mushrooms, sliced
3 tablespoons Parmesan cheese, divided
½ cup ham cubes or 4 slices crumbled bacon

In a heavy saucepan, heat 4 tablespoons olive oil over medium low heat. Add 8 tablespoons butter and melt. Add flour. Cook, stirring continuously, for 3 minutes. Stir in chicken broth. Increase heat and cook 1 minute. Add the mashed garlic, salt, pepper, lemon juice, parsley and cook 5 minutes. Add the artichoke hearts, mushroom slices and 2 tablespoons Parmesan cheese. Simmer this mixture while boiling the linguine according to package directions for 10 minutes. Drain linguine and toss with remaining olive oil, butter and Parmesan cheese. Pour sauce over linguine and sprinkle with ham or bacon. Serves 6.

Artichoke Spinach Casserole

15 ounces canned artichoke hearts
15 ounces canned spinach, drained
1 medium onion, chopped
1 stick butter or margarine
1 cup sour cream
Parmesan cheese

Preheat oven to 375 degrees. Saute' onion in margarine. Cut artichoke hearts in quarters and mix with onions. Place mixture in 1½ quart casserole dish. Mix drained spinach with sour cream and spread over artichoke mixture. Cover with Parmesan cheese. Bake until hot and bubbly. Serves 4.

Note: For a different taste, 8 ounces cream cheese can be substituted for sour cream and topped with croutons.

Vegetables

The Infamous Red Beans and Rice Annual Bazaar

16 ounces red kidney beans
3 large green peppers, chopped
3 large onions, chopped
2 cloves garlic, crushed
1 cup celery leaves, chopped
3 tablespoons butter
2 tablespoons salt, divided
2 pounds Italian sausage, hot or mild
Ham hock, whole
2 level teaspoons thyme
2 level teaspoons oregano
1 level teaspoon bay laurel leaves, chopped
2 tablespoons Worcestershire sauce
8 healthy dashes Tabasco sauce
4 cups water
6 cups rice, cooked

Soak beans in enough water to have an extra inch above them for 3 hours before cooking. Saute' the peppers, onion, garlic and celery leaves in butter for 3 minutes. Add 1 tablespoon salt. Add to beans. Slice sausage in 1 inch slices and add to beans. Add ham hock, spices, thyme, oregano, bay laurel, Worcestershire sauce and Tabasco sauce and 1 tablespoon salt. Add 4 cups water. Cook in cast iron Dutch pot over low heat for 7 to 8 hours. Serve over rice. Serves 10 to 12.

Note: This takes all day to prepare.

French Style Green Bean Casserole

10 ounces frozen French style string beans
¼ teaspoon salt
¼ cup scallions
4 ounces Swiss cheese
4 ounces canned mushrooms, sliced
½ cup sour cream

Slightly cook beans in boiling water with salt according to package directions. Drain beans. Set aside. Chop scallions into small pieces. Cut Swiss cheese into small pieces. Put all ingredients together and add sour cream. Mix well. Place in 350 degree oven until mixture bubbles. Serve immediately. Serves 4.

Calico Beans

½ pound ground round
½ pound bacon, diced
1 large onion, chopped
½ cup catsup
2 teaspoons salt
2 teaspoons prepared mustard
¼ cup barbeque sauce
4 teaspoons cider or white vinegar
¾ cup firmly packed light brown sugar
30 ounces pork and beans
15 ounces garbanzo beans
15 ounces kidney beans
10 ounce package frozen lima beans, thawed

Preheat oven to 350 degrees. Cook beef, bacon and onion in large skillet until meat loses color and onions are tender. Drain only if there is excessive fat. Stir in catsup, salt, mustard and vinegar. Combine remaining ingredients in a 3 quart casserole. Stir in meat mixture; cover. Bake at 350 degrees for 40 minutes or until bubbly.

Note: For variation substitute 1 cup green beans for one of the other beans.

Dill Beans

32 ounces French green beans
3 tablespoons bacon drippings
2 teaspoons dill seed
6 tablespoons flour
6 tablespoons butter
1½ cups milk
3 tablespoons onion, grated
1 teaspoon black pepper
2½ teaspoons Accent
Bread crumbs, buttered

Preheat oven to 350 degrees. Allow 3 hours for beans and dill seed to soak. Cook the beans, bacon drippings and dill seed; let come to boil and then turn down to simmer for 45 minutes. Turn off and let soak for 3 hours. Save 1 cup of the bean juice and drain the rest. Make sauce in a separate pan by combining the cup of bean juice, flour, butter, milk, onion, pepper and accent. Stir over medium heat until thick. Alternate two layers of beans and sauce in a medium casserole dish. Top with buttered bread crumbs. Cook for 30 minutes. Do not cover.

Vegetables

Creole Beans

32 ounces canned whole green beans or cooked fresh beans
Bits of ham or bacon
1 large onion, sliced
1 cup mayonnaise
2 hard-boiled eggs, chopped
1 heaping tablespoon horseradish
1 teaspoon Worcestershire sauce
Garlic salt to taste
1 lemon, juiced

Cook beans with meat and onion for 30 minutes for canned beans or until done for fresh beans. Blend other ingredients. Add to drained beans and serve hot or cold.

Sweet and Sour Green Beans

1 pound fresh green beans, cooked or 1 can green beans
2 strips of bacon
1 large onion, chopped
1 tablespoon flour
½ cup bean liquid
¼ cup vinegar
2 tablespoons sugar
1 teaspoon salt
½ teaspoon pepper

Brown bacon until crisp, remove from pan. Saute' onion in bacon drippings. Stir in flour. Add liquids, seasoning and beans; bring to a boil. Add crumbled bacon before serving. Serves 4 to 6.

Note: For best flavor, combine beans with sauce at least 1 hour before serving.

Broccoli Puff

10 ounces frozen broccoli cuts
1 can cream of mushroom soup
2 ounces sharp cheese
¼ cup milk
¼ cup mayonnaise or salad dressing
1 egg, beaten
¼ cup fine dry bread crumbs
1 ounce butter or margarine, melted

Preheat oven to 350 degrees. Cook broccoli according to directions, omitting salt. Drain thoroughly. Place broccoli in a 10 X 6 X 1½ inch baking dish. Stir together soup and shredded cheese. Gradually add milk, mayonnaise and beaten egg to soup mixture, stirring until well blended. Pour over broccoli, combine bread crumbs and margarine. Sprinkle evenly over soup mixture. Bake for 45 minutes until crumbs are lightly brown. Serves 6.

Greek Broccoli

20 ounces frozen broccoli spears, cooked
1/3 cup butter
1 clove garlic, crushed
2 teaspoons lemon juice, freshly squeezed
Dash black pepper
6 large stuffed olives, sliced
Dash seasoned salt

Heat butter and garlic over low heat in saucepan until butter melts. Add lemon juice, pepper and olives. Heat thoroughly, but do not boil. Cook broccoli according to package directions. Drain and arrange in heated serving dish. Sprinkle lightly with seasoned salt, then pour sauce over all. Serves 6 to 8.

Vegetables

Shredded Cabbage Au Gratin

6 slices bacon
6 cups cabbage
1¼ ounce Cheese Sauce Mix
¾ cup milk
¼ cup dairy sour cream

Shred cabbage. Cook bacon until crisp in a large skillet, saving 2 tablespoons of drippings. Remove bacon from pan and crumble. Add cabbage, contents of cheese sauce envelope and milk to drippings in pan. Bring to a boil. Cook uncovered 5 to 10 minutes, stirring occasionally, just until tender. Stir in sour cream and crumbled bacon. Continue cooking just until hot. Serves 6.

Red Cabbage

4 medium apples
1 large head red cabbage
Salt
1½ cups sugar
2/3 cup wine vinegar
2 whole cloves
8 pieces bacon, cut in tiny strips and fried

Peel and cut apples into quarters. Place in bottom of pot. Shred red cabbage and place in pot. Add salt, sugar, wine vinegar, cloves, bacon and a little of the bacon fat. Cover pot and cook over very low heat, no water, for 2 to 3 hours or until cabbage is done. Serves 6 to 8.

Note: Sugar and vinegar can be increased or decreased to taste depending on the flavor of the apples and cabbage.

Caponata

3 stalks celery, coarsely chopped
1 green pepper, coarsely chopped
1 onion, coarsely chopped
¼ cup oil
1 eggplant, unpeeled and cut into 1 inch cubes
14 ounce can tomatoes, cut up, or 1 pound fresh; peeled, seeded and diced
4 ounces ripe olives, sliced
1 to 2 tablespoons tomato paste
Package of sliced almonds
3 tablespoons wine vinegar
1 tablespoon salt
1 tablespoon sugar
1 tablespoon basil
Dash of pepper

Simmer celery, green pepper and onion in oil until soft. Using a wooden spoon add eggplant, tomatoes, olives, almonds, vinegar, salt, sugar, basil and pepper and stir to combine. Cover and simmer 30 to 40 minutes, stirring occasionally. Stir in tomato paste during last five minutes of cooking.

Note: A cast iron pot gives this an "old world" flavor. Serve this hot, cold or room temperature. Serving ideas; with French bread as an antipasto or hors d'oeuvres at a cocktail party; with greens as a salad; layered with Parmesan and Mozzarella cheese and baked as a super Eggplant Parmesan; fold into an omelet topped with Parmesan cheese; and best, a great low-calorie snack on a cracker. This can be kept in the refrigerator for 2 to 3 weeks.

Carrot Souffle'

1 pound carrots, sliced
Salt
½ cup butter, melted
1 cup sugar
3 tablespoons flour
1 teaspoon baking powder
1 teaspoon vanilla
3 eggs

Cook the carrots until tender in salted water. Drain. Add the butter and mash the mixture. (It is easiest to mash in a blender or processor.) Mix together the sugar, flour, baking powder, vanilla and eggs. Add to the carrots and blend well. Pour into a greased 1 quart casserole and bake at 350 degrees for 45 minutes. Serves 4 to 6.

Note: This recipe may be doubled but cooking time must be increased.

Vegetables

Carrots Cosmopolitan

4 bunches carrots, thinly sliced
1 cup butter
1½ teaspoons sugar
1 teaspoon salt
1/3 cup cognac

In an oblong baking dish, while oven is preheating to 350 degrees, melt butter, sugar and salt. Add carrots and cognac. Cover and bake 45 to 50 minutes or until tender but not brown. Serves 12.

Note: Easy with roast beef — everything can cook at once in the same oven.

Carrot Casserole

2 jars carrots
2 tablespoons carrot juice
1 cup mayonnaise
¼ to ½ bag Pepperidge Farm stuffing
1 heaping tablespoon cream style horseradish
1 heaping tablespoon onion, minced

Preheat oven to 350 degrees. Mix all ingredients except stuffing and put in buttered casserole. Cover carrot mixture with dry stuffing. Cook until bubbly, about 20 minutes. Serves 4.

Carrots A La Down Under

½ pound carrots, cleaned, sliced
6 slices bacon
1 tablespoon butter
½ teaspoon seasoned salt
Dash of pepper
½ teaspoon sugar

Boil prepared carrots in small amount of unseasoned water until tender. Fry bacon until crisp. Just before serving, drain carrots, add butter, salt, pepper, sugar and crumbled bacon. Toss together. Serve immediately. Serves 2 to 4.

Crunchy Celery Casserole

4 cups celery, sliced
4 ounces water chestnuts, sliced and drained
½ teaspoon basil
1 can cream of celery soup
¼ cup pimientos, chopped
½ cup herb seasoned stuffing
1/3 cup slivered almonds, toasted
2 tablespoons margarine, melted

Preheat oven to 350 degrees. Cook celery in salted water until tender but crisp, about 8 minutes. Drain. Combine celery with chestnuts, basil, soup and pimientos. Spoon into lightly greased 2 quart casserole. Combine stuffing, almonds and butter; sprinkle over celery mixture. Bake for 35 minutes. Serves 6 to 8.

Zellwood Corn — To Freeze

3 dozen ears of corn
2 sticks butter
1 pint coffee cream or half and half
Salt and pepper

Wash and shuck corn, cut off cob and scrape out the milk. Put all above in a double boiler and heat through — DON'T BOIL. Let cool. Freeze in serving size portions.

To eat put frozen corn in top of double boiler and cook about 10 to 15 minutes.

You can take frozen corn out of container once frozen solid and put in baggies — air tight — and use containers for more.

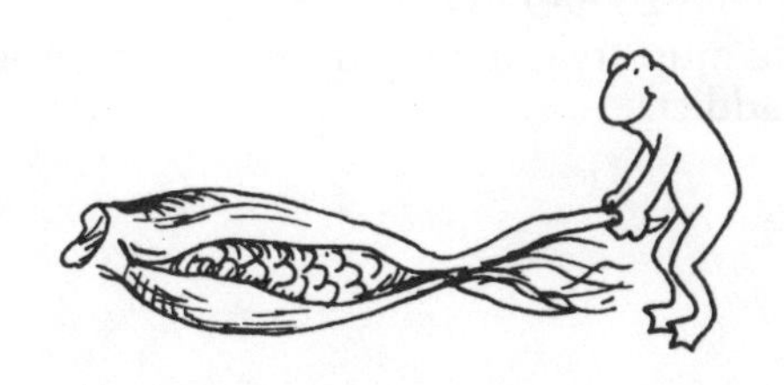

Vegetables

Eggplant Casserole

1 small eggplant
½ pound bulk sausage
1 small onion, chopped
1 egg, well beaten
½ cup dry bread crumbs
1 tablespoon butter, melted
¼ cup cracker crumbs

Preheat oven to 350 degrees. Peel eggplant and cut into 1 inch cubes; cook in a small amount of boiling water 10 minutes or until tender. Drain. Let cool slightly. Cook sausage and onion until onion is tender and sausage is brown. Combine eggplant, sausage mixture, egg and bread crumbs. Mix well and spoon into a greased 1 quart casserole. Combine butter and cracker crumbs; sprinkle over casserole. Bake for 25 minutes. Serves 4.

Note: Can be frozen.

Colelieu

1 hambone with about 1 pound ham on it (or bacon)
1 bunch turnips, bottoms peeled and cut in segments
1 bunch each greens of collards, mustard, turnips (or any mixture)
3 pounds potatoes, peeled and segmented
2 pounds onions, peeled and segmented
1 pound black eyed peas
1 pound navy beans
Spices to taste (vinegar, garlic, pepper)

Cook the hambone, collards, mustard, turnips, potatoes and onions together about 30 minutes. Separately, soak overnight the black eyed peas and the navy beans and then cook them. After cooking the peas and beans, add them to the rest of the mixture and cook an hour longer. Add any spices that your family enjoys.

Note: One must try tasting and eating this three times before becoming a Colelieu addict.

Fabulous Mushroom Casserole

1 pound fresh whole mushroom caps
½ stick butter
2 beef bouillon cubes
½ cup hot water
2 tablespoons flour
½ cup cream
⅛ teaspoon salt
Dash of pepper
¼ to ½ cup bread crumbs
½ to 1 cup grated Parmesan cheese

Preheat oven to 350 degrees. Saute' mushrooms in butter, reserve liquid. Dissolve beef cubes in water. Blend flour into butter liquid. Add cream, salt, pepper and beef broth. Combine all. Top with cheese and bread crumb mixture. Bake in buttered casserole for 30 minutes. Serves 4.

Note: This is good with beef or a roast.

Mushrooms Florentine

1 pound fresh mushrooms
1½ pounds fresh spinach or
 2 boxes frozen leaf spinach
3 tablespoons butter, melted
Garlic salt
¼ cup onion, chopped
¼ cup butter, melted
½ cup Colby cheese, grated
½ cup Swiss cheese, grated

Preheat oven to 350 degrees. Wash and dry mushrooms and spinach. Slice and saute' mushrooms in butter, season with garlic salt to taste. Cook spinach in boiling water 15 minutes. Drain and squeeze all moisture out by handfulls. Line a casserole dish with spinach which has been seasoned with garlic salt, onion and butter. Sprinkle with ½ of the Colby and Swiss cheese mixture. Place the sautéed mushrooms over the spinach and cheese. Cover with remaining cheese and bake for 20 minutes.

Stuffed Mushrooms

1 pound fresh mushrooms
2 tablespoons butter
¼ cup onion, finely chopped
½ teaspoon celery salt
¼ teaspoon pepper
1 tablespoon parsley, chopped
½ cup fine bread crumbs
½ to 1 cup chopped meat
(turkey, ham, chicken, etc.)
½ cup herbed cheese
1 to 2 tablespoons white wine

Preheat oven to 325 degrees. Clean mushrooms, remove and chop stems. Saute' tops quickly (do not let brown). Saute' stems and all other ingredients until thick and well blended. Put mixture in mushroom caps. Top with melted butter just before heating. Warm 10 to 15 minutes or use a microwave oven for warming.

Fabulous Noodle Kugel

8 ounces Pennsylvania Dutch
medium or broad egg noodles
3 eggs
½ cup sugar
1 cup sour cream
¾ cup milk
½ cup seedless raisins
2 tablespoons butter, melted
1 cup cottage cheese
1 teaspoon vanilla extract

Preheat oven to 350 degrees. Cook noodles according to package directions. Drain. In a large bowl beat eggs and sugar; blend in sour cream, cottage cheese, milk, raisins, butter and vanilla. Add noodles and mix thoroughly. Turn into greased 2 quart baking dish and sprinkle, if desired, with cinnamon or crushed cornflakes. Bake 1 hour or until golden brown. Serve hot or cold topped with additional sour cream. Serves 6 to 8.

Note: May be frozen.

To reheat cooked pasta or rice, place it in a strainer over a pan of boiling water. Cover and steam 10 to 15 minutes.

Vidalia Onion Supreme

1 pie crust, baked
3 cups Vidalia onions, thinly sliced
3 tablespoons butter, melted
½ cup milk
1½ cups sour cream
1 teaspoon salt
2 eggs, well beaten
3 tablespoons flour
Bacon slices, fried crisp and crumbled (6 to 8 slices)

Preheat oven to 325 degrees. Brown onion lightly in butter; spoon into pastry shell. In bowl mix milk, sour cream and flour (mix flour with small amount of the sour cream for a better blend). Combine with eggs and pour mixture over onions. Bake in a slow oven for 30 minutes or until firm in center. Garnish with crisp fried bacon. Serves 4 to 6.

Note: Parsley flakes may be sprinkled on top before baking.

Onion Cauliflower Bake

10 ounces frozen cauliflower, thawed
20 ounces frozen onions in cream sauce
¾ cup sharp process American cheese, shredded
¼ cup slivered almonds, toasted
1 tablespoon parsley, snipped
½ cup canned French fried onion rings

Preheat oven to 350 degrees. Cut cauliflower into bite-size pieces. Prepare creamed onions according to package directions. Add cauliflower, shredded cheese, almonds and parsley. Turn into buttered 1½ quart casserole. Bake uncovered for 35 minutes. Top with French fried onion rings and bake 5 minutes more. Serves 8.

Note: Great with roast beef dinner.

When you need a few drops of onion juice for flavor, sprinkle a little salt on a slice of onion; scrape with a knife.

Vegetables

Onion Casserole

6 to 8 medium onions, thinly sliced
3¾ ounce bag potato chips, crushed
½ pound milk Cheddar cheese, grated
2 cans cream of mushroom soup
½ cup milk
⅛ teaspoon cayenne pepper

Preheat oven to 350 degrees. In a buttered 9X13 inch casserole, place alternate layers of onions, crushed potato chips and grated cheese. Mix soup with milk and pour the mixture over the casserole. Sprinkle with cayenne. Bake for 1 hour.

Note: This is a good accompaniment with steak.

Baked Pineapple Casserole

64 ounces pineapple chunks, drained
2 cups sugar
1 cup flour
1 teaspoon cinnamon
1½ cups Cheddar cheese, grated, divided (optional)
½ cup butter
1 packaged roll Ritz crackers, crushed

Preheat oven to 375 degrees. Mix the sugar, flour and cinnamon. Add the pineapple and ¾ cup of cheese, coating it well. Pour into a buttered 9X13 inch pan. Pour the remaining cheese on top of the casserole. Mix the butter with the crackers; cover the top of the casserole. Bake 45 minutes. Serves 10 to 12.

Note: This can be used in place of potatoes and can be prepared ahead of time but can not be frozen.

Pineapple Marshmallow Sweet Potatoes

6 sweet potatoes, baked, or
2 large cans, drained and mashed
1 cup crushed pineapple, undrained
3 to 4 tablespoons butter
1 teaspoon cinnamon
½ cup milk
Marshmallows

Thoroughly mix all the ingredients except marshmallows and beat until light and fluffy. Use more milk or fruit juice if needed. Place in buttered casserole and bake until heated through. Remove from oven and cover top with marshmallows. Run under the broiler, but watch closely, as it only takes seconds to brown. Serves 6 to 8.

Sweet Potato Casserole

3 cups sweet potatoes, mashed
1 cup sugar
½ teaspoon salt
¼ cup sherry
2 eggs
1/3 cup margarine, melted
1 teaspoon vanilla

Topping:
1 cup brown sugar
1/3 cup flour
Dash cinnamon
1/3 cup margarine, melted
1 cup pecans, chopped

Preheat oven to 375 degrees. Mix sweet potatoes, sugar, salt, sherry, eggs, margarine and vanilla. Put in 2 quart casserole dish. Mix topping together and spread over potatoes. Cook for 45 minutes. Serves 6 to 8.

Sweet Potato Boats

6 medium sweet potatoes
Vegetable oil
¼ cup molasses
¼ cup butter, melted
⅛ teaspoon nutmeg
¼ teaspoon cinnamon
¼ teaspoon salt
½ cup whipping cream
Orange peel, cut into long slices and curled

Preheat oven to 400 degrees. Wash potatoes well; rub with oil. Place on baking sheet and bake for 1 hour. Cool potatoes to touch. Slice skin away from top of each potato and carefully scoop out potato leaving shells intact. Combine potato pulp, molasses, butter, nutmeg, cinnamon, salt and whipping cream. Beat until fluffy and spoon mixture back into shells. Bake at 450 degrees 10 to 12 minutes. Garnish with curled orange peel. Serves 6.

Crab Stuffed Potatoes

5 medium Idaho potatoes
1 cup fresh crab meat or 6½ ounces canned crab meat
8 ounces butter
½ cup light cream
1 teaspoon salt
4 teaspoons onion, grated
2 cups Cheddar cheese, grated
½ teaspoon paprika
¼ teaspoon white pepper

Bake potatoes until tender. Cut lengthwise and scoop out pulp. Whip together potatoes, butter, cream, salt, pepper, onion and cheese. Add a little more cream if necessary. With a fork mix in crab meat and refill four halved shells. (The extra potato is to ensure plenty of stuffing.) Sprinkle with paprika and reheat in a 400 degree oven for about 15 minutes. Serves 8.

Note: Freezes well.

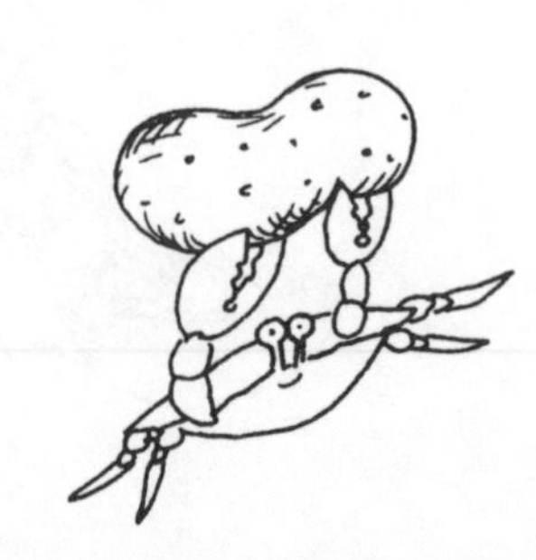

Meals in a Peel

A great way to use baked potatoes as a hearty main dish. Here are two recipes to start. Your imagination will bring you other delicious meals!

Serve one potato per person. Scrub the potatoes and pat dry. Wipe them with a small amount of cooking oil and prick them several times with a fork. Bake in a preheated 450 degree oven for 1 hour. Remove from the oven, split open and fluff the insides with a fork. Add topping and serve.

Mushroom topping:

1 pound mushrooms, washed and sliced
6 tablespoons butter, divided
½ cup cooked ham, diced
½ cup scallions, sliced
½ tablespoon seasoned salt
¼ teaspoon tarragon
¼ teaspoon marjoram
¼ teaspoon chives
1 cup chicken stock
2 tablespoons corn starch
¼ cup water
Sour cream

Saute' mushrooms in 4 tablespoons butter until tender. Remove from skillet and set aside. In the same skillet add 2 tablespoons butter and saute' ham, scallions, seasoned salt, tarragon, marjoram and chives for 2 minutes. Add chicken stock and simmer 3 minutes. Mix together corn starch and water and add mushrooms and simmer 1 minute longer. Garnish potato with mushroom topping and 1 heaping tablespoon sour cream.

Chicken topping:

4 chicken breasts, fileted and cubed
1 small onion, chopped
1 cup celery, chopped
3 tablespoons butter
1 can cream of celery soup
¼ cup mayonnaise
¾ cup buttermilk
Paprika

Saute' onion and celery in butter until tender. Add chicken and saute' for 2 minutes. Set aside. In a bowl, mix soup, mayonnaise and buttermilk. Add chicken to mixture and transfer to a casserole dish. Bake at 350 degrees for 30 minutes. Remove from oven and let set for 5 to 10 minutes. Serve over prepared potato. Sprinkle with paprika.

Vegetables

Twice Baked Potatoes

4 good shaped baking potatoes
¼ cup butter
1 cup cottage cheese
2 tablespoons mayonnaise
Salt and pepper to taste
2 tablespoons chives, optional
1 cup Cheddar cheese, grated
Paprika

Preheat oven for baking potatoes. After potatoes are cooled enough to handle, cut a hole in the top and scoop out potato. Mix with butter, cottage cheese, mayonnaise, salt and pepper and chives. Put mixture back into potato shells. There will be enough to mound up on top. Top with grated cheese and sprinkle with paprika. Bake at 450 degrees to heat through. Can be done hours or even a day or so ahead.

Potato Supreme

6 to 8 medium potatoes
½ teaspoon salt
¼ cup butter, melted
2 cups Cheddar cheese, shredded
1/3 cup onion, chopped
8 ounces sour cream
¼ teaspoon pepper

Cook potatoes in a small amount of salted water. Drain, peel and refrigerate overnight in a covered saucepan or bowl. (DO NOT DICE OR CUT POTATOES BEFORE COOKING.) The next day grate potatoes coarsely. Mix with salt, butter, cheese, onion, sour cream and pepper. Put in a casserole or baking dish. Bake 35 to 45 minutes at 350 degrees. Serves 6.

Note: For variation add bell pepper.

Italian Baked Potatoes

3 to 4 Idaho baking potatoes, unpeeled
8 tablespoons butter
1 package dry Good Seasons Italian salad dressing mix

Preheat oven to 350 degrees. Cut potatoes in half lengthwise. Then in 4 to 6 lengthwise slices. Melt butter in a glass baking dish. Place potato slices in bottom of dish and roll in butter making sure all slices have butter on them. Sprinkle Italian dressing mix on potatoes. Bake about 45 minutes or until potatoes are done and golden brown. Serves 6 to 8.

Optional: Can sprinkle with ½ cup Parmesan cheese before baking.

Scalloped Potatoes

5 to 7 medium size potatoes, sliced and cooked
4 or 5 slices bacon, cooked crisp
1 large onion, sliced
½ pound Velveeta cheese, cubed
1 stick butter, chopped
Salt and pepper to taste

Mix all ingredients together in casserole. Bake at 350 degrees for 1 hour. Stir once or so. Serves 8.

Note: Green olives can be added for a different taste.

Delicious Swiss Cheese Potatoes

6 large baking potatoes
¼ pound butter, melted
½ teaspoon salt
Pepper, freshly ground
½ cup heavy cream
¾ cup Swiss cheese, coarsely shredded

Preheat oven to 375 degrees. Cut slice off top of each baked, cooled potato and scoop out pulp. Do not mash, but break up coarsely in a bowl. Add melted butter, salt and pepper. Turn into a 9 inch glass pie pan, pour cream over and let stand for 30 minutes. Sprinkle top evenly with cheese. Bake for 20 minutes or until the cheese is melted and crusty. Serves 6.

Note: The potatoes may be baked earlier in the day if desired. This does not freeze well. Also, more butter may be used.

Pasta Primavera

8 tablespoons unsalted butter
1 medium onion, finely chopped
2 large cloves of garlic, pressed
1 pound thin asparagus, tough ends trimmed, cut diagonally into ¼ inch slices, tips left intact
6 ounces cauliflower, broken into small florets
1 medium zucchini, cut into ¼ inch rounds
1 small carrot, halved lengthwise and cut into ⅛ inch slices
½ pound mushrooms, thinly sliced
1 cup half and half or whipping cream
½ cup chicken stock
2 tablespoons fresh basil, chopped or 2 teaspoons dried
1 cup frozen tiny peas, thawed
5 ounces ham, chopped
5 green onions, chopped
1 pound spaghetti or linguine, cooked and drained
1 cup freshly grated Parmesan cheese
1 pound shrimp, cooked and shelled (optional for variation)

Heat wok or skillet. Add butter and saute' onion about 2 minutes. Add garlic, asparagus, cauliflower, zucchini and carrot and stir fry 2 minutes. Add mushrooms and saute' additional minute. Increase heat to high. Add cream, stock and basil and allow to boil until liquid is slightly reduced, about 3 minutes. Stir in peas, ham and green onion and cook 1 minute more. Season to taste with salt and pepper. Add pasta and cheese, tossing until thoroughly combined. Turn into large serving platter. May garnish with wedges of tomatoes.Serve immediately. 6 to 8 main course servings.12 side dish servings.

Wild Rice and Spinach Casserole

6 ounce package long grain and wild rice
4 ounce can sliced mushrooms, drained
2 teaspoons prepared mustard
½ teaspoon salt
10 ounces frozen chopped spinach
2¼ cups water
¾ cup onion, chopped
1 tablespoon butter
8 ounces cream cheese, cubed

Preheat oven to 375 degrees. Place rice mix, mushrooms, mustard and salt in casserole dish. In saucepan, combine spinach, water, onion and butter. Bring to a boil. Pour over rice mixture. Cover and bake for 30 minutes. Uncover. Stir in cheese and bake for 10 to 15 minutes more.

Florida Rice

1 cup Uncle Ben's Converted Rice (long grain)
2 cups water
3 to 4 tablespoons orange juice concentrate
1 teaspoon salt
1 tablespoon butter
3 tablespoons golden raisins
2 tablespoons slivered almonds (optional)

Bring 2 cups water to a boil; stir in 1 cup rice, salt, butter, orange juice concentrate, raisins and almonds. Cover tightly and simmer 20 minutes. Remove from heat; let stand covered until all water is absorbed. If not enough orange, you may stir in more concentrate after rice is cooked.

Note: This is delicious with poultry!

Bake rice instead of cooking it on top of the stove when baking a roast or chicken, etc. in the oven. Use same ingredients suggested on package, place in casserole, cover and bake for 1 hour. Stir once. This not only saves energy, but the rice never sticks and it reheats beautifully.

Vegetables

Fried Rice

3 cups rice, cooked
  (1½ cups uncooked)
1 onion, chopped
½ cup oil
3 eggs
Dash soy sauce
Green onion tops, chopped
½ cup lettuce, shredded
1 tomato, cut into small pieces

Saute' onion in oil. Add eggs and scramble; add rice. Mix together about 5 minutes. Add soy sauce, green onions, lettuce and tomato. Toss until hot. Serves 4.

Green Rice

2 cups raw rice
2 cups milk
2/3 cup Crisco oil
Dash of salt
2 cups sharp Cheddar cheese,
  grated
2 green peppers, chopped
3 medium yellow onions, chopped
1 clove garlic, mashed
1 cup fresh parsley, chopped
2 eggs, beaten

Cook rice according to directions. Add all other ingredients. Pour into covered casserole. Bake at 325 degrees for 45 minutes. Serves 10.

Cheesy Rice

1 cup rice, uncooked
15 ounces tomatoes
½ cup sharp cheese, shredded
¼ cup olive oil
1 onion, cut in rings
1 cup water
1 small jar green or black olives,
  pitted and chopped

Mix all ingredients and place in a 10 inch pan. Cook at 350 degrees for 45 minutes covered, remove cover and bake an additional 45 minutes. Serves 4.

Note: This is good with turkey, chicken or pheasant.

Soubise

2/3 cup rice
1½ teaspoons salt
4 quarts rapidly boiling water
6 tablespoons butter, divided
2 pounds yellow onions, thinly sliced
Salt and pepper to taste
¼ cup whipping cream
¼ cup Swiss cheese, grated
1 tablespoon parsley, finely chopped

Preheat oven to 300 degrees. Drop rice into rapidly boiling water with salt and boil for exactly 6 minutes. Drain immediately. Melt 4 tablespoons of butter in a heavy 3 quart ovenproof casserole. When butter is foaming over medium heat, stir in the onions. Toss until well coated with butter and stir in the rice. Cover and bake for 1 hour or more, stirring occasionally. Rice and onions should be very tender and light golden yellow. Salt and pepper to taste. Just before serving, stir in the cream, cheese and 2 tablespoons softened butter. Correct the seasonings. Serve in a hot vegetable dish and sprinkle with parsley. Serves 4.

Note: This recipe can be prepared in advance to the point of adding the cream, cheese and butter.

Brown Rice and Barley

1/3 cup brown rice
1/3 cup hulled barley
1/3 cup bulgar
2 chicken or beef bouillon cubes or 2 tablespoons instant bouillon
2 tablespoons instant onion
2 tablespoons parsley, fresh or dried
4 ounces canned mushrooms

Soak bulgar in 3 to 4 tablespoons of water for 30 minutes. Bring 2 cups water to a boil. Add bouillon, onion, parsley, mushrooms and any other spice or vegetable you wish to try. Add the 3 grains. Reduce heat; cover and simmer for 1 hour. Add a pat of butter before serving. Serves 6 to 8.

Note: This makes a tasty healthy change from plain old white rice. The grain ingredients are available at a health food store. This recipe can not be prepared ahead.

Vegetables

Spicy Rice

1 cup rice, uncooked
2 tablespoons butter or margarine
2/3 cup onion, coarsely chopped
¾ cup celery, sliced
1½ teaspoons salt
¼ teaspoon black pepper
2 cups apple juice
¼ teaspoon ground cinnamon
⅛ teaspoon ground allspice
1 tablespoon brown sugar
½ cup raisins
1/3 cup nut meats, chopped, optional

Melt butter in a 2 or 3 quart saucepan. Add onion and celery. Cook until tender crisp. Add remaining ingredients except nuts. Bring to a boil; stir once or twice. Reduce heat, cover and simmer 20 to 25 minutes or until rice is tender and liquid is absorbed. Remove from heat and fluff with a fork. Replace cover and let stand 5 to 10 minutes. Add nuts before serving. Serves 6.

Wild Rice

8 ounces wild rice, cooked according to directions
¼ pound butter
½ cup onion, chopped
½ cup green onions, chopped
3 cloves garlic, crushed
4 ounces canned mushrooms, chopped (reserve liquid)
½ cup water
2 teaspoons chicken stock
½ cup celery, chopped
2 teaspoons Worcestershire sauce
2 dashes Tabasco sauce
Salt to taste
½ pound bacon, fried crisp

Melt butter in skillet and saute' onions, green onions, garlic and mushrooms. Add chicken stock and celery to water in small saucepan and bring to a boil. Combine with onion mixture, then add mushroom liquid, Worcestershire sauce, Tabasco sauce and salt to taste. Sauce may be made in advance to this point and reheated. Just before serving add bacon and pour over warm rice. Serves 8.

Rice with Pine Nuts

4½ cups rice, cooked and hot
½ cup olive oil
1 cup onion, finely chopped
1 teaspoon paprika
¼ teaspoon Tabasco sauce
1 cup pine nuts
1 teaspoon salt
½ teaspoon black pepper, freshly ground
¼ cup parsley, chopped
3 pimientos, chopped

Put olive oil in a medium size saucepan. Saute' onion, pine nuts, paprika and Tabasco sauce for 6 to 8 minutes. Use two forks to toss with hot rice. Season to taste with salt and pepper. Garnish with chopped parsley and chopped pimiento. Serves 6.

Trader Vic's Rice

2 cups long grain rice
2/3 stick butter
4 cups liquid (chicken broth, clam juice or bouillon, depending on entree)
¾ cup carrots, finely chopped
¾ cup parsley, chopped
½ cup onion, finely chopped
½ cup nuts, chopped, optional

Saute' the rice and butter for about 5 minutes to coat. Add the broth. Bake, covered, at 375 degrees for 30 minutes. Add vegetables and nuts. Stir. Cook 30 more minutes. Serves 8.

Note: This may be cooked on top of the stove, in an electric skillet or a large pan.

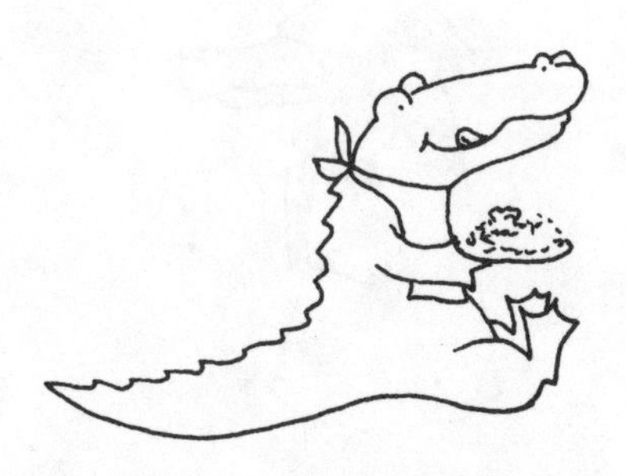

Vegetables

Wild Rice and Sausage Casserole

1 pound mild sausage
1 large onion, chopped
6 ounce box long grain and wild rice mix
2 ounces pimiento
1 small can mushroom pieces, drained
6 ounces water chestnuts, sliced and drained

Saute' sausage with chopped onion. Drain. Prepare rice according to package direction. Mix all ingredients together. Place in an 11¾ X 7½ X 1¾ inch pyrex dish and cook in slow oven until heated through. Serves 8.

Maitland Wild Rice

2 cups cooked wild rice
3 tablespoons green onion, chopped
3 tablespoons bacon, chopped
3 tablespoons slivered almonds, blanched or toasted
3 tablespoons butter

Saute' the green onion, bacon and almonds in butter. When the mixture is hot, add the cooked wild rice and stir until blended with the other ingredients. Serves 4.

Note: This is an excellent accompaniment to beef tenderloin. Use the wild rice as a bed for a butterflied beef tenderloin and serve with mushroom sauce.

Cold Curried Rice

2 cups rice
4 cups chicken stock or broth
1 inch piece of fresh ginger
1 teaspoon curry powder
½ teaspoon turmeric
Salt to taste
Pepper, freshly ground to taste
¼ cup olive oil
Juice of 2 small lemons
½ cup white raisins
½ cup black raisins or currants
1 cup green pepper, chopped
Mayonnaise
Sour cream
Toasted almonds, sliced
½ cup parsley, minced

Cook rice in stock with ginger, curry powder, turmeric, salt and pepper according to directions on the rice package. Toss cooked rice with olive oil and lemon juice and let stand overnight if possible. The morning you plan to serve, toss the rice with raisins, currants, green pepper and enough mayonnaise and sour cream so rice is rich and moist. Taste for seasoning and add pepper and lemon if necesary. Sprinkle almonds and parsley on top. Serves 8 generously.

Note: This is also excellent served hot; omit the lemon juice, mayonnaise, sour cream and green pepper. Especially good with curries.

Old Fashioned Turkey Stuffing

1 loaf whole wheat bread
Water
4 ounces butter
1 medium onion, chopped
3 stalks celery, chopped
1 cup dried apricots
1 cup pecans, chopped
½ pound fresh mushrooms, sliced
1 cup slivered almonds
4 ounce package wild rice, cooked
Salt and pepper to taste

Tear bread and crusts into small pieces. Add enough water to cover bread. Let stand until soft. Squeeze out excess liquid. Melt butter in a large pan over moderate heat. Add onion, celery, apricots, pecans, almonds and mushrooms. Cook over medium heat, stirring frequently until celery and onion are just soft. Add bread and rice to onion mixture. Mix lightly but thoroughly. If necessary, add water to hold mixture together. Add salt and pepper to taste.

Note: Stuffing may also be used for chicken or game hens, as well as a side dish for duck or dove.

Vegetables

Spinach and Spaghetti

10 ounces frozen chopped spinach
1 egg, beaten
½ cup sour cream
¼ cup milk
½ cup grated Parmesan cheese
2 tablespoons minced dried onions
Salt and pepper to taste
2 cups Monterey Jack cheese, shredded
4 ounces spaghetti, cooked and drained

Preheat oven to 350 degrees. Cook spinach according to package directions; drain well. Combine egg, sour cream, milk, 2 tablespoons of the Parmesan cheese, onion and ½ teaspoon salt and pepper. Add Monterey Jack cheese and mix well. Add the drained spinach and spaghetti; mix well. Turn mixture into an ungreased 10 X 6 X 2 inch baking dish. Sprinkle with the remaining 2 tablespoons Parmesan cheese. Bake covered for 15 minutes; uncover and bake 15 to 20 minutes more or until hot. 6 to 8 servings.

Spinach Parmesan

40 ounces frozen chopped spinach
6 tablespoons Parmesan cheese
6 tablespoons onion, minced
6 tablespoons heavy cream
5 tablespoons butter, melted
½ cup Ritz cracker crumbs

Cook spinach according to directions. Drain thoroughly. Add cheese, onion, cream and 4 tablespoons of butter. Arrange in shallow baking dish or a glass pie plate and sprinkle with the crumbs mixed with the remaining butter. Bake at 350 degrees for 10 to 15 minutes. Serves 6 to 8.

Spinach Ring

20 ounces frozen spinach, cooked and drained
6 eggs
½ teaspoon salt
⅛ teaspoon pepper
¼ teaspoon celery salt
¼ teaspoon cayenne, optional
¼ cup Worcestershire sauce
¼ teaspoon onion juice
½ pint whipping cream
6 ounces Monterey Jack cheese with Jalapẽno, shredded
6 ounces Swiss cheese, shredded

In a bowl whip eggs with spices, Worcestershire sauce and onion juice. Add cream and mix well. Stir in cheeses and spinach. Pour into buttered ring mold and bake at 350 degrees for 35 minutes or until inserted knife comes out clean. Let stand 4 minutes and unmold. Serves 6 to 8.

Spinach Malino

30 ounces frozen spinach, cooked and drained
¼ cup flour
¼ cup margarine, melted
3 eggs, beaten
4 slices American cheese, cubed
4 slices natural brick cheese, cubed
12 ounces cottage cheese
Salt and pepper, to taste

Preheat oven to 350 degrees. Blend flour into the margarine. Then add cooked and drained spinach and the remaining ingredients. Put in a 1½ quart greased casserole. Bake for one hour. Serves 8.

Vegetables

Park Avenue Squash

1 to 2 pounds yellow squash
¼ cup green onions, chopped
2 tablespoons butter
Salt and pepper to taste
1 cup sour cream
1 tablespoon flour
Dill, chopped
Paprika

Peel squash, cut in small pieces and cook in microwave until tender, about 6 to 7 minutes. Turn bowl and stir squash several times while cooking. Drain. Saute' onion in butter until tender. Add squash, salt and pepper. Combine sour cream and flour in pan and bring to a boil. Pour over squash. Serve garnished with dill and paprika. Serves 4 to 6.

Baked Squash

6 medium squash, zucchini or summer
1 cup dry bread crumbs, divided
3 tablespoons water
½ cup onion, minced
12 slices bacon
½ cup Cheddar cheese, grated

Wash and cut squash lengthwise. Cover squash with boiling water and cook in covered saucepan until nearly tender, about 5 minutes. Drain well. Roll squash in ¾ cup bread crumbs and place in a greased, oven proof dish to which water has been added. Mix remaining bread crumbs and onions for topping and sprinkle over squash. Place a piece of bacon on each squash and bake in a 375 degree oven for 30 minutes or until bacon is done. Top with cheese and heat until cheese melts. Serves 12.

Note. This can be prepared a day ahead and baked at the last minute.

Butternut Squash Casserole

2 cups butternut squash
3 eggs
¾ stick butter
1 teaspoon ginger
1 cup milk
½ teaspoon nutmeg
1 cup sugar
2 teaspoons coconut

Preheat oven to 350 degrees. Cook squash, mash and drain. Combine ingredients in large bowl and mix well. Bake in a greased casserole which has been set in a pan of water. Bake for 45 minutes to 1 hour or until set. Serves 6 to 8.

Squash Casserole

1½ pounds yellow squash, sliced
1 small onion, sliced
1 stick butter
1 small package Pepperidge Farm Dressing
1 cup sour cream
4 small carrots, grated
1 small can pimientos
1 can cream of chicken soup

Preheat oven to 350 degrees. Cook squash and onion, drain and mash with fork. Melt butter. Add ½ package of stuffing. Add remaining ingredients to squash. Line casserole with stuffing. Fill with squash and sprinkle with remaining stuffing. Cook for 30 minutes. Serves 6 to 8.

Vegetables

Squash Stuffed with Spinach

4 to 5 summer squash
1 package spinach, chopped
6 ounces sour cream
Salt and pepper to taste
1/3 cup bread crumbs, buttered

Preheat oven to 300 degrees. Boil squash until tender. Cool until you can handle with fingers. Split squash and scoop out seeds. Prepare spinach by package directions; then drain spinach well. Mix in sour cream, between 4 to 6 ounces, then add salt and pepper to taste. Top with the buttered bread crumbs. Bake for 20 to 25 minutes or until hot. Serves 6.

Optional: One small onion, chopped, added to spinach.

Tomatoes Rockefeller

15 thick slices tomatoes (5 tomatoes, sliced into thirds)
20 ounces frozen chopped spinach
1¾ cups seasoned bread crumbs
1 cup green onions, chopped
5 eggs, slightly beaten
¾ cup butter, melted
½ cup Parmesan cheese
½ teaspoon garlic powder
1 teaspoon salt
1 teaspoon thyme
Tabasco sauce to taste

Preheat oven to 350 degrees. Arrange tomatoes on greased jelly roll pan. Cook spinach according to package directions, place in colander and squeeze out excess water. Combine remaining ingredients, add spinach and mix well. Mound mixture on tomato slices. Bake for 15 minutes. Serves 15.

Note: This can be prepared several hours ahead and baked at the last minute. Also makes surprisingly good leftovers.

Tomato Pudding

28 ounces canned tomato purée
2½ cups brown sugar
½ teaspoon salt
¾ cup butter or margarine, melted
8 regular slices of fresh white bread, do not remove crust and cut in 1 inch squares

Add sugar and salt to purée and boil 5 minutes. Place bread in casserole, put melted butter over it and mix. Add hot tomato mixture. Bake 30 to 45 minutes at 375 degrees. Serves 8 to 10.

Note: This is good with beef and can be made in the morning and allowed to sit at room temperature during the day.

Gourmet Turnips and Peas

6 small turnips, peeled and thinly sliced
1 tablespoon onion, chopped
2 tablespoons butter, melted
½ teaspoon granulated sugar
½ cup whipping cream
1 cup green peas, cooked and drained
½ teaspoon sherry

Cook and drain the turnips and set aside. Saute' the onion in the butter and add sugar. Add the rest of the ingredients and heat through. Serves 4 to 6.

Note: Even non-turnip lovers like this one!

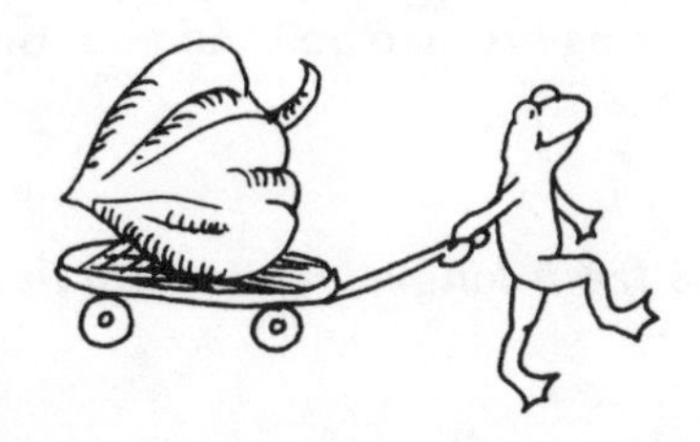

Vegetables

Vegetables Italiano

14 ounces canned artichoke hearts, sliced
6 ounces green olives, sliced
2 small onions, sliced
6 ounces canned mushrooms, sliced
16 ounces canned seasoned French-style green beans

Dressing:
1 clove garlic, minced
½ cup red wine vinegar
¾ cup salad oil
1 teaspoon salt
¼ teaspoon pepper

Combine the vegetables. Mix together the dressing ingredients and pour over the vegetables. Marinate overnight. Serves 4 to 6.

Oven Vegetables

½ cup celery, sliced
½ cup onion, sliced
½ cup green pepper, cut in chunks
½ cup peas
1 cup carrot chunks
1 zucchini, sliced
1 yellow squash, sliced
½ cauliflower in pieces
1 cup broccoli pieces
1 carton cherry tomatoes

Place these vegetables in a large shallow baking dish. Mix together and pour over vegetables:

1/3 cup olive oil
3 cloves garlic, chopped
2 teaspoons salt
½ bay leaf
½ teaspoon savory
½ teaspoon tarragon
1 cup beef bouillon

Preheat oven to 350 degrees. Bake 50 minutes lightly covered with foil.

Note: May be prepared the day before. Cover vegetables with a damp towel in refrigerator. Bring broth to boil and pour over just before baking.

To keep mushrooms fresh longer, refrigerate in a brown paper bag.

Zucchini Cheese Casserole

1½ pounds zucchini, cut into ½ inch slices
1 pound ground chuck
1 medium onion, chopped
1½ cups cooked rice
1 can cream of mushroom soup
1 teaspoon oregano
½ teaspoon salt
¼ teaspoon garlic powder
2 cups cottage cheese,
1 cup Cheddar cheese, shredded

In saucepan cook zucchini in boiling salted water about 3 to 4 minutes or until crisp-tender. Drain well. In skillet cook meat and onion until meat is browned and onion is tender. Drain. Stir in rice, soup, oregano, salt and garlic powder. In a 12X7½X2 inch baking dish arrange half of the zucchini. Top with meat mixture, cottage cheese and remaining zucchini. Bake in 350 degree oven for 1¼ hours. Sprinkle with Cheddar cheese. Return to oven and bake 2 to 3 minutes more. Serves 8.

Note: This can be made in advance and frozen.

Italian Zucchini

7 to 8 medium zucchini, cut into ¼ inch slices
1 cup water, salted
8 slices bacon, diced
1 large onion, chopped
1 large garlic clove, minced
4 slices white bread, diced
2 cups Cheddar cheese, shredded
1 teaspoon salt
1 teaspoon Italian seasoning
Dash of pepper
15 ounces tomato sauce
¼ cup Parmesan cheese, grated

In large saucepan cook zucchini in 1 cup boiling, salted water until tender, about 5 minutes; drain. In medium skillet cook bacon until crisp; remove from pan. Add onion and garlic to skillet and saute' until onion is tender; drain. Preheat oven to 350 degrees. Stir onion-bacon mixture into drained zucchini; add remaining ingredients except Parmesan cheese and toss until well coated. Spoon zucchini into a 13X9 inch baking dish or 2 quart casserole. Sprinkle with Parmesan cheese. Bake for 20 minutes or until bubbly. Serves 10 to 12.

Vegetables

Zucchini Custard

4 to 5 cups zucchini, shredded and packed
1¼ teaspoons salt
1 cup Cheddar cheese, shredded
⅛ teaspoon garlic powder
⅛ teaspoon pepper
¼ cup fresh parsley or ⅛ cup dry parsley
¼ cup biscuit mix
4 eggs, beaten
1 tablespoon margarine
Olives or bacon

Sprinkle shredded zucchini with salt and set aside for 1 hour. Then put into a colander and squeeze out liquid. Combine zucchini, cheese, pepper, garlic, parsley and biscuit mix. Stir in eggs, blending thoroughly. Melt margarine in 10 inch dish, spread over bottom and sides of dish. Pour zucchini mixture into dish. Cook uncovered in microwave on high for 10 minutes, stirring halfway through cooking time. Add olives or bacon for garnish. Serves 6 to 8.

Baked Zucchini Parmesan

4 medium sized zucchini
2 to 4 ounces butter
Garlic salt
Parmesan cheese, grated

Melt butter and set aside. Wash zucchini and cut both ends off each. Cut each zucchini lengthwise. Place zucchini halves (inside section face-up) on a baking pan. Brush butter on each. Generously shake garlic salt and Parmesan cheese over each zucchini. Broil until brown. Then turn off oven but leave zucchini in oven for about 20 minutes to finish cooking. Serve immediately. If you have large zucchini, bake at 350 degrees without topping or butter for 20 minutes and then proceed according to recipe. Serves 8.

Garlic bulbs last longer if left uncovered in pantry.

Seafood

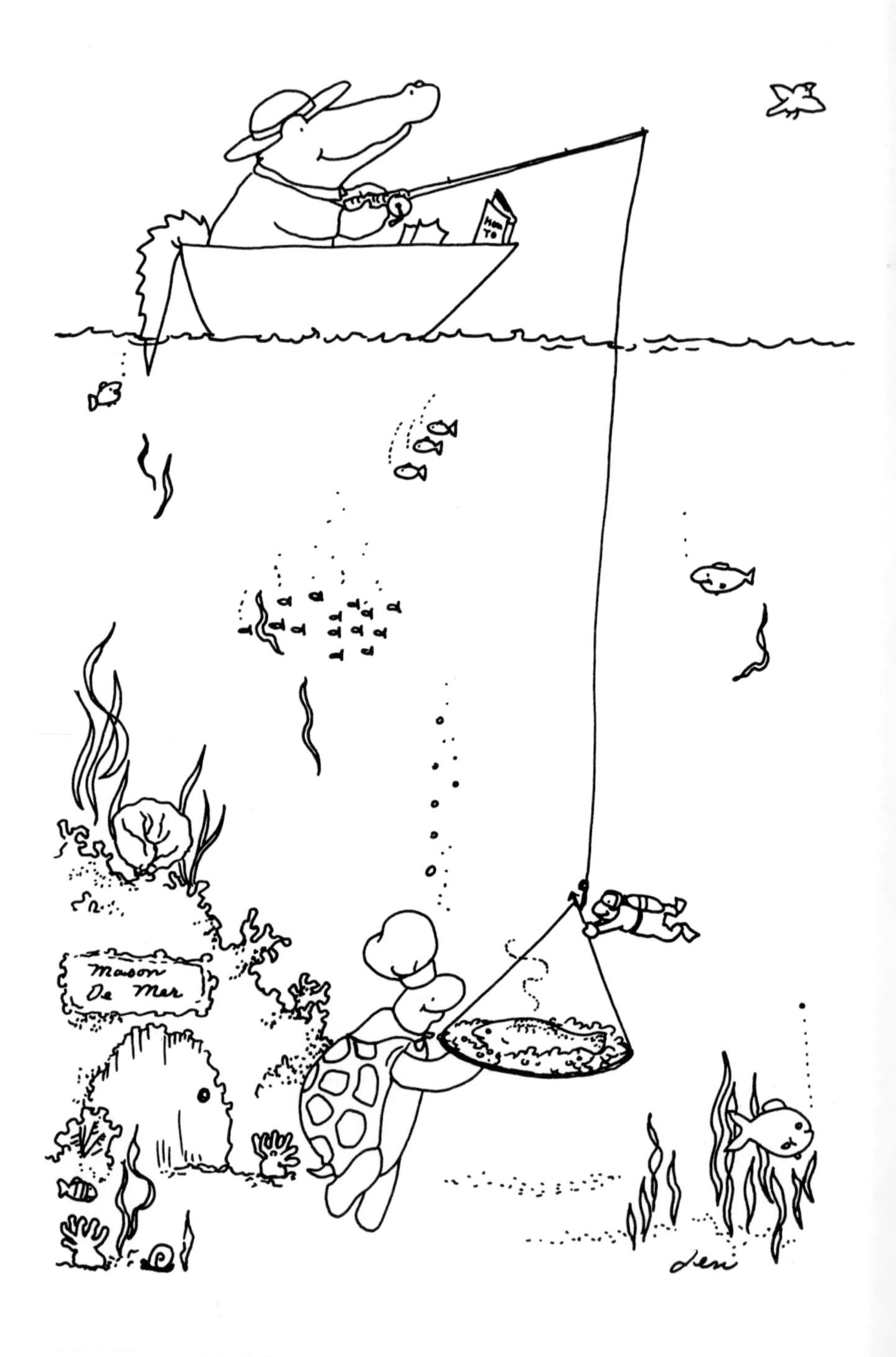
How To
Mason De Mer

Spaghetti with White Clam Sauce

8 ounces spaghetti
6½ ounces canned chopped clams with juice
3 ounces olive oil
3 cloves garlic, chopped
½ tablespoon oregano
1 tablespoon parsley, chopped
Juice of 2 lemons
Pepper, freshly ground

While cooking spaghetti, put oil, garlic, oregano and parsley in a 10 inch skillet and saute' for 1 minute. Add the clams with their juice and the lemon juice and allow to simmer on low heat for 3 to 5 minutes. Serve hot over the drained spaghetti. Sprinkle with pepper. Serves 4.

Crab Imperial

1 pound lump crab meat
2 tablespoons butter
1 cup cream
½ teaspoon salt
½ teaspoon red pepper
½ teaspoon dry mustard
1 teaspoon vinegar
1 tablespoon Worcestershire sauce
½ cup green pepper, finely chopped
1 cup fine fresh bread crumbs
Dry bread crumbs
Mayonnaise, ½ teaspoon per shell
Olive for garnish
Crab shells (may use ceramic)

Preheat oven to 400 degrees. Melt butter, add cream, salt, red pepper, dry mustard, vinegar and Worcestershire sauce. When thoroughly heated, add green pepper. Cook 1 minute. Add bread crumbs. Mix well. Remove from heat and mix in crab meat. Stuff into shells. Sprinkle with dry bread crumbs, top with mayonnaise and olive. Cook in hot oven until brown. Serves 4 to 6.

Note: Mixture may be placed in ramekins or casserole dish for serving. For an elegant dish, prepare a meringue topping as follows:

Topping:
6 egg whites, stiffly beaten
½ cup mayonnaise

Make meringue by folding mayonnaise into stiffly beaten egg whites. Spread over casserole. Bake at 350 degrees until lightly browned. Approximately 15 minutes. Serves 4.

Seafood

Crab Meat Mornay in Shells

1 pound white lump crab meat
½ cup butter
½ pound fresh mushrooms or 8 ounce can of mushrooms
1 small bunch green onions, finely chopped
2 tablespoons fresh parsley or 1½ teaspoons dried
2 tablespoons flour
1½ cups light cream or 13 ounce can of evaporated milk
½ pound Swiss cheese, grated
1 tablespoon white wine
1 teaspoon salt
½ teaspoon cayenne pepper
Seasoned pepper

Microwave butter in a 2 quart measuring cup for one minute. Saute' mushrooms, onions and parsley on high for 5 minutes. Blend in flour and cream. Cook on high for 3 minutes or until mixture thickens. Stir in cheese and cook on high for 1 minute or until cheese is melted. Add wine, salt and pepper and gently fold in the crab meat. Spoon mixture into shells or ramekins and sprinkle with bread crumbs. When ready to serve, place 3 to 4 filled shells in the microwave at a time. Cook on high for 1½ minutes or until heated thoroughly. Serves 6.

Note: 2 teaspoons of creole seasoning may be substituted for the salt and cayenne pepper. A 7 X 11 inch casserole dish may be used or a 2 quart round dish. Increase cooking time to 8 to 10 minutes. Slivered almonds may be sprinkled on top of casserole, if desired.

Crab Mornay

1 pound crab meat, cleaned
6 tablespoons butter or margarine
3 tablespoons flour
1 teaspoon pepper
1 teaspoon salt
2 cups milk
1 egg yolk, slightly beaten
6 ounces sharp Cheddar cheese, grated

Preheat oven to 350 degrees. To make a thick, rich cream sauce, melt butter, add flour and blend thoroughly. Do not brown. When smooth, add seasonings and slowly add milk. Stir constantly about 3 to 4 minutes until mixture boils. After cooked, add egg yolk. In a greased baking dish, place a layer of crab meat. Then follow by placing a layer of grated cheese and sauce. Repeat with cheese on top. Bake for about 25 minutes. Serves 4.

Crab Cakes

1 pound claw crab meat
1 level tablespoon prepared mustard
2 cups cracker meal
2 eggs, beaten
6 dashes Tabasco sauce
½ cup onion, finely chopped
3 heaping tablespoons mayonnaise
Salt and pepper to taste
¼ cup oil

Mix all ingredients except oil and 1 cup of cracker crumbs together. Make into patties, 2½ to 3 inches in diameter. Bread with remaining 1 cup of cracker crumbs. Fry in hot oil slowly until brown. Makes 9 to 10, 3 inch diameter patties. Serves 4.

Note: It is easier to form patties when hands are wet. Crab cakes can be frozen on a plate and then wrapped securely. For a different taste, add 1 tablespoon of horseradish with only 1 dash of Tabasco sauce.

Sherried Crab Souffle'

8 ounce package frozen Alaskan King Crab or 7½ ounce can Alaskan King Crab
2 envelopes unflavored gelatin
½ cup dry sherry
2 tablespoons butter
2 tablespoons flour
2 cups milk
4 eggs, separated
1 tablespoon onion, grated
½ teaspoon dried tarragon
1 teaspoon salt
¼ teaspoon pepper
1 cup heavy cream, whipped
Parsley for garnish

Drain and slice crab, reserving some for garnish. Soften gelatin in sherry. In saucepan, melt butter and blend in flour. Add milk gradually and cook, stirring constantly, until thickened and bubbly. Beat egg yolks until light. Blend a small amount of hot mixture into yolks. Return to hot mixture and cook several minutes longer. Stir in softened gelatin and heat until dissolved. Add onion, tarragon, salt, pepper and sliced crab. Chill until mixture mounds slightly. Fold in whipped cream. Beat egg whites until stiff but not dry. Fold into gelatin mixture. Pour into collared 1 quart souffle' dish. Chill several hours until firm. Remove collar. Garnish with parsley and reserved crab. Serves 6 to 8.

Seafood

Spaghetti a la King Crab

1 pound king crab meat
½ cup butter
2 tablespoons olive oil
8 cloves garlic, pressed
1 bunch green onions, sliced
2 medium tomatoes, diced
½ cup parsley, chopped
2 tablespoons lemon juice
½ teaspoon Italian seasoning
12 ounces thin spaghetti
Parmesan cheese

Drain and slice crab. Heat oil and butter. Add garlic and saute' gently. Add crab, green onions, tomatoes, parsley, lemon juice, Italian seasoning and dash of salt. Heat gently 8 to 10 minutes. Cook spaghetti and drain. Toss with crab mixture and Parmesan cheese. Pass additional grated Parmesan cheese. Serves 4.

Hot Crab Souffle'

15 ounces canned crab meat or
  16 ounces frozen crab meat
8 slices thinly sliced bread
½ cup mayonnaise
1 onion, chopped
1 green pepper, chopped
1 cup celery, chopped
4 eggs, beaten
1 cup milk
1 can cream of mushroom soup
1 cup sharp cheese, grated
Paprika

Cut bread to fit the bottom of 8 X 12 X 2 baking dish. Mix crab, mayonnaise, onion, pepper and celery. Spread over the bread. Cover with remaining bread cut in small cubes. Pour eggs and milk over top. Refrigerate until the next day. When ready to bake, spoon warmed soup over mixture. Cover with cheese and sprinkle with paprika. Bake for 1 hour in a 350 degree oven. Serves 8.

Note: This can be prepared ahead of time, but do not freeze. This is excellent for luncheons served with salad and rolls. For a different taste, substitute 1½ pounds fresh mushrooms, sliced, for the crab meat.

Mother Buck's Deviled Crabs

Two crabs are required for each deviled crab. The following makes 8 deviled crabs.

16 blue crabs

Steam crabs. If you do not have a steamer, use big pot or turkey roaster placing a riser made from a grill, a pie tin on a couple of large spoons or anything else to keep the crabs up and out of the water. Add a couple of tablespoons salt to the water or use your favorite crab boil mixture. Do not boil crabs directly in the water. Steam for 15 to 20 minutes. Cool the crabs and break the claws off with a twisting motion. Set aside. Remove the legs in the same way and discard. Pull back on the flap on the bottom of the crab and pry the body out of the shell carefully. Set the shell aside. Scrub out (inside and out) the shells. Save the 8 best. Allow to dry. Discard the lungs (finger like items on side of body). Discard white material in the center of the body. (Roe can be saved and mixed into the stuffing later). Break the body in two. Take a knife (sharp and small) and split the body section in two. Pick out the white meat being careful to discard all shell. Crack and shell the claws. This is the standard method of picking crabs.

Stuffing:

4 slices of bread (use heels)
½ teaspoon of dried tarragon
½ cup heavy cream
4 tablespoons butter
¼ teaspoon cayenne pepper or
Tabasco sauce to taste

Chop bread in blender or processor (steel blade) until you have fine crumbs. Blend in tarragon. Mix crumbs with crab meat. Fold in cream. Stuff shells and place small chips of butter on top. Heat in 300 degree oven for 10 minutes, switching to broil for browning for another 3 minutes.

Note: The crabs can be prepared a day ahead, wrapped in plastic or foil, and heated for serving. If just removed from the refrigerator, extend the heating 5 minutes.

Seafood

Elegant Luncheon Crab Quiche

6½ ounces crab meat
1 cup Swiss cheese, shredded
9 inch pie shell, unbaked
5 large eggs
1¼ cups half and half cream
⅛ teaspoon black pepper
½ teaspoon salt
½ cup mushrooms, sliced

Sprinkle cheese into pie shell. Beat eggs. Mix with cream, seasonings and mushrooms. Pour over cheese. Sprinkle crab meat over pie. Bake in a 350 degree oven 35 to 40 minutes or until firm. Cut in wedges. Serves 6.

Note: Lobster may be substituted for crab meat and this can be frozen.

Fish a la Crème

1 pound fish fillet (snapper, grouper or haddock)
¼ cup lemon juice
½ cup butter, melted
½ cup shrimp soup
½ cup sour cream

Marinate fish in lemon juice for 10 minutes. Mix butter, soup and sour cream and pour over fish. Broil for 10 minutes. Bake in 350 degree oven until it starts to bubble or turn brown. Serves 2.

Onion Baked Fish

2 pounds fish fillets
1 teaspoon salt
1 cup sour cream
1 cup mayonnaise
1 package Ranch House dressing mix
2 cans French fried onion rings, crushed

Preheat oven to 350 degrees. Salt the fish. Mix sour cream and mayonnaise with the dressing mix. Dip the fish in the mixture and roll in crushed onion rings. Bake for 20 to 25 minutes. Serves 4.

Captain Pizzani's Italian Stuffed Fish

6 medium flounder, cleaned
1 pound fresh crab meat, cleaned
Imported olive oil
2 bunches of parsley leaves, finely chopped
2 celery stalks, chopped
2 to 3 bunches green onions, chopped
1 clove garlic, pressed
1 tablespoon oregano
1 bay leaf
1 large onion, chopped
1 stick butter, melted
Few dashes Tabasco sauce
1 cup Italian style bread crumbs

Preheat oven to 375 degrees. In 3 tablespoons of olive oil, saute' until softened the parsley, celery, green onion, garlic, oregano, bay leaf and onion. Add crab meat to the mixture and cook until heated. Add the butter, Tabasco sauce and bread crumbs. Rub the inside of the flounder and outside with olive oil and stuff. Cook for 20 to 30 minutes, basting with olive oil.

Note: Captain Pizzani was a riverboat pilot on the run from New Orleans up the Mississippi River.

Fish Italiano

Flounder fillets (may use grouper or snapper)
2 tomatoes
2 to 3 tablespoons wine or tarragon vinegar and water
Salt
Italian spice, garlic and onion powder to taste

Thinly slice tomatoes and simmer in non-stick pan with vinegar, water, spices, onion and garlic powder. Cover and cook 2 to 3 minutes. Add fish, cover and simmer until fish is cooked, about 4 minutes. Keep fish firm, do not overcook. Serves 2.

Note: The fish and tomato sauce can be served over hot cooked rice. This is a low calorie recipe.

Seafood

Fabulous Flounder

1 pound flounder fillets, fresh or frozen
1/3 cup mayonnaise
Salt and pepper to taste
Parmesan cheese
1/6 cup dry Vermouth

Preheat oven to 350 degrees. Pat fish dry. Cover fillets with mayonnaise after putting them in a casserole dish. Sprinkle with salt and pepper. Pour Vermouth over fillets and sprinkle with Parmesan cheese. Bake uncovered for 30 minutes. Serves 2.

Note: This is also good with other kinds of fish fillets.

Fish Supreme

3 pounds fillet of flounder, pompano or trout
1 cup stale bread crumbs
Juice of 1 lemon
Salt to taste
Pepper, freshly ground, to taste
Worcestershire sauce, to taste
6 ounces Swiss cheese
2 cups sour cream

Place 1/3 of bread crumbs in the bottom of a buttered oblong baking dish and add a layer of fish. Sprinkle with lemon juice, salt, pepper and Worcestershire sauce; cover with a layer of cheese. Cover all with 1 cup of sour cream. Repeat layers. Cover top with buttered bread crumbs and bake at 325 degrees for 40 minutes. Serves 6.

Grilled Fish

6 medium speckled trout or
  Spanish mackerel
Oil
Salt and pepper to taste
6 bacon slices

Fillet fish lengthwise. Wipe both sides of each piece well with cooking oil. Salt and pepper well. Wrap a slice of bacon several times around each piece. Place fish in a wire hamburger rack and grill over charcoal fire until bacon is done. When the bacon is done, the fish will be also. Serves 6.

Beer Batter Fry

Fish fillets, shelled shrimp
  or scallops
Self-rising flour
Salt and pepper to taste
Cooking oil

Batter:
12 ounces beer
1 cup self-rising flour
¼ teaspoon paprika

Slice fish into chunks or fingers. Roll seafood in flour, then dip in a batter made of beer, flour and paprika. Drop coated seafood into a pan of hot cooking oil (380 to 400 degrees) until golden brown. Fish fingers cook quickly, so watch carefully.

Seafood

Frog Legs Provencale

6 pair large frog legs
Juice of 1½ lemons
1/3 cup oil
5 garlic cloves, crushed
Lemon-pepper seasoning to taste
Salt to taste

Combine all of the above ingredients and marinate for 1 hour. Grill over low charcoal heat. Reserve marinade. Cook 15 to 20 minutes or until done.

Sauce:
Reserved marinade from frog legs
4 fresh tomatoes, quartered
Beurre (1 tablespoon soft butter mixed with 2 tablespoons flour until crumbly)
Parsley, chopped

Heat the reserved marinade in a skillet. Add the tomatoes. When the tomatoes are tender, add the beurre to thicken. Add parsley. Pour over the barbecued frog legs and serve. The sauce should be prepared while grilling the legs. Serves 4 to 5.

Note: To thin the sauce, add ½ cup white wine, Tabasco sauce to taste and ½ cup V-8 juice.

Abaco Inn Grouper

2 pounds grouper fillets
2 tablespoons butter
1 onion, sliced
2 cloves garlic, pressed
1/3 cup white wine
½ cup Parmesan or Swiss cheese, grated
10 ounces frozen chopped broccoli
½ cup sour cream
Salt
Pepper

Preheat oven to 350 degrees. Place fish in an oven-proof dish with butter. Put the onion slices around fish and smooth the garlic on top. Pour on the white wine and cover the fish with cheese. Bake uncovered about 25 minutes, then broil for 5 minutes until lightly browned. While fish is broiling, cook the broccoli according to package directions. Drain and mix with the sour cream and heat 1 minute more. Serve with the broccoli on top of the fish. Salt and pepper last if desired. Serves 6.

Superb Oysters

½ to 1 pint oysters
20 ounces frozen chopped spinach
6 ounces cream cheese
Juice of 1 lemon
Pepperidge Farm herb stuffing mix
Salt and pepper to taste
2 tablespoons butter

Preheat oven to 400 degrees. Cook the spinach according to package directions. Drain very well. While still hot, crumble the cream cheese over the spinach. Stir until melted and a smooth cream. Add the lemon juice. Adjust seasonings to taste. Spoon into casserole. Top with oysters. Salt and pepper to taste. Sprinkle top with stuffing mix and dot with butter. Bake until butter is melted and oysters are to desired firmness, approximately 20 minutes. Serves 4 to 6.

Oyster and Spinach Casserole

2 pints oysters
40 ounces frozen chopped spinach
2 cans cream of mushroom soup
1 tablespoon lemon juice
1 teaspoon onion, grated
½ teaspoon Maggi seasoning
¼ teaspoon nutmeg
Garlic and white pepper to taste
1 pound bacon, fried crisp and chopped
Parmesan cheese
Bread crumbs, buttered

Cook spinach. Combine next 6 ingredients, seasoning heavily. Drain and mash cooked spinach to eliminate the water. Spread in bottom of 3 quart casserole dish. Add 1½ cups of the sauce mixture and mix well with the spinach. Spread the well drained oysters on top of spinach mixture. Sprinkle with bacon. Spread remaining sauce over all and sprinkle top with Parmesan cheese and bread crumbs. Bake at 350 degrees for 30 minutes. Serves 8 for dinner and 10 to 12 as a side dish.

Note: This is good served with fresh fruit. This recipe can be frozen.

Oysters Bienville

Broil 4 dozen oysters on the half shell for 3 or 4 minutes. Cover each oyster with Bienville Sauce. Bake in hot oven (400 degrees) until top is brown and crisp.

Bienville Sauce:

6 ounces boiled shrimp, chopped
2 slices bacon
1/3 cup fresh mushrooms, chopped
2 cloves garlic, chopped
¼ cup shallots or green onions, chopped
3 tablespoons butter
2/3 cup flour
1 quart hot milk
2/3 cup oyster juice
1/3 lemon juice
1/3 cup sherry
¼ cup parsley, chopped

Cut bacon into small pieces and fry until brown. Add mushrooms, garlic and shallots and cook until done. Add butter to pan, stirring until melted. Blend in flour and cook for 5 minutes. Gradually add hot milk and stir until thick and smooth. Add the shrimp, oyster juice, lemon juice, sherry and parsley. Cook over low heat for 15 minutes and use for topping the oysters.

Hot Panned Oysters

1 quart oysters
¼ pound butter
¼ cup celery, chopped
¼ cup green pepper, chopped
3 tablespoons Worcestershire sauce
20 drops Tabasco sauce
Salt and pepper to taste
1 tablespoon lemon juice
¼ pound soda crackers, crushed

Preheat oven to 350 degrees. Drain oysters in a colander. Melt the butter in a 2 quart casserole dish. Place oysters in bottom of dish; place remaining ingredients on top of oysters. Top with crackers. Bake for 1 hour. Serves 4.

Rub hands with parsley or lemon to remove any odor.

New Orleans Oysters Mosca

2 pints oysters, reserve liquid
8 to 10 spring onions, chopped
¼ pound butter
¾ teaspoon oregano
¼ teaspoon red pepper
½ teaspoon thyme
Salt and pepper to taste
1 teaspoon garlic, minced
1 cup seasoned bread crumbs
Parmesan cheese

Preheat oven to 350 degrees. Saute' onion in butter, add seasonings, then add oysters. When edges of oysters begin to curl, add reserved oyster liquid and fold in bread crumbs. Place in a casserole dish. Sprinkle with cheese. Bake for 15 to 20 minutes. Serves 4.

Paella

2 packages frozen lobster tails
3 pounds chicken, cut up
1 tablespoon flour
3 tablespoons olive oil
1½ teaspoons salt
¼ teaspoon pepper
½ cup onion, chopped
1 pound uncooked shrimp, peeled and deveined
10 ounces frozen peas
2 pimientos, chopped
1 tomato, cut in eighths
½ teaspoon garlic powder
2 cups chicken broth
¾ cup yellow rice

Partially thaw lobster tails. Break backs and remove meat. Set aside. Sprinkle chicken with flour and brown in oil. After browning, salt and pepper the chicken. Add onion, shrimp, peas and pimientos. Cook for 30 minutes on medium heat. Add lobster, tomato, garlic and chicken broth, cover and simmer 10 minutes. Add rice and simmer 20 minutes. Serves 6 to 8.

Seafood

Western Scalloped Salmon

2 cups canned red salmon
4 tablespoons butter
¼ cup flour
1½ cups milk
¼ teaspoon salt
⅛ teaspoon black pepper
1 tablespoon onion, grated
½ bay leaf
1 tablespoon parsley, chopped
2 beef bouillon cubes
½ cup ripe olives, cut in large pieces
½ cup dry bread crumbs
½ cup cheese, grated

Preheat oven to 350 degrees. Melt butter and blend in the flour. Add milk, salt, pepper, onion, bay leaf, parsley and bouillon cubes. Cook and stir until thickened. Remove bay leaf. Place layer of salmon, which has been drained and flaked, in bottom of greased 1½ quart casserole. Cover with part of the sauce. Sprinkle with olives, bread crumbs and cheese. Repeat until all is used - top with crumbs and cheese. Bake for 30 minutes. Serves 6.

Salmon Loaf

16 ounces red salmon
1 teaspoon salt
½ teaspoon pepper
½ cup hot milk
¼ teaspoon paprika
2 tablespoons lemon juice
2 egg yolks, well beaten
½ cup cracker crumbs
2 egg whites, stiffly beaten
Lemon, thinly sliced, optional

Remove small bones and bits of skin from salmon. Drain and mash well. Add all of the above ingredients except egg whites. Fold in beaten egg whites. Bake in a buttered loaf pan (8½ X 4½ X 2½ inch or smaller) at 350 degrees for 1 hour. Thin lemon slices may be arranged on top during the baking. Serves 4 to 6.

Note: This makes a good oven dinner with baked potatoes and a green salad.

A whole lemon heated in hot water for 5 minutes will yield about 1 tablespoon more juice than an unheated lemon.

Salmon in a Blanket

15 ounces salmon, boned
¼ teaspoon salt
¼ teaspoon pepper
1½ teaspoons dry mustard
2 tablespoons lemon juice
¼ cup dill
1 pie crust mix or 2 crust pastry
Egg yolk
Sesame seeds

Preheat oven to 425 degrees. Prepare pie crust and roll out into large square, approximately 16 X 16 inch. Mix rest of ingredients and place in center of pie crust. Fold corners over to make envelope. Brush with egg yolk and sprinkle with sesame seeds. Bake for 20 to 25 minutes. Serve with lots of tartar sauce and lemon slices. Serves 6.

Wonderful with fruit salad, broiled tomato and glass of wine for a supper that's tasty and elegant. Pastry decorations may be added to top.

Coquilles St. Jacques

1 pound fresh scallops, preferably bay scallops
¾ cup water
1/3 cup Sauterne
½ teaspoon salt
Dash of cayenne
3 tablespoons flour
3 tablespoons butter
2 tablespoons onion, finely chopped
1 teaspoon parsley, chopped
1 egg yolk, well beaten
¼ pound mushrooms, sautéed in butter
¾ cup soft bread crumbs

If using large scallops, cut into small pieces with scissors. Combine water, Sauterne, salt, cayenne and scallops. Simmer 5 minutes. Drain and reserve liquid. In same pan, make sauce of butter and flour and reserved liquid. Add onion, parsley and cook until thick, about 5 minutes. Quickly blend in egg yolk. Add scallops and mushrooms. Spoon into 6 buttered shells. Top with crumbs and bake at 425 degrees for 5 minutes, or until golden brown. Serves 6.

Note: For an elegant dish, garnish with parsley and lemon or lime slices. This recipe can be put into smaller shells and used as an hors d'oeuvre or fruit course.

Seafood

Scallops Provencale

1½ pounds scallops
2 tablespoons fresh lemon juice
4 tablespoons butter
4 to 6 cloves garlic, minced
4 shallots, minced
3 medium ripe tomatoes, peeled, seeded and chopped
½ cup dry Vermouth
¼ teaspoon salt
¼ teaspoon white pepper
Fresh parsley, finely chopped

Marinate scallops in lemon juice for at least 15 minutes. In large skillet, melt butter until foamy and quickly saute' scallops, turning to lightly brown on both sides. (Do not crowd scallops or they will stew rather than brown.) Remove scallops with slotted spoon and set aside. To the skillet add garlic, shallots, tomatoes, wine, salt and pepper. Cook uncovered, stirring occasionally, for 15 minutes. Return scallops to skillet; cover and cook gently, just long enough to heat thoroughly, shaking pan frequently to avoid sticking. Correct seasonings and spoon onto heated individual serving dishes. Sprinkle with parsley and serve immediately. Serves 4.

English Muffin Scallops

1 to 1½ pounds scallops
½ cup butter
1 cup parsley to make 1/3 cup chopped
2 cloves garlic
2 English muffins
2 tablespoons butter in small pieces
¼ cup lemon juice
Clam juice
1/3 cup Parmesan cheese, freshly grated

Preheat oven to 450 degrees. Place rack in upper third of oven. Generously butter 9 X 13 inch baking dish. Process parsley. Set aside. Process garlic and muffins. In skillet, melt butter over low heat. When foam subsides, increase heat slightly; add crumbs and garlic. Toss together 3 to 6 minutes or until crisp and golden. Stir in parsley and lemon juice. Spread 2/3 mixture in dish. Sprinkle with clam juice to moisten. Arrange scallops over crumbs. Blend cheese with remaining crumbs and spread on top of scallops. Dot with butter. Bake 10 to 12 minutes until golden brown and tender.

Seafood Holly

1 pound seafood (shellfish or fillets, flaked)
4 ounces pimento cheese, sliced
½ cup butter or margarine
2 cups coffee cream
4 ounces thin noodles
Salt, pepper, paprika to taste
Sherry to taste

Preheat oven to 350 degrees. In double boiler, melt cheese and butter. Add cream, stirring until thickened and smooth. Meanwhile, cook noodles according to package; drain and pour into greased baking dish. Add seasonings, sherry and seafood to sauce. Pour over noodles but do not mix. Bake for 30 minutes. Serve with salad and rolls. Serves 6.

Seafood Casserole

1 cup fresh shrimp, pre-cooked
1 cup crab meat, rinsed and cleaned
1 cup fresh oysters, rinsed and drained
1½ cups cooked rice
1 cup mayonnaise
2 tablespoons Worcestershire sauce
1 cup celery, chopped
½ cup green pepper, chopped
½ cup onion, chopped
1 teaspoon salt
⅛ teaspoon pepper
Potato chips, crushed

Preheat oven to 350 degrees. Mix togther all ingredients except potato chips. Pour into casserole. Top with potato chips. Bake 35 minutes. Serves 8.

Seafood

Magnolia Seafood Curry

1½ pounds shrimp, cooked and deveined
½ pound crab meat
7 ounces curry rice
½ cup celery, chopped
¾ cup onion, chopped
1 small green pepper, chopped
½ pound mushrooms, sliced
¼ cup butter or margarine
½ cup milk
21 ounces cream of mushroom soup
2 ounces pimiento, chopped
2 teaspoons curry, optional
½ cup almonds, slivered

Prepare rice according to package directions. Set aside. Saute' celery, onion, pepper and mushrooms in butter. Avoid browning. Add cooked rice, milk, canned soup, seafood, pimiento and curry. Mix thoroughly. Pour into 3 quart casserole and top with almonds. Bake in 350 degree oven until bubbling hot, about 20 to 30 minutes. Serves 8.

Shrimp Florentine

3 pounds shrimp, cooked, shelled and deveined
4 10-ounce packages frozen chopped spinach
½ cup butter or margarine
½ cup flour
3 cups milk
1 cup dry white wine
½ cup scallions, sliced
Salt, pepper and paprika to taste
2 cups Cheddar cheese, shredded

Preheat oven to 350 degrees. Thaw, drain and squeeze dry spinach. Spread ½ of spinach in each of two 9 inch pie pans. Top with shrimp. In a saucepan, melt butter and stir in flour. Gradually add milk, wine and scallions stirring constantly over low heat until sauce bubbles and thickens. Add salt and pepper to taste and paprika for rosy color. Pour sauce over shrimp. Sprinkle each pie with shredded cheese. Bake at 350 degrees for 30 to 35 minutes or until bubbly. Serve with noodles almondine, tossed salad and French bread.

Note: Recipe makes two 9 inch pie pans. Each serves 4 to 6. Second can be frozen in pie pan. When frozen solid, lift from pan and wrap in heavy duty aluminum foil and put back in freezer. When ready to bake, remove foil, replace frozen pie back in pan and bake at 350 degrees for 1 hour. Serve with lemon wedges.

Shrimp Marseillaise

2 pounds shrimp, cooked and cleaned
1 package long grain and wild rice mix
½ pound fresh mushrooms
¾ cup celery, chopped
1 medium onion, chopped
1 green pepper, chopped
Butter for sautéing
2 ounces pimiento, cut up
21 ounces cream of shrimp soup
1 can cream of mushroom soup
½ cup sherry
Almonds, slivered and toasted

Preheat oven to 350 degrees. Cook rice according to package directions. Set aside. In a large saucepan, saute' mushrooms, celery, onion and pepper in butter. Drain off any excess butter. Add shrimp, pimiento, soup and sherry to the mushroom mixture and blend. Add rice, mix and turn into casserole dish. Bake for 45 minutes to 1 hour. Garnish with almonds before serving. Serves 8.

Note: Serve with stuffed squash, green salad and hot rolls for a delicious meal.

Shrimp Perlo

2 pounds shrimp, shelled and deveined
8 slices bacon
1 large onion, chopped
1 large green pepper, chopped
2 large cloves garlic, finely chopped
2 28-ounce cans tomatoes, mashed with fork
2 teaspoons thyme
4 bay leaves
2 cups uncooked rice
4 hot Datil peppers or ¼ teaspoon cayenne pepper and Tabasco sauce to taste

Fry bacon until crisp. Remove from pan and save. Saute' onion and green pepper in bacon fat until transparent. Add garlic, tomatoes, bacon, thyme and bay leaves. Simmer 15 minutes. Add rice and cook until rice is tender. Add raw shrimp and cook 20 minutes longer. About 5 minutes before serving, add the Datil peppers but do not stir into rice and shrimp. Before serving, remove peppers and bay leaves.

Seafood

Baked Stuffed Shrimp

16 large raw shrimp
½ pound fresh crab meat, shell and cartilage removed
3 slices stale bread, finely crumbled
¼ cup celery, finely chopped
1 tablespoon pimiento, finely chopped
2 teaspoons parsley, chopped
¼ teaspoon Worcestershire sauce
3 drops Tabasco sauce
2½ heaping tablespoons mayonnaise
Paprika
1 stick butter
2 cloves garlic, minced

Shell, devein and butterfly shrimp. Combine crab meat, bread crumbs, celery, pimiento, parsley, Worcestershire sauce, Tabasco sauce and mayonnaise. Place a heaping tablespoon on top of each shrimp. Sprinkle each with paprika. In a small skillet, melt butter and add minced garlic. Saute' for 3 minutes. Place shrimp in baking dish and pour garlic butter over and around shrimp. Bake in 400 degree oven for 12 minutes. Spoon the garlic butter over shrimp when serving. Serves 4.

Pub Shrimp

3 pounds fresh shrimp
24 ounces beer
1 teaspoon thyme
1 tablespoon dry mustard
2 bay leaves
1 tablespoon chives, chopped
1 tablespoon salt
2 cloves garlic, chopped
2 tablespoons parsley, chopped
½ teaspoon pepper

Place all ingredients except shrimp in large boiler and let come to a boil. Cut off legs of shrimp but leave shells on. Add shrimp and when mixture has returned to a boil, simmer for 5 minutes.

Sauce:
4 tablespoons lemon juice
2 tablespoons chives or onions
2 teaspoons salt
2 tablespoons parsley, minced
8 tablespoons butter or margarine, melted

Mix sauce ingredients together. Serve shrimp hot, with sauce and plenty of napkins and maybe a wet towel for sticky fingers. Serves 4.

Shrimp Newberg

1 pound fresh shrimp, shelled and deveined
2 tablespoons butter
1 teaspoon Spanish paprika
1 pint heavy cream
Salt and pepper to taste
3 egg yolks
3 or 4 tablespoons sherry

Heat butter in skillet until hot. Do not burn. Add shrimp and fry for 2 minutes. Add paprika and fry another 2 minutes. Add enough heavy cream to cover shrimp and bring to boil. Season with salt and pepper. Put 3 egg yolks in a cup and mix with a little cream. Add this to the shrimp while it is boiling. Stir constantly. When mixture thickens, take off heat and add sherry. Serve over steamed rice. Serves 4.

Shrimp Creole

3 pounds raw shrimp
1½ green peppers, minced
3 to 4 cloves garlic, minced
3 large onions, minced
6 tablespoons oil
1 tablespoon salt
⅛ teaspoon pepper
½ teaspoon dried rosemary
½ teaspoon paprika
6 dashes Tabasco sauce
58 ounces canned tomatoes

Clean shrimp. Boil in salted water 6 to 8 minutes. Drain. Saute' green pepper, garlic and onion in oil until tender. Add salt, pepper, rosemary, paprika, Tabasco sauce and tomatoes. Add shrimp and simmer until flavored through, about 45 minutes. Serve shrimp over hot, parsley-seasoned rice. Serves 8 to 10.

Seafood

Luncheon Shrimp

¾ pound shrimp, cooked and cleaned
6 slices bread, crusts removed
6 eggs, hard-boiled and halved

Egg stuffing;
¼ teaspoon dry mustard
¼ to ½ teaspoon curry powder
½ teaspoon paprika
½ teaspoon salt
½ cup mayonnaise

Sauce:
4 tablespoons butter
4 tablespoons flour
2 cups half and half
1 cup sharp Cheddar cheese, grated
1 tablespoon onion, grated
½ teaspoon dry mustard
½ teaspoon Worcestershire sauce

Mash the egg yolks and mix with the dry mustard, curry powder, paprika, salt and mayonnaise. Pile this into the egg whites.

For the sauce, melt the butter; add the flour and stir. Gradually add half and half, stirring until thick. Add the remaining sauce ingredients and stir until melted and blended. Add the shrimp.

Toast and butter the bread. Dry it out in a 250 degree oven for 1 hour.

Arrange 2 halves of eggs on each piece of toast and spoon shrimp over all.

Charcoaled Marinated Shrimp

2 pounds raw shrimp in shells
3 cloves garlic, chopped
1 medium onion, chopped
1 teaspoon dry mustard
1 teaspoon salt
½ cup olive or peanut oil
3 tablespoons lemon juice
½ cup parsley, chopped
1 teaspoon dry basil

Rinse shrimp, snip shell down back. Combine remaining ingredients; pour over shrimp. Marinate shrimp for at least five hours. Place shrimp on grill over hot coals. Cook 5 to 8 minutes turning once. Serve in shell with plenty of napkins. Serves 4 to 6.

Shrimp Lagoon

1½ pounds raw shrimp
1½ pounds self-rising flour
1 pint ice water
2 teaspoons salt
1½ teaspoons white pepper
2 tablespoons salad oil
2 eggs
1 cup coconut, shredded

Mix flour, water, salt, pepper, oil and eggs together. Dip shrimp in batter. (Batter will be medium thick.) Roll battered shrimp in coconut. Deep fry for approximately 4 minutes at 350 degrees, then place in 300 degree oven for 5 minutes to complete cooking of shrimp.

Shrimp and Crab Quiche

Pastry:
1 cup all-purpose flour
½ teaspoon salt
1/3 cup plus 1 tablespoon shortening
2 to 3 tablespoons cold water

Quiche:
6 ounces frozen crab meat and shrimp combination, thawed and drained
½ cup mayonnaise
2 tablespoons all-purpose flour
2 eggs, beaten
½ cup milk
½ pound Swiss cheese, cut into ¼ inch cubes
1/3 cup green onions, chopped

To prepare pastry: Combine flour and salt; cut in shortening until mixture looks like coarse cornmeal. Sprinkle cold water evenly over surface; stir with fork until all is moistened. Shape into a ball and chill for 45 minutes. Roll to fit a 9 inch quiche or pie pan. Place a piece of buttered foil, buttered side down over pastry and gently press into pastry shell. This prevents the sides of the shell from collapsing. Bake at 400 degrees for 10 minutes. Remove foil, prick shell lightly and bake 3 to 5 additional minutes or until very lightly browned. Cool and fill with quiche mixture.

To prepare Quiche: Preheat oven to 350 degrees. Combine mayonnaise, flour, eggs and milk; mix thoroughly. Stir in crab meat and shrimp. Add cheese and onion, stirring to combine. Spoon into pastry shell and bake for 30 to 40 minutes. Serves 4.

Seafood

Lake Virginia Bouillabaisse

1½ pounds shrimp
3 seabass or halibut steaks,
cut into 1 inch pieces
1 pound crab meat, cleaned
4 medium lobster tails
1 pound clams or scallops
¼ cup oil
½ cup onion, chopped
1 tablespoon garlic, chopped
½ cup celery, chopped
16 ounces canned tomatoes
8 ounces tomato sauce
2 teaspoons salt
1 tablespoon paprika
½ cup sherry or white wine
2 cups water
Pinch of dried basil or thyme

Place oil, onion, garlic, celery, tomatoes, tomato sauce, salt, paprika, sherry or wine, water and basil or thyme in a Crock Pot. Cover and cook on high for 2 to 4 hours, or on low heat for 6 hours. If you do not have a Crock Pot, a saucepan can be used, and cook for 30 to 45 minutes. Add seafood and cook an additional 1 to 3 hours on high heat in the Crock Pot. If using a saucepan, cook approximately 30 minutes or until seafood is done.

Note: To make this a more economical dish, substitute 16 ounces canned clams, chopped; 24 ounces frozen shrimp, cooked and cleaned; and halibut or flounder fillets. If using cooked shrimp and canned clams, place in the Crock Pot the last hour, or, if using a saucepan, add the last 10 to 15 minutes of cooking time.

Barbecued Shrimp

5 pounds shrimp, in shells
1 pound butter
2 ounce can black pepper
2 packages Good Seasons Italian dressing, mixed according
to package directions
Juice of 4 lemons

Preheat oven to 350 degrees. Melt butter. Add pepper, Italian dressing and lemon juice. Place shrimp in large roasting pan. Pour sauce over shrimp. Cover pan and bake for 45 minutes. Serves 6 to 8.

Note: Less pepper may be used. Sauce can be frozen. Serve extra sauce in a pitcher. Peel and dip shrimp. Hot but wonderful.

Shrimp Linguine

12 jumbo shrimp, diced
8 ounces linguine or thin spaghetti
½ cup butter
4 to 6 cloves garlic, minced
4 ounces canned mushrooms, or ¼ pound fresh, diced
6 tablespoons Romano cheese, grated
½ teaspoon salt
Pepper, freshly ground
Parsley sprigs for garnish

Cook linguine or spaghetti in rapidly boiling salted water for 10 minutes. Drain, rinse with cold water and set aside. Melt butter in a 10 inch skillet. Add garlic, shrimp and mushrooms and cook slowly in hot butter for 5 minutes. Add linguine or spaghetti to the skillet. Sprinkle with cheese, salt and pepper. Toss until linguine is very hot but do not let butter brown. Turn onto warm serving dish, sprinkle with more cheese and garnish with sprigs of parsley. Serves 4.

Shrimp and Artichoke Casserole

1½ pounds shrimp, cooked, peeled and deveined
2 cans artichoke hearts, cut into fourths.
½ pound fresh mushrooms, sliced in half
6 tablespoons butter, divided
¼ cup flour
1½ cups half and half
½ cup dry sherry
1 tablespoon Worchestershire sauce
Salt and pepper to taste
¼ teaspoon paprika
½ cup Parmesan cheese, grated

Preheat oven to 350 degrees. Saute' mushrooms in 2 tablespoons butter until soft. Layer the shrimp, mushrooms and artichoke hearts in an oblong 2 quart casserole. Melt the remaining butter until foamy, add flour; cook and stir for 3 minutes. Gradually add half and half, cook and stir until sauce is well blended and thickened. Add sherry, Worcestershire sauce, salt, pepper and paprika. Pour sauce over casserole ingredients and sprinkle with Parmesan cheese. Bake until bubbly, about 30 to 40 minutes. This may be made the day before and left in the refrigerator overnight. Serve with broiled tomatoes, plain white rice and Caesar salad for a nice company dinner. Serves 4 to 6.

Seafood

Rock Shrimp

1½ pounds rock shrimp,
  deveined and split open
Salt and pepper
1 cup Italian bread crumbs
½ cup oil, divided
½ teaspoon garlic salt

Preheat oven to 350 degrees. Grease large baking pan (15 X 10 X 1 inch) and lay shrimp flat. Sprinkle with salt and pepper. Prepare paste of bread crumbs and ¼ cup oil. Add garlic salt to taste. Sprinkle oil on top of shrimp, then divide paste on top of each shrimp, pressing paste down. Sprinkle more oil on top. Bake for 40 minutes. Serves 6.

Sizzling Shrimp

3 pounds shrimp
1½ cups oil
1 tablespoon salt
½ cup catsup
2 cloves garlic, minced
½ small onion, minced
1 tablespoon lemon juice
1 teaspoon parsley

Combine all ingredients except shrimp. Peel and clean shrimp, leaving on tails. Marinate shrimp in sauce for 1 hour in refrigerator.

Arrange shrimp on skewers; place on broiler tray and brush with sauce. Broil 4 inches from heat for 10 minutes. Turn and baste shrimp at least once during broiling time. Serves 6.

Shrimp Floridian

2 pounds fresh shrimp, cleaned
  and deveined
8 ounces bleu cheese
8 ounces cream cheese
1 tablespoon chives, chopped
1 tablespoon parsley, chopped
1 clove garlic, minced
¾ cup dry white wine

Preheat oven to 400 degrees. Cream cheeses; blend in remaining ingredients except shrimp. Pour over shrimp in casserole and bake, covered, for 30 minutes. Serves 4.

Shrimp Kabobs

For each serving, alternate about 5 shelled and deveined jumbo shrimp, 5 pineapple cubes, and 5 green pepper slices. Brush with the following sauce:

Shrimp Kabob Sauce:
¼ cup brown sugar
1 teaspoon chili powder
½ teaspoon seasoned salt
1 teaspoon A-1 or Worchestershire sauce
1 cup onion, chopped
¼ cup lemon juice
¼ cup salad oil
8 ounce can tomato sauce

Combine in order given and simmer ½ hour or until mixture thickens. Makes 2 cups.

Brush Kabobs with sauce and broil 5 to 8 minutes, basting frequently and turning slowly to cook thoroughly. Serve as appetizer or main course!

Sherried Shrimp with Tangy Sauce

1½ pound raw shrimp
¼ cup dry sherry
4 tablespoons butter
½ teaspoon garlic salt
¼ cup Parmesan cheese, grated

Peel and devein shrimp. Place in bowl and pour sherry over them. Let marinate for several hours. Melt butter in fry pan over low heat. Add shrimp and sherry. Sprinkle with garlic salt and simmer for 10 to 15 minutes. Just before serving, sprinkle cheese over shrimp and place under broiler for 2 to 3 minutes until cheese is lightly browned. Turn into chafing dish and keep warm. Serve with Tangy Dip. Serves 6 to 8.

Tangy Sauce
½ cup mayonnaise
2 teaspoons lemon juice
1 tablespoon catsup
2 teaspoons Worcestershire sauce
2 teaspoons prepared mustard

Mix ingredients and chill until ready to use. Makes ½ cup sauce.

Seafood

Shrimp Au Vin

5 pounds fresh or frozen shrimp
12 tablespoons butter
2 teaspoons flour
1 cup whipping cream
½ cup light cream
1 teaspoon salt
Red and white pepper
1 bunch green onions, chopped
1 cup dry white wine
½ cup Cheddar or Parmesan cheese, grated

Peel and devein shrimp; chop. Melt 4 tablespoon butter, blend in flour. Add creams and seasonings. Cook over low heat, stirring constantly, until thick. Keep warm. Saute' shrimp in remaining butter until pink. Add green onion. Stir in cream sauce and simmer 15 minutes. Add wine, remove from heat and let stand 10 minutes. Place in buttered casserole. Spinkle with cheese. Broil until cheese melts, about 2 to 3 minutes. Serves 8.

Dip for Shrimp

1 pint Hellman's mayonnaise
2 cloves garlic, minced
1 teaspoon dry mustard
1 teaspoon prepared mustard
1 teaspoon Worcestershire sauce
1 tablespoon capers, chopped
1 tablespoon tarragon vinegar
1 pinch tarragon
2 teaspoons horseradish
Salt and pepper to taste
Dash Tabasco sauce
Dash paprika
1 tablespoon parsley, chopped

Mix all ingredients together and allow to marinate several hours. This is a welcome change from red sauce.

Shrimp Sauce

1 egg yolk
2 teaspoons anchovy paste
½ teaspoon dry mustard
1 cup mayonnaise
1 tablespoon red wine vinegar
Scant tablespoon onion, grated
½ clove garlic, pressed
2 tablespoons dry white wine

Mix all the above ingredients and let stand in the refrigerator for 24 hours. Serve with shrimp or other seafood.

Sarasota Shrimp

1 pound shrimp per person
½ gallon water
2 to 3 tablespoons shrimp boil
2 celery stalks with leaves
½ lemon, quartered
1 onion, chopped
1 teaspoon salt

Simmer water, shrimp boil, celery, lemon, onion and salt for 30 minutes. Add shrimp and cook until done. Serve with sauce.

Sauce:
Juice of 2 lemons
1 tablespoon tarragon vinegar
1 tablespoon Worcestershire sauce
2 tablespoons soy sauce
8 dashes Tabasco sauce
1 tablespoon salt
3 sticks butter, melted

Combine all ingredients in a saucepan and heat.

Baked Red Snapper

1 large red snapper, cleaned and dried, salt and peppered

Stuffing:
8 ounce package Pepperidge Farm corn bread stuffing
1 to 1½ pounds raw shrimp, cleaned

Prepare stuffing according to package directions and add shrimp. Stuff the snapper with dressing.

Sauce:
½ cup onion, chopped
½ cup celery, chopped
½ cup green pepper, chopped
32 ounces tomato sauce
6 ounces tomato paste
2 cups or more catsup
Salt to taste
Pepper to taste
Soy sauce to taste
Garlic salt to taste
Parsley

Preheat oven to 375 degrees. Brown the onion, celery and green pepper in oil. Add tomato sauce, tomato paste and catsup. Add seasonings and parsley last for color. Pour over the snapper and bake for 45 minutes, basting occasionally.

Note: The sauce makes this dish, so be sure to prepare plenty.

Seafood

Baked Snapper with Everything

2 pounds snapper or grouper fillets, 1 inch thick
1 banana
1 large firm tomato
1 large apple
8 tablespoons butter
1 clove garlic, crushed, optional
Juice of ½ lemon
Pinch of tarragon

Preheat oven to 450 degrees. Peel and chop banana into ½ inch pieces (no more than 1/3 cup). Remove seeds from tomato and chop into ¼ inch pieces. Peel and core apple and chop into ¼ inch pieces. Melt butter in bottom of Dutch oven or any deep ovenware with lid. Cook banana, apple, tomato and optional garlic until slightly soft. Stir in lemon juice to taste. Add pinch of tarragon. Put fish in Dutch oven, spooning sauce over and around it. Bake for 20 minutes. If fillets overlap, bake an additional 2 to 3 minutes. Serve with a little white rice on the side. Serves 4.

Red Snapper Almondine

1 pound red snapper
1 teaspoon lemon juice
Seasoning salt

Place snapper in glass baking dish. Rub lemon juice on top and salt lightly. Cover with plastic wrap. Microwave on high for 5 minutes or until fish flakes easily. Let stand covered while making sauce.

Sauce:
1/3 cup almonds, slivered
1/3 cup butter or margarine

Combine almonds and butter in 2 cup measuring cup. Cook on high for about 2 minutes or until melted. Stir and continue cooking on high for 3 to 5 minutes or until lightly browned. Serve over fillets.

Note: Flounder, bass, grouper or any fish fillets that are in season may be used.

Stuffed Red Snapper

2 pounds red snapper fillets
¼ cup butter, melted

Using a sharp knife, cut a pocket in the fillet. Be careful not to cut completely through the fillet.

Stuffing:
8 tablespoons butter, divided
2 small carrots, minced
½ medium onion, minced
¼ cup whipping cream
1 celery stalk, minced
½ pound shrimp, cleaned, deveined and minced (can mix ¼ pound shrimp and ¼ pound crab)
1 egg, lightly beaten
½ teaspoon Worcestershire sauce
Salt
Pepper, freshly ground
1¼ to 1½ cups bread crumbs, freshly made

Melt 2 tablespoons butter in small skillet over medium-high heat. Add carrot and onion and saute' for 2 minutes. Reduce heat, cover and simmer gently until vegetables are soft. Transfer to food processor or blender. Add cream and purée. Transfer to medium mixing bowl. Melt 2 tablespoons butter in separate skillet over medium-high heat. Add celery and saute' until softened, about 4 to 5 minutes. Add shrimp and saute' just until pink, about 10 seconds. Fold in carrot and onion purée . Blend in egg. Stir in Worcestershire sauce or herbs and season with salt and pepper. Add enough bread crumbs so mixture holds together but is not overly moist. Spoon stuffing into fillets and fasten with toothpicks. Transfer fish to baking dish and spoon 4 tablespoons melted butter over top. Season with salt and pepper. Bake 45 minutes to 1 hour in a preheated 400 degree oven. If fillets are extra thick, bake 1 hour.

Crispy Fish

Fish fillets
1 stick butter or margarine
8 ounces Pepperidge Farm Stuffing, plain or cornbread
Salt and pepper to taste

Melt butter. With rolling pin, finely crumble the stuffing mix. Dip fish in butter until covered and roll in stuffing mix. Put in baking dish and bake at 350 degrees for 30 to 45 minutes, depending on the thickness of fish. Salt and pepper to taste.

Seafood

Fish

Fresh fish are available year 'round. Approximately 240 species including both fish and shellfish are harvested commercially and of these about 67 are found in Florida waters.

"Lean fish" is a designation given to fish with a low fat content. Sea trout, drum, flounder, snapper, grouper, whiting, spot, Jewfish and tilefish are common in this category. Due to low oil content, these fish maintain quality during freezing up to six months and the very leanest can be held up to a year.

"Fat fish" have an oil content of more than 5 percent. These should be used within three months when frozen. Mackerel, mullet, bluefish, croaker and pompano are a few of the fat fish found in Florida.

Lean fish may be substituted for fat fish in a recipe but more frequent basting may be required.

Spiny Lobster

The spiny lobster, also called Florida lobster, sea crawfish or crayfish, is available live or frozen. If purchased live, it must show movement.

Allow a one pound whole lobster per person. When used in combination with other ingredients, one pound will serve six.

Lobster may be baked and should be frequenly basted or completely covered with stuffing during baking.

When boiling lobster, be sure to keep the water just below the boiling point. Boiling will toughen an dry out moisture and destroy delicate texture.

Broiling cooked lobster is a common practice but steaming retains the moisture and texture of the meat and is the preferred method. Steam just long enough to heat the lobster meat. Serve immediately in the shell.

Many recipes used for crab and shrimp are excellent with lobster substituted. It is also delicious served with drawn butter, garlic butter or hollandaise.

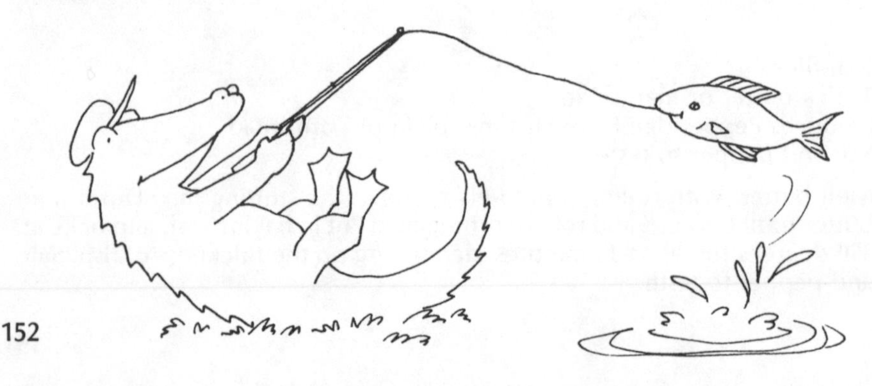

Meats

Jeni

Sauces
THE GRAVY BOAT
Jeni

Jeni

Beef Wellington

4 to 4½ pound tenderloin
Salt and pepper

Preheat the oven to 425 degrees. Salt and pepper the beef. Bake for 30 minutes. Let stand to cool. Trim all fat. Serves 8 people at ½ pound per person.

Butter pastry:
1 cup cold butter
2 tablespoons shortening (Crisco)
3¾ cups flour
1 teaspoon salt
¾ cup ice water (approximately)

Cut butter and shortening into the flour. Add salt. Add water 1 tablespoon at a time to make stiff dough. Cover and chill. Roll butter pastry 3 inches larger than the roast (approximately 12 to 13 inches wide).

Duxelle:
1 pound mushrooms, finely chopped
¼ cup green onion, chopped
¼ cup butter
½ teaspoon salt
¼ teaspoon marjoram
2 teaspoons flour
Dash of pepper
¼ cup beef broth
2 teaspoons parsley, chopped
½ to 1 cup ham, finely chopped

Saute' mushrooms, onions and butter until liquid evaporates. Stir in everything but parsley and ham. Cook and stir constantly until thickened (boil). Mixture is like paste. Remove and add parsley and ham. Let cool. Press duxelle into pastry, leaving one inch uncovered at edges. Place beef on pastry. Close. Press edges tightly. Trim and have a single layer of dough on ends. Place seam side down in pan. Cut decorations (flowers and petals) from remaining dough.

Topping:
1 egg
1 tablespoon water
Sesame seeds

Brush pastry with egg and water mixture. Sprinkle with sesame seeds.

Bake at 400 degrees 30 to 35 minutes until dough is brown. Let stand 15 minutes before cutting.

When slicing thin slices of raw meat, place in freezer for half an hour to make slicing easier.

Beef

Steak au Poivre

2 tender steaks, ½ inch thick
Whole black peppercorns
2 shallots or green onions, minced
2 tablespoons beef fat or salad oil
Approximately 3 ounces cognac
3 tablespoons red wine, cream or broth

Preheat the frying pan - high heat is essential. Coarsely crush the peppercorns by placing them in a plastic bag and using a rolling pin. (Allow approximately 1 teaspoon pepper per steak.) Press the pepper into each side of the steak with your hands. Saute' the shallots in oil. When tender, push to one side and add the steaks. Cook quickly on one side; turn and cook the other side. When steaks are done to your liking, pour in cognac and light. As soon as the flames die down, put the meat on heated plates and add wine to the pan. Ladle pan drippings over the steaks. Serves 2.

Favorite Swiss Steak

2 pounds round steak, cut into serving pieces
Flour seasoned with garlic salt, accent, lemon pepper
1 medium onion, sliced
½ green pepper, chopped
1 to 2 stalks celery, finely chopped
2 cloves garlic, minced
16 ounces canned tomatoes
1 cup bouillon
½ teaspoon sweet basil
½ teaspoon marjoram

Pound steak well with a meat mallet; dredge in seasoned flour. Saute' steak, onion, green pepper, celery and 1 clove of garlic in cooking oil; drain to remove excess grease when steak is well browned. Place steaks in baking dish. Put tomatoes in blender for 10 to 15 seconds on low speed. Combine with bouillon, remaining garlic, basil and marjoram in saucepan and heat to a full boil. Pour sauce over steaks; cover tightly and bake in 300 degree oven for 2 to 2½ hours. Serves 6.

Note: This recipe can be prepared in advance and can also be frozen.

Orange Beef Fondue

2 pounds beef tenderloin, cubed, or other cut of beef

Marinade:
½ cup water
2 bay leaves, crumbled
6 whole peppercorns, crushed
2 teaspoons sugar
½ cup onion, chopped
1 clove garlic, crushed
¾ cup orange juice
¼ cup peanut oil

Combine water, bay leaves, peppercorns, sugar, onion and garlic in a small saucepan. Boil slowly for 5 minutes. Cool and pour into a jar with orange juice and oil. Shake well and pour over beef. Marinate for at least 1 hour.

Note: Serve beef fondue with Curry Sauce (curry mixed with mayonnaise) and Fire Pot Sauce. Use peanut oil for cooking beef fondue. The marinade will tenderize tougher cuts.

Fire Pot Sauce:
1 cup soy sauce
1 tablespoon salad oil
6 drops Tabasco sauce
1 tablespoon scallions, finely chopped
1 teaspoon sesame seeds

Combine soy sauce, salad oil and Tabasco sauce. Sprinkle with scallions and sesame seeds. Makes 1¾ cups.

Fast Flank Steak

1 flank steak
4 whole cloves
1 to 2 teaspoons garlic salt
2 to 3 tablespoons catsup
1 teaspoon butter

Preheat broiler. Place flank steak in broiler pan and stud with cloves. Sprinkle top all over with garlic salt to taste. Cover surface with a thin layer of catsup. Dot with butter. Broil without turning until top begins to blacken, or about 12 to 15 minutes, depending on desired degree of doneness (rare will be more tender). Remove cloves and slice thinly on the diagonal. Serves 4 to 6.

Note: While steak is broiling, microwave baked potatoes, toss a salad and dinner will be ready in less time than it takes to go for fast food.

Beef

Filet Steak with Mustard Glaze

4 filet steaks, 1 inch thick
Salt
Freshly ground black pepper
4 tablespoons butter
2 tablespoons olive oil
4 teaspoons Dijon mustard
2 tablespoons brown sugar

Season steaks generously with salt and freshly ground pepper. Heat butter and olive oil in a thick bottomed frying pan and saute' steaks on each side until tender (3 to 6 minutes on each side for rare to well done). Spread 1 teaspoon Dijon mustard on top of each steak; sprinkle with brown sugar. Transfer steak to a gratin dish and glaze under a preheated broiler until golden brown. This will take only a short time. Serves 4.

Marinated Roast Beef

4½ to 5 pound eye of round roast

Paste: Made of fresh garlic, salt and pepper

Sauce:
3 tomatoes with seeds
1 green pepper, chopped
1 red bell pepper, chopped
½ cup green olives, chopped
2 slices of dill pickle
2 tablespoons Worcestershire sauce
½ cup good quality oil
¾ cup white vinegar
1 tablespoon salt
1 tablespoon prepared mustard

For the sauce, mix the above ingredients. Taste and adjust seasoning. It should be spicy.

Two or three days before serving, cover the meat with the paste. Refrigerate in a covered dish.

One or two days before serving, bake at 350 degrees until cooked to your taste. Cool and slice as thinly as possible. In a 2 quart dish begin with a layer of sauce, then meat, etc. Refrigerate at least 24 hours.

Recipes often call for small amounts of tomato paste. Spoon the rest into a freezer container and freeze.

Carne Asade

2 pounds tenderloin, sliced
2 cups vegetable oil
1 cup soy sauce
Juice of 1 lemon
2 teaspoons cracked black pepper
1 teaspoon garlic powder
1 teaspoon oregano

Marinate meat for no longer than one hour, otherwise it is too salty. Heat oil in large skillet and saute' beef quickly. Serve immediately in warm, buttered soft flour tortillas. Top with guacamole and/or salsa fresco and/or refried beans.

Beef Burgundy

2 pounds steak, cubed
2 large red onions, chopped
1 garlic clove, chopped
4 ounces butter
21 ounces canned beef gravy
1 tablespoon flour
2 tablespoons water
Salt and pepper to taste
¼ teaspoon oregano
½ cup Burgundy wine
¼ teaspoon marjoram
½ pint sour cream
Parsley, chopped

Saute' the onion and garlic in butter until tender. Brown the meat in the drippings. When the meat is brown, add the gravy which has been heated, then thicken with paste made from flour and water. When the meat mixture is well blended, add the salt and pepper and the onions and garlic. Cover and simmer gently one hour, or until meat is tender. Stir in the oregano, marjoram and the wine. Simmer, uncovered, for 15 minutes. Then slowly stir in the sour cream. Heat but do not boil. Serve over noodles or rice. Sprinkle with parsley. Serves 8.

Sauerbraten

4 pound roast
1 lemon, cut into ¼ inch slices
3 tablespoon butter
½ cup sour cream
Flour

Marinade:
2 cups vinegar
1 large onion, quartered
2 teaspoons salt
¼ cup sugar
2 bay leaves
2 cups water
10 peppercorns
3 whole cloves

Mix marinade ingredients and heat but do not boil. Pour over raw roast and allow to cool. Add lemon slices. Cover and refrigerate for 3 to 4 days, turning meat once or twice a day.

Strain and save all the marinade. Brown the meat on all sides in butter over medium heat. Add 2 cups marinade slowly; cover kettle and cook over medium heat for 2½ to 3 hours. Remove meat to platter and keep warm. To prepare gravy, add sour cream and flour to remaining liquid and cook over low heat until thickened.

Roquefort London Broil

2 pounds flank steak
3 ounces Roquefort cheese
4 tablespoons butter
1 teaspoon Worchestershire sauce

Put the Roquefort cheese and butter in a bowl and pour the Worcestershire sauce on top. Do not blend. Let this soften for several hours. Then broil the steak under a high flame 5 minutes per side. Remove. Mix the softened ingredients together and spread on top of the steak. Return to the broiler for 1 or 2 minutes. Remove to a platter. Carve the steak against the grain in ½ inch slices. Serves 4. This is also good cooked outside on the grill.

Bul Kogi

2 pounds flank steak

Marinade:
½ cup onion, chopped
4 garlic cloves, crushed
5 tablespoons soy sauce
5 tablespoons oil (preferably sesame seed oil
1 tablespoon sugar
2 teaspoons black pepper
3 tablespoons sherry

Mix the above ingredients for the marinade. Add the meat; cover and let stand in the refrigerator for 2 hours.

If using wok: Partially freeze the flank steaks to make it easier to slice across the grain in very thin (¼ inch) slices. Add to marinade. Cook 3 minutes on each side.

If using grill: Place meat in marinade. Grill 3 to 4 minutes on each side 4 inches from the coals for rare.

Barbecue Brisket

4 to 5 pounds of brisket
Liquid smoke

Sauce:
1 cup catsup
¼ cup Worcestershire sauce
1 teaspoon chili powder
1 cup water
1 teaspoon celery seed
1 cup brown sugar

Mix the above ingredients for the barbecue sauce.

Preheat oven to 325 degrees. Rub brisket with liquid smoke. Bake in oven 3 hours covered. Cool and refrigerate overnight. The next day you may thinly slice the meat. It may be frozen at this time. Place the beef in a pan and cover with sauce. Simmer in oven for 1 hour. Good alone or as a sandwich. Serves 6 to 8.

Note: This is great for a cocktail buffet!

Beef

Rolled Steak

1 pound round steak, thinly sliced
Mustard
Dill pickle, thinly sliced
Onion, thinly sliced

Spread meat with mustard. Place pickle and onion slice on meat. Roll and fasten with a toothpick. Brown in large skillet in butter. Cover and simmer about 30 minutes. Salt and pepper may be added.

Note: May use top sirloin or flank steak, cut on diagonal. Roll will be 1 to 1½ inches wide.

Hot Chili

1 pound ground beef
½ pound Italian sausage, casing removed
1 onion, chopped
1 bell pepper, chopped
1 celery stalk, chopped
1 small clove garlic, crushed
2 tablespoons butter
1 jalapeño pepper, diced
1 cup red kidney beans
16 ounces stewed tomatoes
12 ounces tomato paste
¼ cup chili powder
2 dashes Tabasco sauce
1 tablespoon Worcestershire sauce
1 tablespoon white vinegar
½ teaspoon red pepper, crushed
1 teaspoon bay leaves, crushed
6 ounces beer
1 cup water

Saute' the onion, bell pepper, celery and garlic in butter until tender. Add the ground beef and sausage and cook over medium heat until brown. Add the jalapeño pepper, kidney beans, tomatoes, tomato paste, chili powder, Tabasco sauce, Worcestershire sauce, vinegar, red pepper and bay leaves. Stir in the beer and the water and simmer for 2 hours. Serves 6 to 8.

Favorite Casserole

2 pounds ground beef
12 ounces tomato sauce
10 ounces tomatoes and green chilies
1 teaspoon oregano
Salt and pepper to taste
1 tablespoon sugar (optional)
16 ounces sour cream
8 ounces Cheddar cheese, grated
8 ounces cream cheese, softened
16 ounces large noodles

Brown the ground beef. Add tomato sauce, tomatoes and green chilies, oregano, salt, pepper and sugar. Simmer for 20 minutes. Cream the sour cream, 2/3 of the Cheddar cheese and the cream cheese together. Cook the noodles as directed for casseroles. Do not over cook. In a large casserole dish, layer the meat sauce, noodles and cheese mixture. Repeat, ending wth meat sauce. Garnish with remaining cheese. Cover and bake at 350 degrees for 30 minutes or until bubbly. Serves 8 to 10.

Note: This can be prepared in advance, refrigerated and cooked just before serving.

Streamlined Lasagna

1 pound ground beef
1/3 cup onion, minced
1 tablespoon salad oil
¾ teaspoon salt
¼ teaspoon pepper
1 clove garlic, minced
¼ teaspoon oregano
3 tablespoons parsley, divided
20 ounces canned tomatoes, cut up
12 ounces tomato paste
6 ounces lasagna (6 pieces)
¼ pound Swiss cheese, thinly sliced
1½ cups cottage cheese

Brown beef and onion in oil; add salt, pepper, garlic, oregano, 1 tablespoon parsley, tomatoes and tomato paste. Simmer uncovered for 30 minutes. Cook lasagna by package directions; drain. Preheat oven to 350 degrees. Layer lasagna, half of the sauce, half of the cottage cheese and half of the Swiss cheese in a greased oblong dish. Repeat layers. Sprinkle with 2 tablespoons parsley. Bake uncovered for 30 minutes, or until hot and bubbly. Serves 8 to 10.

Portia's Lasagna

1 pound ground beef
10 ounces lasagna noodles, cooked
1 pound Mozzarella cheese, thinly sliced

Sauce:
1 clove garlic, minced
1 tablespoon parsley, chopped
1 tablespoon basil
½ teaspoon salt
Pepper to taste
16 ounces canned tomatoes
12 ounces tomato paste
Pinch of onion salt

Brown ground beef slowly; spoon off fat. Add the sauce ingredients and simmer, uncovered for 30 minutes. Cook noodles, drain and rinse in cold water.

Filling:
24 ounces creamed cottage cheese
½ cup Parmesan cheese, grated
2 eggs, beaten
2 tablespoons parsley, chopped
2 teaspoons salt
2 teaspoons pepper

Combine ingredients for filling and mix well.

To assemble lasagna, place half the noodles in the bottom of a 13 X 9 X 2 inch pan. Spread half the filling on top of the noodles, top with half of the Mozzarella cheese, then half of the sauce. Repeat layers. Bake at 350 degrees for 30 minutes. Let stand 10 minutes before cutting.

Note: This may be assembled ahead of time and refrigerated. If lasagna is cold before baking, allow an additional 15 minutes of baking time. This also freezes well.

Manicotti Verde

Sauce:

½ pound ground beef
1 or 2 tablespoons butter
1 small clove garlic, mashed
16 ounces canned tomatoes
8 ounces tomato sauce
½ teaspoon salt
Pepper

Brown meat in butter with garlic; add remaining ingredients and heat to boiling. Cover and cook over medium heat about 20 minutes. Uncover and simmer 1 to 2 hours.

Filling:

¼ cup onion, chopped
2 tablespoons butter
10 ounces frozen chopped spinach, cooked and well drained
2 cups Ricotta cheese
½ cup Parmesan cheese, grated
2 eggs, lightly beaten
½ teaspoon each of salt and pepper

Lightly cook onion in butter. Stir in spinach, Ricotta cheese and Parmesan cheese. Add eggs and seasonings and mix well.

3 to 10 Manicotti shells, cooked according to package directions.

Using a small spoon, fill shells with spinach filling. Pour half of sauce into 11¾X7½X1¾ inch baking dish. Arrange filled shells in a row; pour remaining sauce over. Bake at 350 degrees for 30 minutes. Serves 4.

Note: Serve with antipasto, tossed salad and garlic bread for a complete dinner. This is a good buffet dish and can be prepared ahead of time and frozen.

Gougère De Gibier

Choux Paste Pastry:
1 cup water
½ cup butter
1 cup flour
4 eggs, beaten
½ cup Cheddar cheese, diced

Pastry can be mixed ahead and refrigerated, but allow to soften to room temperature before baking. Bring water and butter to a boil. Remove from heat and add flour all at once, stirring vigorously until smooth. Cool, then add eggs, a little at a time, beating in thoroughly. Stir in cheese and season to taste.

Filling:
1 medium onion, sliced
1 tablespoon butter
½ cup mushrooms, sliced
2 tablespoons flour
1 cup stock
1 cup meat, cooked
1 teaspoon herbs, chopped
1 tablespoon Cheddar cheese, grated
Bread crumbs
Chopped parsley

Preheat oven to 400 degrees. Saute' onion in butter, adding mushrooms. Stir in flour and pour in stock. Stir until boiling. Add meat and herbs. (A diced, peeled and pitted tomato may be added).

Butter an ovenproof dish (round) and arrange pastry around sides, leaving a hollow in the center; then pour filling in. Sprinkle with grated Cheddar cheese and bread crumbs. Bake for 30 to 40 minutes. When risen and browned, sprinkle with chopped parsley. Serve immediately.

Short Ribs Supreme

3 pounds beef short ribs
2 teaspoons salt
½ cup water
½ cup onion, chopped
1 clove garlic, minced
6 ounces tomato paste
1 cup catsup
¾ cup brown sugar
½ cup vinegar
2 tablespoons prepared mustard

Brown the ribs in their own fat. Cover and simmer for 1 hour. Pour off the drippings. Mix the other ingredients and add to the meat. Cover tightly and cook 1½ hours or until tender. Serves 4.

Note: This is a good family meal.

Stir Fried Beef and Vegetables

1 pound flank steak
2 tablespoons soy sauce
2 tablespoons dry Vermouth
2 garlic cloves, crushed
⅛ teaspoon red pepper, crushed
1½ cups beef broth, divided
3 teaspoons corn starch
3 teaspoons salad oil, divided
2 medium onions, cut in wedges
1 bunch broccoli, cut in 2 inch pieces
1 green pepper, cut in 1½ inch chunks
½ pint cherry tomatoes, cut in half

With a sharp knife, cut the flank steak lengthwise into 1½ inch strips. Cut the strips diagonally across the grain into ⅛ inch thick pieces. In a medium bowl combine the soy sauce, Vermouth, garlic and red pepper. Add the beef strips and toss to coat well. In a small bowl combine 1 cup beef broth and the corn starch. Set aside. In a medium skillet over high heat, heat 2 teaspoons oil until very hot. Add the beef strips and cook, stirring quickly and frequently for 3 to 5 minutes. With a slotted spoon, remove the beef strips to a bowl and set aside. In the same skillet heat 1 teaspoon more of salad oil. Stir-fry the onion, broccoli and green pepper 2 to 3 minutes. Add the remaining beef broth, cover and reduce the heat and cook for 5 minutes or until the vegetables are tender-crisp. Add the cherry tomatoes, beef strips and broth. Cook, stirring gently, until sauce thickens. Serves 4.

Note: This is a low calorie dish with only 260 calories per serving. Serve with steamed rice and a salad for a complete meal.

Chop Soupy

1 pound round steak or sirloin, cut into very thin strips
3 tablespoons salad oil
4 ounces mushrooms, sliced and drained
1½ cups celery, sliced
1 cup green pepper pieces
1 can onion soup or beef broth
2 tablespoons soy sauce
2 tablespoons corn starch
½ cup water

Brown round steak in oil. Add mushrooms, celery, green pepper, onion soup and soy sauce. Cook 20 minutes until meat is tender. Mix corn starch and water until smooth and then add to meat mixture until juices thicken. Serve over cooked rice. Serves 6 to 8.

Note: This recipe can be frozen.

Salpicon Al Queso

- 2 pounds ground beef
- 3 strips bacon
- 2 tablespoons olive oil
- 3 tablespoons butter, divided
- 1 medium onion, minced
- 1 garlic clove, minced
- 1 slice American bread, crust removed
- ½ cup evaporated milk, heated
- 1 teaspoon salt
- 3 tablespoons tomato sauce
- ½ teaspoon Tabasco sauce
- 2 egg yolks, slightly beaten
- 1 cup Cheddar cheese, cubed
- 1 tablespoon fresh parsley, chopped
- ¼ cup toasted almonds, finely crushed
- ½ cup seasoned bread crumbs, divided
- 2 egg whites
- 2½ ounce jar of mushrooms, drained
- 1 bouillon cube
- 1 cup water
- ½ cup tomato sauce
- ½ cup Burgundy wine

Preheat oven to 325 degrees. Use a shallow baking pan, 11½X8½ inch, greased lightly with butter. Place bacon strips, evenly spaced, at an angle. Place meat in a large mixing bowl. In a skillet, heat oil and 2 tablespoons butter, add onion and saute' until transparent. Add garlic and cook until onion is limp. Pour saute' over meat in bowl but do not mix. Place bread in a saucer and add hot milk. Crumble bread as it soaks up the milk. Set aside.

To meat in bowl, add salt, tomato sauce, Tabasco sauce, egg yolks, cheese, parsley, almonds and 2 tablespoons of seasoned bread crumbs. With 2 wooden spoons mix thoroughly but lightly all ingredients in bowl. Add soaked bread and mix again. Beat egg whites until soft peaks form and fold into meat mixture.

On a long strip of wax paper, spread the remaining bread crumbs, place meat mixture on top of the bread crumbs and mold into a well shaped meat loaf about 14 inches long and 4 inches in diameter. Do not handle too much or press the meat mixture. Give it room to cook deliciously light and juicy. Roll meat loaf carefully into the pan with bacon. Bring bacon up and around the meat loaf and secure ends of bacon with a toothpick. Bake uncovered for 30 minutes.

Meanwhile, in a skillet, saute' the mushrooms in 1 tablespoon of butter for 2 or 3 minutes. Dissolve the bouillon cube in hot water and combine with the tomato sauce and wine. Add to skillet, bring to a boil, then simmer for 15 minutes. Remove from heat and, when meat loaf has been in the oven for 30 minutes, pour sauce over it and bake another 30 minutes, basting occasionally. Serves 6 to 8.

Note: An envelope of dried onion soup may be added to the hot water instead of the bouillon cube. This also makes a superb sauce for the salpicon. Slice leftover meat thinly for sandwiches. Exceptionally good on hamburger buns calientes!

Mushroom Filled Meat Loaf

Filling:

1 cup fresh mushrooms, sliced
1 cup onion, chopped
2 tablespoons butter
½ cup sour cream

Saute' mushrooms and onion in butter. Remove from heat and stir in sour cream. Set aside.

Meatloaf:

1½ pounds ground beef
2 eggs
½ cup milk
¾ cup bread crumbs
2 teaspoons salt
1 tablespoon Worcestershire sauce

Preheat oven to 350 degrees. Combine ingredients and place half of the meat loaf mixture in a 9 X 5 X 3 inch loaf pan. Make shallow trough down the center of the meat for filling. Spoon filling into this crevice. Shape the rest of the meat loaf mixture over the filling, making sure all the filling is covered. Seal the meat loaf well around the edges. Bake 1 hour. Let stand 15 minutes before slicing. Serves 4 to 6.

Topping:

1 cup fresh mushrooms, thinly sliced

Garnish top with mushrooms before serving.

Sour Cream Sauce:

1 cup sour cream
1 teaspoon Dijon mustard
1 teaspoon prepared horseradish
½ teaspoon salt
Pinch of nutmeg
White pepper

Stir together ingredients in a saucepan over low heat. Pour sour cream sauce over hot meat loaf.

Beef

Meat Loaf in the Round

2 pounds ground beef
1½ cups Cheddar cheese, shredded and divided
2 cups soft bread crumbs
1 egg, slightly beaten
½ cup celery, chopped
½ cup onion, chopped
1 teaspoon Worcestershire sauce
1 teaspoon salt
1 teaspoon pepper
8 ounces tomato sauce

Preheat oven to 350 degrees. Combine ground beef, 1 cup cheese, bread crumbs, egg, celery, onion, Worcesterhsire sauce, salt and pepper. Mix well and shape into a ball. Flatten ball slightly and place in a shallow 9 inch pan and bake for 1 hour. Pour off drippings and pour tomato sauce over meat. Sprinkle with remaining cheese and bake an additional 15 minutes. Serves 8.

Note: This recipe can be frozen before or after cooking.

Meal in a Squash

5 medium to large yellow squash
½ pound sausage, mild
½ cup onion, chopped
1 rib celery, chopped
¼ cup seasoned stuffing mix
3 tablespoons Parmesan cheese
½ teaspoon salt
½ teaspoon pepper
¼ teaspoon Italian seasoning
¼ cup Mozzarella cheese, grated
8 ounces tomato sauce or Italian sauce with mushrooms

Preheat oven to 350 degrees. Cook whole squash in water until tender. Cool, split length-wise, scoop out pulp and reserve. Saute' meat, onion and celery. Add squash pulp, stuffing mix, Parmesan cheese, salt, pepper and Italian seasoning. Stuff squash shells. Place in greased 9 X 13 inch dish. Top with Mozzarella cheese. Pour sauce over squash and cheese. Bake for 35 minutes. Serves 4 to 5.

Pouring a strong solution of salt and hot water down the sink will help eliminate and remove grease from drainer.

Mexican Meatballs

1 pound ground beef
1 pound ground pork
3 slices fresh bread
¼ cup milk
2 teaspoons salt
1 teaspoon chili powder
½ teaspoon oregano
2 eggs, beaten

Soak bread in milk. Add to remaining ingredients. Mix well. Form small (1½ inch) meatballs. Set aside.

Sauce:
2 tablespoons olive oil
½ cup onion, chopped
1 clove garlic, chopped
1½ tablespoons chili powder
1 teaspoon salt
¼ teaspoon oregano
¼ teaspoon cumin
10½ ounces tomato purée

In oil brown onion and garlic. Add remaining sauce ingredients and bring to a boil. Simmer covered for 15 minutes. Add 1 cup water and bring to boil. Drop in meatballs, one at a time. Simmer for 35 minutes covered, stir several times. Serves 4 to 6.

Note: Serve this recipe over rice or tiny noodles for a different dinner idea.

Island Teriyaki

½ cup soy sauce
¼ cup brown sugar
2 tablespoons olive oil
1 teaspoon dry ginger
¼ teaspoon pepper
2 cloves garlic, minced

Combine and mix well.

1½ pounds sirloin steak, cut into strips ¼ inch thick by 1 inch wide
Water chestnuts

Add to sauce. Stir to coat. Let stand 2 hours. Lace meat in accordian style on skewers. Add a water chestnut on the end of each. Broil over hot coals about 10 minutes turning often and basting with marinade. Serves 4.

Burgers Mexicale

1 pound lean ground beef
½ medium onion, finely chopped
¾ teaspoon salt
⅛ teaspoon pepper
8 ounces taco sauce
4 pineapple slices, drained
2 roasted red peppers, cut in half
4 ounces Monterey Jack cheese, grated
1 cup iceberg lettuce, finely shredded
4 slices whole wheat bread

In a medium bowl mix the ground beef, onion, salt, pepper and ½ cup taco sauce; shape into 4 patties. Preheat the broiler. Arrange the patties on a rack in a broiling pan. With a pastry brush, brush some of the remaining taco sauce on the patties. Broil 5 to 6 minutes, turn, baste again with more taco sauce; continue broiling for 3 to 4 minutes, or until desired doneness. Place pineapple slices on rack in broiling pan; brush with remaining taco sauce. On each meat patty arrange a roasted red pepper half; sprinkle with cheese. Broil burgers and pineapple slices 1 to 2 minutes or until cheese has melted. Arrange shredded lettuce on each bread slice. Top with pineapple ring, then a hamburger patty. Serve with avocado-tomato salad. Serves 4.

Barbecued Chuck Roast

4 pound chuck roast
3 tablespoons flour
3 tablespoons brown sugar
1 teaspoon salt
1 teaspoon pepper
½ teaspoon dry mustard
¾ cup catsup
1½ tablespoons Worcestershire sauce
1 tablespoon vinegar
5 feet aluminum foil

Brown roast over charcoal fire for 20 to 30 minutes. Mix flour, brown sugar, salt, pepper, dry mustard, catsup, Worcestershire sauce and vinegar. Double the foil and place the roast on it. Top with 1/3 to ½ of the sauce. Seal and bake over coals for 1½ to 2 hours. Potatoes, carrots and onions may be cooked in foil with the roast. Heat remaining sauce and serve with roast. Serves 6 to 8.

Barbecued Bourbon Pot Roast

Chuck roast with blade
1 5-ounce bottle soy sauce
½ cup water
¼ cup brown sugar, packed
¼ cup bourbon
Juice of ½ lemon

Combine the soy sauce, water, brown sugar, bourbon and lemon juice. Pour over the chuck roast and marinate in the refrigerator overnight. The next morning, remove the roast from the refrigerator and allow it to sit out all day, turning occasionally in the marinade. To cook, place over charcoal fire and cook approximately 20 minutes per side, basting continuously with the marinade. Cut into thin slices and serve with the heated left over marinade.

Italian Pot Roast

1 chuck roast
1 carrot, chopped
1 stalk celery, chopped
1 onion, ringed
Salt and pepper to taste
Garlic salt to taste
1 can mushrooms
1 cup red wine
1 small can tomato paste
2 cups beef broth or consomme', warmed
2 bay leaves

Put all ingredients in a crock pot on low and cook all day. Thicken gravy and serve over pasta.

Venison Stroganoff

1½ pounds venison, fat removed and cut in 2X1½ inch strips
Salt and pepper
2 small onions, thinly sliced
5½ tablespoons margarine, divided
Small amount of flour
1 teaspoon hot prepared mustard
1 cup beef bouillon
½ cup sour cream at room temperature

Salt and pepper the venison and brown in 4 tablespoons margarine with sliced onions. In 1½ tablespoons margarine blend flour, then add mustard and bouillon. Stir and cook until thick and smooth. Add sour cream and heat to boiling. Add meat and onions. Heat until hot. Serve over cooked noodles. Serves 3 to 4.

Note: To remove the gamy taste of the venison, soak in 1 cup vinegar at room temperature for 1 hour before cooking.

Sunshine Fondue Sauce

¼ cup butter
½ cup catsup
¾ cup fresh Florida orange juice
¼ cup Florida lime juice
½ cup brown sugar
1 clove garlic, minced
1 tablespoon soy sauce
½ teaspoon ginger
1 teaspoon corn starch
1 tablespoon cold water

Melt butter in small saucepan over medium heat. Add remaining ingredients except corn starch and water. Heat mixture, stirring until smooth. Add corn starch to water and mix well. Remove sauce from heat and add corn starch mixture. Stir well and return to heat. Simmer for 10 to 15 minutes. Serve as a dip for beef fondue. Makes approximately 2 cups.

Ham Loaf

1½ pounds lean pork, ground
1 pound ham, ground
2 eggs
1 cup milk
10 slices bread, torn
1 can tomato soup
1 teaspoon pepper or more to taste

Preheat oven to 350 degrees. Mix ingredients together and bake for 1 hour and 30 minutes. Serves 4 to 6.

Note: Have the pork and ham ground together. This may be made in a ring mold and served with vegetables in the center and mustard sauce on the side. This can be frozen.

Ham and Artichoke Bake

12 thin slices ham, boiled or baked
2 pounds canned artichoke hearts, drained
4 tablespoons butter
4 tablespoons flour
2 cups warm milk
Generous dash seasoned salt
Generous dash cayenne pepper
¼ teaspoon ground nutmeg
Paprika
Pinch of white pepper
2/3 cup Swiss and Parmesan cheese, grated and mixed
4 tablespoons dry sherry

Melt the butter in a saucepan over medium heat. Gradually stir in the flour and warm milk; when smooth return to heat. Stir constantly until thickened. Add the seasonings, then cheese. Stir over low heat until melted. Remove from heat; stir in sherry.

If the artichoke hearts are large, cut in half and wrap two halves in a slice of ham, allowing two rolls per person. Arrange in a buttered casserole dish with sides touching; pour sauce over all.

Topping:
2/3 cup buttered bread crumbs
2/3 cup Parmesan and Swiss cheese, grated and mixed

Mix the above ingredients and put on top. Bake at 350 degrees for 25 to 30 minutes until brown and bubbly. Serves 6.

Ham and Asparagus Bake

2 cups ham, cubed
2 cups Minute Rice, uncooked
½ to 1 cup Cheddar cheese, grated
1 can cream of asparagus soup
1 cup half and half
3 tablespoons onion, chopped
1 cup corn flakes
5 tablespoons butter, melted
1 large can asparagus or a frozen package of asparagus spears

Preheat the oven to 375 degrees. Combine the first six ingredients and pour in a round buttered casserole dish. Top with corn flakes tossed in the melted butter and bake for 20 to 25 minutes or until corn flakes are lightly browned. Arrange heated asparagus spears in a pin wheel design on top of the casserole and serve immediately.

Really good with a congealed, frozen or fresh fruit salad and garlic bread.

Jambalaya

2½ cups ham, cooked and cubed
½ pound raw shrimp, shelled
5 bacon strips
1½ cups uncooked rice
1 medium onion, minced
1 green pepper, chopped
1 clove garlic, crushed
16 ounces canned tomatoes
13¾ ounces canned chicken broth
1 bay leaf
1 teaspoon salt
½ teaspoon thyme
3 to 4 drops Tabasco sauce

Fry bacon until crisp in a large skillet. Drain bacon, crumble and set it aside. In the same skillet, in bacon grease over medium heat, cook the rice, onion, green pepper and garlic until the rice is lightly browned. Stir in tomatoes with their liquid, chicken broth, bay leaf, salt and thyme. Cover and simmer 20 minutes. Stir in ham, shrimp and Tabasco sauce. Cook covered for 15 to 20 minutes until the rice is tender. Stir occasionally. Spoon onto platter and top with crumbled bacon. Serves 6.

Stuffed Ham Rolls with Creamed Chicken

2 cups creamed chicken:
4 or 5 chicken breasts or 1 hen
1 onion
1 carrot
1 stalk celery
1 can cream of chicken soup
1/3 cup chicken stock
1/3 cup milk
Sauteed mushrooms, sliced
Pimiento, chopped
1 teaspoon curry powder
¼ cup sherry

Stuffing:
½ cup rice, cooked
3 tablespoons butter
½ cup almonds or walnuts, toasted
2 tablespoons parsley, chopped
Pinch of poultry seasoning or mixed herbs
Salt and pepper to taste

16 thin slices cooked ham
Paprika

For creamed chicken, boil a hen with the onion, carrot and celery until it is tender. Remove the meat from the bones and chop it into bite sized pieces. Use undiluted soup, thinned with the chicken stock and milk. Add the chicken to the liquid. Add the mushrooms and pimiento. Add curry and sherry. Mix all together.

Mix the stuffing ingredients well and spread on the ham slices. Roll up and place flat side down in a baking pan. Cover with creamed chicken. Sprinkle with paprika. Bake at 350 degrees until hot and bubbly.

For a ladies lunch, serves 16. For a buffet or brunch, serves 8. This can be prepared ahead of time.

Pork Chop Casserole

4 pork chops
1 cup raw rice
1 green pepper, sliced
1 medium onion, sliced
2 cans beef consomme', undiluted

Place rice on bottom of casserole and lay pork chops over rice. Cover with green pepper and onions. Pour soup over top. Bake in 325 degree oven for 1½ to 2 hours. You may wish to sprinkle with thyme and pepper.

Pork

Oriental Pork Chops with Vegetables

6 pork chops, cut 1 inch thick
1/3 cup soy sauce
2 tablespoons lemon juice
½ teaspoon dry mustard
½ teaspoon ginger
¼ teaspoon garlic powder
⅛ teaspoon pepper
½ cup water
2 cups celery, diagonally sliced
2 small onions, sliced in rings
2 tablespoons corn starch
8 ounces water chestnuts, sliced
1 cup fresh mushrooms, sliced
10 ounces frozen pea pods

Combine soy sauce, lemon juice, mustard, ginger, garlic powder and pepper in a small saucepan. Stir in water and cook 5 minutes, stirring to blend. Cool. Place chops in plastic bag or dish; add marinade, turning to coat chops on both sides. Tie bag securely or cover dish and marinate in refrigerator 4 hours or overnight. Pour marinade from chops into saucepan and place chops on rack in broiler pan so surface of meat is 4 to 5 inches from heat. Broil 8 minutes, turn and broil 8 additional minutes. Continue broiling 5 to 10 minutes or until done. Add celery and onions to marinade, cover tightly and cook 10 minutes. Blend ¼ cup cold water with corn starch, stir into vegetables and stir until thickened. Add water chestnuts and mushrooms and cook slowly for 5 minutes. Fold in pea pods, warm through and serve. Serves 6.

Tangy Barbecued Pork Chops

6 to 8 pork chops
½ cup maple syrup
½ cup catsup
1 tablespoon Worcestershire sauce
1 tablespoon steak sauce
1 teaspoon vinegar
1 tablespoon prepared mustard
1 tablespoon salad oil
1 teaspoon butter, melted
1 teaspoon lemon juice
Dash of ground cloves
Salt and pepper to taste

Combine all ingredients except pork chops in a small saucepan; bring to boil. Simmer over low heat 5 to 10 minutes. Grill chops over medium heat, basting frequently. Serves 6 to 8.

Cheese Stuffed Pork Chops

4 double rib pork chops
3 ounce can mushrooms, sliced
¾ cup processed Swiss or Velveeta cheese, diced
2 tablespoons parsley flakes
⅜ teaspoon salt, divided
½ cup bread crumbs, seasoned
Dash pepper
1 egg, beaten
Hot shortening
Parsley, sage or thyme, optional

Trim excess fat from chops. Cut pocket in fat side of each chop. Drain mushrooms, reserving liquid. Combine mushrooms, cheese, parsley and ½ of the salt and stuff into pockets. Use toothpicks to close chops. Mix crumbs, remaining salt and dash of pepper. Dip chops into egg, then into crumbs and brown slowly in hot shortening. Add water (or wine) to reserved mushroom liquid to make ½ cup liquid. Pour over chops. Cover tightly and simmer for 1 hour or until tender. Serves 4.

Ham Stuffed Pork Chops

6 (½ inch thick) pork chops with pocket
1½ teaspoons salt
1½ teaspoons sage
1½ teaspoons thyme
1½ cups bread crumbs
½ cup ham, chopped
Dash pepper
⅛ teaspoon nutmeg
1 egg
10½ ounces canned condensed beef broth
2 tablespoons salad oil

Preheat oven to 450 degrees. Rub pork chops with salt, sage and thyme on all sides. Filling: Combine bread crumbs, ham, pepper, nutmeg, egg and ¼ cup beef broth. Stuff pork chops with filling and secure pockets with toothpicks. Completely brush chops with salad oil. Place side by side in baking pan. Bake uncovered 30 minutes, turning once. Reduce heat to 400 degrees. Add enough water to fill the broth can and pour over chops. Cover and bake 1½ to 2 hours. Serves 6.

Pork

Pork Chop and Apple Bake

6 pork chops
3 or 4 unpeeled apples, cored and sliced
¼ cup brown sugar, packed
½ teaspoon cinnamon
2 tablespoons butter

Preheat oven to 400 degrees. Brown chops on all sides in hot fat. Place apple slices in greased baking dish. Sprinkle with sugar and cinnamon; dot with butter. Top with chops. Cover; bake 1 hour 30 minutes. Serves 6.

Note: To prepare in the microwave, cook 40 minutes at 60% power.

Orange Sauced Pork Chops

4 pork loin chops, cut ½ inch thick
1 tablespoon cooking oil
1 tablespoon brown sugar
¼ teaspoon ground ginger
½ teaspoon orange peel, finely shredded
2/3 cup orange juice
2 tablespoons corn starch

Trim excess fat from chops. In a skillet brown the chops slowly in hot oil. Preheat oven to 350 degrees. Remove the chops to a 9 X 9 X 2 inch baking dish. Combine brown sugar, ginger and orange peel; stir in orange juice. Pour over chops. Cover and bake for 45 to 50 minutes or until chops are tender. Transfer chops to a warm platter and keep warm. Skim fat from the cooking liquid. Measure the cooking liquid and add water, if necessary, to make ¾ cup liquid. In a saucepan combine 1 tablespoon cold water and corn starch; add the ¾ cup liquid. Cook and stir until thickened and bubbly; cook and stir 2 minutes more. Spoon some sauce over the chops.

Hot Mustard

1/3 cup sugar
1/3 cup cider vinegar
1/3 cup dry mustard
1 tablespoon mayonnaise

Beat all ingredients thoroughly. Pour into jar with lid. Let sit 10 days in the refrigerator.

Orange Pork Chops

4 lean pork chops
Flour
Salt and pepper to taste
1 tablespoon fat
4 orange slices
2 tablespoons sugar
2 tablespoons corn syrup
⅛ teaspoon allspice
1 cup hot water
2 tablespoons lemon juice
¼ cup orange juice

Coat pork chops with flour seasoned with salt and pepper. Brown in fat in skillet. Put an orange slice on each chop. Mix sugar, syrup and allspice in saucepan. Gradually stir in hot water. Cook, stirring over low heat, until smooth and thick. Add fruit juices. Pour over chops. Cover and simmer 1 hour or until meat is tender. Serves 4.

Sweet and Sour Pork

1 to 1½ pounds pork
1 egg, beaten
¼ cup flour
½ teaspoon salt
¼ cup corn starch
1½ cups chicken broth, separated
Vegetable oil
1 green pepper, chopped
½ cup carrots, thinly sliced
1 clove garlic, minced
¾ cup sugar
½ cup red wine vinegar
3 teaspoons soy sauce
¼ cup cold water
3 tablespoons corn starch
8 ounces pineapple chunks, drained
2 small tomatoes, cut into wedges

Prepare batter of egg, flour, salt, corn starch and ¼ cup of the chicken broth. Beat until smooth. Trim fat from pork, cut into ½ to 1 inch cubes. Dip pork into batter, deep fry in large skillet in vegetable oil for 5 to 6 minutes. Remove from skillet and drain. Heat 2 tablespoons oil in skillet. Add pepper, carrots and garlic. Cook until tender, but not browned, stirring often. Stir in remaining chicken broth, sugar, vinegar and soy sauce. Boil rapidly 1 minute. Mix water and corn starch and add to vegetables. Cook until thickened and bubbly. Add pork, pineapple and tomatoes. Cook until just well-heated. Serve over rice. Serves 6 to 8.

Pork

Pork Turnovers

2 cups cooked pork, chopped
½ cup green pepper, chopped
¼ cup onion, chopped
1 tablespoon butter
8 ounces applesauce
2 tablespoons Dijon style mustard
½ to ¾ teaspoon ground ginger
¼ teaspoon salt
2 packages (6 biscuits each) refrigerated biscuits
Milk
Sesame seeds, optional

Preheat oven to 400 degrees. In a medium saucepan cook green pepper and onion in butter until tender. Remove from heat; stir in pork, applesauce, mustard, ginger and salt. On a floured surface roll each biscuit to a 5 inch circle. Place the pork mixture on 6 of the dough rounds, spreading mixture to within ½ inch of the edge. Top with remaining dough rounds. Moisten and press edges together; seal with tines of a fork. Brush with milk and sprinkle with sesame seeds if desired. Place on an ungreased baking sheet and bake for 10 to 12 minutes or until brown. Serves 6.

Pork Sate's

2 cups lean pork cubes
15 ounces crushed pineapple
¼ cup soy sauce
¼ cup vinegar
½ teaspoon ground ginger
1 large clove garlic, crushed
½ cup vegetable oil
12 wooden skewers

Marinate pork cubes in next six ingredients for at least four hours. Soak wooden skewers in water for 20 minutes. Heat coals of grill or hibachi, or use indoor grill. Thread pork cubes on skewers, allow 2 skewers per person. Grill over moderately hot coals 5 minutes, then turn for another 3 to 4 minutes grilling time. Baste frequently with marinade. Serve over bed of Chinese fried rice, wild rice or brown rice cooked in chicken broth. Serves 6.

Pork Mandarin

5 to 6 pound pork roast
½ cup vinegar
⅛ cup soy sauce
¾ cup pineapple juice
½ teaspoon dry mustard
Salt and pepper
Juice of 1 orange
¼ cup molasses
1 teaspoon ginger

Blend above ingredients and marinate pork overnight. Next day, bake at 350 degrees for 3½ hours. Baste every 15 to 20 minutes. Be sure to keep at least ¼ inch of liquid in pan to keep from sticking. Add water if needed. Serves 6.

Marinated Pork Roast

4 to 5 pound pork loin roast, boned and rolled
2 tablespoons dry mustard
2 teaspoons thyme
½ cup dry sherry
½ cup soy sauce
¼ teaspoon garlic powder or 2 cloves garlic, mashed
1 teaspoon ground ginger

Sauce:
10 ounces orange or apricot preserves
2 tablespoons soy sauce
2 tablespoons dry sherry

Combine the dry mustard, thyme, ½ cup sherry, soy sauce, garlic and ginger. Marinate the pork roast in this mixture 3 to 4 hours in the refrigerator. You may roast it in the oven 40 to 45 minutes per pound at 350 degrees, but it is better cooked on a rotisserie grill. The timing depends on the heat of coals, the height of the grill, etc. Cook no less than 3 hours. When done, glaze with sauce made from mixing the preserves, soy sauce and dry sherry. Heat the remaining sauce after glazing and serve. Serves 12 to 14. Excellent buffet attraction.

Pork

Pork Loin Roast with Cherry Sauce

3 pound boneless, rolled and tied pork loin
Salt and pepper to taste

Sauce:
12 ounces cherry preserves
2 tablespoons light corn syrup
¼ cup red wine vinegar
¼ teaspoon salt
¼ teaspoon ground cinnamon
¼ teaspoon ground nutmeg
¼ teaspoon ground cloves
¼ cup slivered almonds

Preheat oven to 325 degrees. Rub roast with a little salt and pepper. Place on rack in shallow baking pan. Roast, uncovered, about 2 to 2½ hours. Meanwhile combine cherry preserves, corn syrup, vinegar, salt, cinnamon, nutmeg and cloves. Heat to boiling, stirring frequently. Reduce heat and simmer 2 minutes. Add almonds. Keep sauce warm. After meat has cooked 2 to 2½ hours, spoon enough hot cherry sauce over roast to glaze. Return to oven for 30 minutes. Baste roast with sauce several times during the 30 minutes. Pour the remaining sauce with the roast at the table. Serves 4 to 6.

Sausage Casserole

1 pound sausage, fried and crumbled
16 ounces cream style corn
1 small jar pimientos, diced
10 ounces Chedddar cheese, grated and divided
4 slices bread, crumbled
2 eggs
Salt, pepper, garlic salt to taste

Preheat oven to 325 degrees. Mix sausage, corn, pimientos, 6 ounces of cheese and bread. Beat eggs with salt, pepper and garlic salt to taste. Combine all ingredients. Put in greased casserole and top with remaining grated cheese. Cover with foil. Bake for 1 hour. Uncover the last 10 minutes. Serves 4 to 6.

Curry Sauce

1 cup sour cream
½ cup mayonnaise
1 tablespoon fresh parsley, chopped
2 teaspoons curry powder
1 teaspoon fresh lemon juice
½ teaspoon Worcestershire sauce
½ clove garlic, crushed
¼ teaspoon salt

Blend all ingredients until smooth. Chill. Makes 1½ cups.

Mustard Sauce

¾ cup sugar
4 tablespoons flour
¼ teaspoon salt
8 tablespoons margarine
¾ cup prepared mustard
¼ cup water
¼ cup horseradish
¾ cup vinegar
¾ cup Miracle Whip

Mix sugar, flour, salt, margarine, mustard, water and horseradish in pan. Heat and stir until thick. Then add vinegar and cook 5 minutes or more. Let cool, add Miracle Whip. Keeps in the refrigerator for a long time. This is excellent for ham.

Jezebel Sauce

18 ounces pineapple preserves
18 ounces apple jelly
2 ounces dry mustard
5 ounces horseradish

Mix all the above ingredients together. Chill. Serve over cream cheese as a spread for crackers or serve with roast beef or pork. Makes about 1 quart.

Lamb

Minty Lamb Chops with Herb Butter

8 loin lamb chops
1/3 cup fresh mint, chopped
1 clove garlic, minced
Juice of 1 lemon
½ cup olive oil
Salt and pepper to taste

Combine all ingredients except lamb in food processor. Pour over lamb chops. Marinate several hours at room temperature. Remove chops from marinade. Broil until desired doneness is reached. Serve each chop with a dollop of herb butter. Serves 4.

Herb Butter:
½ cup butter, room temperature
2 tablespoons fresh mint, minced
1 tablespoon parsley, minced
2 cloves garlic, minced

Combine all ingredients and chill until ready to use.

Note: This can be prepared 3 to 4 hours in advance.

Mint Glazed Leg of Lamb

6 to 7 pound leg of lamb
1 clove garlic, slivered
Salt and freshly ground pepper
10 ounces mint jelly
½ cup brown sugar
½ cup catsup
1 tablespoon Worcestershire sauce
Dash of Tabasco sauce
Dash of ginger

Wipe the lamb well and place on a rack in a roasting pan, fat side up. Place the slivers of garlic in different tiny pockets of the lamb. Salt and pepper well. For a pink and juicy lamb, roast the meat in a preheated 325 degree oven for approximately 2 hours or until a meat thermometer registers 165 degrees. For a medium to well-done lamb, roast the meat 2½ to 2¾ hours or until the thermometer registers 180 degrees. The last hour of baking, baste the lamb with the glaze consisting of the remaining ingredients. Serve the remaining warm sauce with the lamb. Serves 8 to 10.

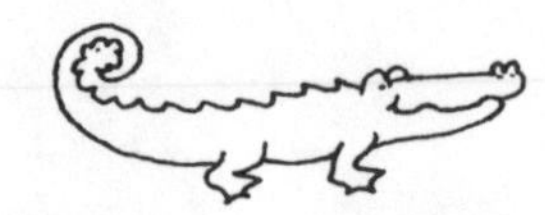

Leg of Lamb

6 pound leg of lamb
1 teaspoon ground ginger
2 tablespoons olive oil
2 cloves garlic, pressed
1 tablespoon each of marjoram, thyme and rosemary, mixed together
Salt, pepper, flour and paprika
1 cup white wine and
1 cup water, mixed together

Rub lamb with ground ginger. Then rub in the olive oil that has the garlic pressed in it. Sprinkle the marjoram, thyme and rosemary over the top of the roast. Then sprinkle salt, pepper, flour and paprika on top. Cook in 325 degree oven for 25 minutes per pound, but for at least 3 hours. Baste every 20 minutes with the water and wine mixture and then from the drippings in the bottom of the pan. Serves 6 to 8.

Note: To serve oven browned potatoes with the lamb, boil red potatoes for 30 minutes and then add to the pan for the last 30 minutes of cooking. Rubbing lamb with the ground ginger removes the "muttony" flavor. Remove as much of the fat and "fell" as possible before preparing. The lamb can be frozen after cooking.

Rack of Lamb Persillé

2 racks of lamb, 6-rib
2 cups bread crumbs
¼ cup parsley, chopped
Salt and pepper to taste
1 clove garlic, minced
Olive oil
½ cup butter, clarified

Preheat oven to 500 degrees. Mix bread crumbs, parsley, salt, pepper and garlic. Trim all fat from ribs. Place racks in an oiled roasting pan, bone side up, and brush thoroughly with olive oil. Be sure meat is at room temperature. Roast for 10 minutes, then turn over and cover with bread crumb mixture. Spoon clarified butter over racks. Continue to cook the racks for another 6 to 8 minutes. Serve immediately. Serves 6.

Note: Ask your butcher to trim fat and cut in French manner, then intertwine the two racks for an elegant presentation.

Soudzoukakia Smyrnayka
Greek Meat Loaves

1 pound ground lamb
½ cup soft bread crumbs
½ cup dry white wine
2 cloves garlic, minced
¼ teaspoon caraway seeds
Olive oil or butter
8 ounces tomato sauce
½ cup water
Salt and pepper to taste

Mix lamb, bread crumbs, wine, garlic and caraway seeds. Shape into rolls about 5 inches long and 2 inches in diameter. Brown rolls lightly in olive oil or butter. Add tomato sauce and water. Heat slowly to boiling. Simmer 5 minutes or until done. Serve with mashed potatoes or rice. Serves 4.

Veal Parmesan

4 veal patties, 4 ounces each
2 cups tomato sauce, no sugar added
½ pound mushrooms, sliced
⅛ teaspoon oregano
⅛ teaspoon garlic powder
Salt and white pepper to taste
1 ounce Parmesan cheese, divided
3 ounces Mozzarella cheese, grated

Make thin veal patties and broil for 5 minutes on each side. Preheat oven to 375 degrees. In a medium saucepan combine tomato sauce, mushrooms, oregano, garlic powder, salt and white pepper and ½ ounce Parmesan cheese. Cook over medium heat until mushrooms are tender. In a 10 inch casserole layer veal, cheese, sauce and remaining Parmesan cheese. Bake for 15 minutes. Serves 4.

Note: This makes a great dinner served with spaghetti, green salad and garlic bread.

Veal

Veal Amelio

2 pounds veal, cut into 1½ ounce slices
Flour
Salt and pepper
2 tablespoons olive oil
1 cup butter
6 tablespoons dry white wine
1 tablespoon lemon juice
1 pound fresh mushrooms, sliced

Pound veal gently with a wooden mallet. Sprinkle lightly with flour, salt and pepper. Heat olive oil and 2 tablespoons butter. When pan is hot, saute' veal on both sides (without browning). Remove and set aside, keeping veal warm. Add wine to pan and heat slightly. Add remaining butter and lemon juice. Saute'mushrooms briefly. Place several veal slices on each plate and top with mushrooms and sauce. Serves 6.

Note: This recipe should not be prepared in advance nor should it be frozen.

Veal Scallopini

1½ pounds veal, thinly sliced
2 tablespoons olive oil
1 clove garlic
¼ cup flour
½ cup Parmesan cheese, grated
½ teaspoon salt
⅛ teaspoon pepper
½ cup dry white wine
½ cup consomme' or stock
1 tablespoon lemon juice

Heat oil and garlic in largest skillet available. Dredge veal in flour, Parmesan cheese, salt and pepper mixture. Brown veal on both sides; remove garlic, add liquid to pan. Cover and simmer slowly. Sprinkle with parsley and serve on small egg or spinach noodles. Serves 4 to 6.

Veal

Wiener Schnitzel

6 veal cutlets (4 ounces each)
½ cup all-purpose flour
2 eggs, beaten
1½ cups packaged bread crumbs
½ cup butter
Parsley, stuffed olives and lemon slices for garnish

Pound cutlets with a mallet until they are ¼ inch thick. Put flour, eggs, and bread crumbs into separate flat dishes. Dip each cutlet in flour, then in egg and finally in bread crumbs. Coat the cutlets well. Press bread crumbs into the meat by pounding lightly with a mallet. Refrigerate cutlets 20 to 30 minutes. This helps to keep the coating on during cooking. Heat butter in each of two large skillets. Saute'cutlets 3 to 4 minutes on each side or until golden brown. Garnish. Serves 6.

Cumberland Sauce

1 lemon rind, grated
Juice of 1 lemon
1 orange rind, grated
1 tablespoon confectioners' sugar
1 teaspoon prepared mustard
½ cup red currant jelly
1 tablespoon port wine

Combine all ingredients in a small saucepan and heat over low heat, stirring frequently until well blended. This is a delicious variation to mint jelly as an accompaniment to roast lamb. You can also combine this sauce with thickened pan drippings (from lamb) to make a hearty gravy as well. Makes ¾ cup.

Menus

Wild Game Dinner

Onion Puffs

Smoked Fish Log with Crackers

Mushroom Rolls

Romaine Lettuce with Garlic-Cheese Dressing

Venison Stroganoff | *Quail Supreme*

Wild Rice | *Oven Vegetables*

Cornbread for a Crowd

Amaretto Souffle' | *Waldorf-Astoria Cake*

Menus

Lakeside Dining

Texas Crab Grass with Fritos

Mock Boursin with Crackers

Barbecued Bourbon Pot Roast

Scalloped Potatoes *Baked Zucchini Parmesan*

Romaine Leaves with Curried Caesar Salad Dressing and Croutons

Seasoned Bread

Luscious Florida Lime Souffle'

"Almost Pecan Pie" Cookies

Poultry

Jeni

Spanish Spaghetti

5 pound hen, cooked and cut into pieces
46 ounces V-8 juice
15 ounces tomato purée
8 ounces mushrooms, drained
30 ounces canned English peas, drained
2 cups chicken broth
Salt, pepper and garlic to taste

Combine all ingredients in a big pot and simmer for 2 to 3 hours or until thick. Serve over spaghetti. Serves a crowd.

Chicken Crepes Elegante

3 cups chicken, cooked and diced
3 tablespoons onion, chopped
6 tablespoons butter
½ cup flour
2 cups milk
4 ounce can mushrooms, sliced
1 cup Swiss cheese, grated
6 tablespoons sherry
3 tablespoons chives
Salt and pepper to taste
Dash of paprika

Saute' onion in butter. Blend in flour and slowly add milk. Cook and stir until the mixture boils thoroughly. Add mushrooms, cheese, chicken, sherry, chives, salt, pepper and paprika. Lightly mix together. Chill the mixture for easier handling — should be very thick. Preheat the oven to 375 degrees. Spoon filling into crepes and roll up. Place in a buttered dish. Cover with sauce. Bake for 15 to 20 minutes. Sprinkle the crepes with Parmesan cheese before serving.

Sauce: Same as the filling except delete the chicken and increase the milk to 2-2/3 cups.

Serve with broccoli with hollandaise, broiled tomatoes and curried fruit. Really delicious!

Poultry

Basic Crepes

1¼ cups of flour
Pinch of salt
3 eggs, beaten
1½ cups of milk
2 tablespoons butter, melted

Place all ingredients in a blender or mixer and beat well. Let batter stand at room temperature 1 hour before using, or let it refrigerate overnight. The addition of onion, garlic or celery salt can also create a tasty crepe. Season the surface of a crepe pan or small non-stick frying pan. Use ½ teaspoon or less of oil and apply with a paper towel. Pour in a small amount of batter, just enough to lightly coat the bottom of the pan. Tilt the pan to even the batter. Cook only until the bottom is lightly browned. It is not necessary to cook both sides as the lighter side is either filled or folded inward. An 8 inch pan makes 16 to 20 crepes. A 7 inch pan makes 20 to 24 crepes. Crepes will keep 2 or 3 days in the refrigerator or 1 to 2 months in the freezer.

Dessert Crepe Batter:
Prepare basic crepe batter and add 2 tablespoons sugar and 1 tablespoon Brandy. Blend for 10 seconds. Crepes will be sweeter and cook slightly faster.

Buffet Casserole

2½ to 3 pounds boned chicken breasts
1 pound pork sausage
1 pound fresh mushrooms, sliced
2 medium onions, sliced
1 box Uncle Ben's wild rice (not instant), cooked
¼ cup flour
½ cup heavy cream
2½ cups chicken broth
1 tablespoon salt
Pepper

Preheat oven to 350 degrees. Saute' sausage and remove with slotted spoon. In fat, saute' mushrooms and onion. Cook chicken and save broth. Separate chicken into bite size pieces. Add sausage, chicken and rice to mushrooms and onion. Mix flour and cream. Add remaining ingredients and cook over medium heat until sauce thickens. Put all ingredients into casserole. Bake for 25-30 minutes. Serves 4.

Can be frozen.

Curry Chicken Casserole

1 hen or 2 large fryers, cooked, skinned and chopped into bite size pieces
½ cup dry sherry
½ teaspoon salt
½ teaspoon curry (or more if you like curry)
1 onion, chopped
2 stalks celery, chopped
1 pound button mushrooms (canned)
2 packages Uncle Ben's wild rice, cooked according to directions
1 cup sour cream
1 can cream of mushroom soup

Preheat oven to 350 degrees. Mix all the above ingredients and put into a casserole. Bake for 1 hour. Serves 8 to 12.

Citrus Chicken Niberia

1 chicken, cut up
2 tablespoons flour
½ teaspoon salt
⅛ teaspoon pepper
2 tablespoons margarine
2 tablespoons olive oil
1 clove garlic, minced
½ cup chicken broth
6 ounces orange juice concentrate, thawed and undiluted
1 teaspoon dried oregano
1 green pepper, cut in strips
1 onion, sliced
½ pound fresh mushrooms, sliced
½ cup black olives, sliced

Preheat electric skillet to 325 degrees. Wash the chicken and pat dry. Combine the chicken, flour, salt and pepper in a plastic bag. Coat the chicken with mixture. Heat the margarine and olive oil in the skillet. Add the garlic and stir. Brown the chicken on all sides. Combine the broth, orange concentrate and oregano. Pour over the chicken. Cover and cook 15 minutes. Baste the chicken with pan juices. Add the green peppers and onion. Cook 5 minutes. Add the mushrooms and olives. Cover and cook 5 minutes or until the chicken is tender. Serves 6.

Note: This can be prepared a day in advance, but be sure to reheat thoroughly.

Poultry

Dijon Chicken

1 chicken, cooked and deboned
3 tablespoons butter
2 tablespoons all-purpose flour
1 cup chicken broth
5½ ounces evaporated milk
2 tablespoons Dijon mustard
¼ teaspoon marjoram
¼ teaspoon tarragon
¼ teaspoon parsley
2 cups egg noodles, cooked

Melt butter in saucepan. Add flour and mix well. Gradually add chicken broth and milk. Cook over medium heat until thickened. Stir in mustard and seasonings. Add chicken and simmer 10 minutes. Serve over noodles. Serves 4. Pretty sprinkled with extra parsley.

Chicken Scallopini

2 pounds chicken breasts, boned
Salt and freshly ground pepper
¾ cup onion, coarsely chopped
1 clove garlic, finely chopped
4 tablespoons butter
2 tablespoons olive oil
4 to 6 tablespoons Madeira
Juice of ½ lemon
½ cup heavy cream
Cooked rice or noodles
4 to 6 tablespoons almonds, coarsley chopped

Cut chicken breasts diagonally across the grain into slices about ¼ inch thick. Season chicken slices generously with salt and pepper. Saute' chopped onion and garlic in butter and olive oil until soft. Remove from pan with a slotted spoon and reserve. Add sliced chicken to the pan and saute' in remaining fat, stirring constantly, until chicken is golden brown on all sides. Return vegetables to pan, stir once. Add Madeira and cook over a high heat, stirring, until Madeira is reduced to half its original quantity. Then add lemon juice, stir once and add thick cream. Cook for a few minutes longer, stirring, until sauce is heated through. Correct seasonings. Serve immediately with cooked rice or noodles, garnished with almonds and served with a green salad. Serves 4.

Russian Chicken

6 breasts of chicken
1 bottle of Russian salad dressing
½ small jar apricot preserves
¼ cup water
1 package Lipton dry onion soup

Preheat over to 350 degrees. In a saucepan combine the Russian dressing, apricot preserves, water and soup; bring to a boil. Pour the sauce over the chicken breasts and cover with foil. Bake for 1 hour. Then uncover, baste and bake for 30 minutes uncovered. Serves 6.

Tangy Chicken

1 chicken, cut up
1 teaspoon salt
¼ cup butter, melted
¼ cup lemon juice
¼ cup vinegar
½ teaspoon garlic, minced
1 medium onion, chopped
½ teaspoon pepper
½ teaspoon thyme

Preheat oven to 350 degrees. Combine all ingredients except chicken and mix well. Place chicken in baking dish and pour ingredients over it. Cover and cook for ½ hour. Uncover and cook additional ½ hour. 4 servings.

Chicken Supreme

6 chicken breasts, deboned
5 ounces chipped beef
6 strips of bacon, uncooked
1 cup sour cream
10¾ ounces of mushroom soup

Preheat oven to 250 degrees. Butter a 2 quart casserole dish. Spread beef over bottom in bite size pieces. Wrap 1 strip of bacon around each breast. Place chicken on beef. Mix sour cream and mushroom soup together and pour over chicken. Bake for 3 hours. Serves 6. May be frozen.

Poultry

Chicken Tetrazzini

4 pounds chicken breasts
1 teaspoon salt
1 small onion, sliced
1 clove garlic, crushed
1 bay leaf, crushed
½ pound butter
1 cup flour
4 cups light cream
3 cups chicken stock
1 pound mushrooms, sliced
2 tablespoons butter
12 ounce package noodles
¼ tablespoon curry powder
1 tablespoon Worcestershire sauce
2 tablespoons sherry
½ cup Parmesan cheese, grated

Preheat oven to 350 degrees. Cover chicken with water in a covered baking pan. Add salt, onion, garlic and bay leaf. Cook for about 1 hour. Cool enough to handle, then remove meat from bones and cut into bite size pieces.

Preheat oven to 325 degrees. In a saucepan, melt ½ pound butter. Blend in flour; add cream and chicken stock. Cook, stirring, until thick. Saute' mushrooms in 2 tablespoons butter. Cook noodles according to package directions. Drain. Add curry powder, Worcestershire sauce and sherry to the sauce mixture. Combine the chicken, sauce, mushrooms and noodles in a large casserole, mixing well. Sprinkle the cheese on top. Bake until heated through, about 30 minutes. This is best when made a day ahead. If dry before heating, add a bit of cream and sherry while heating. Serves 12.

Divine Chicken

4 large chicken breasts, deboned
1 teaspoon salt
3 tablespoons flour
1 cup sour cream
1 can mushroom soup
½ cup Sauterne wine
½ cup almonds, sliced
1 teaspoon paprika
Small jar pimientos

Preheat over to 325 degrees. Sprinkle chicken with ½ teaspoon salt. Mix flour and ¼ cup sour cream and other ½ teaspoon salt, rest of sour cream, soup and wine. Pour over chicken. Sprinkle with almonds, paprika and pimientos. Bake for 1 to 1½ hours. Serve over rice. Serves 4.

Chicken Curry

1 chicken, large enough to make about 2 cups chopped chicken
1 celery stalk
1 bay leaf
1 small onion, chopped
3 cups rice, cooked

Stew the chicken with the celery, bay leaf and onion. Save the stock and remove the chicken meat from the bones. Chop the meat.

Sauce:
2 large onions, chopped
2 teaspoons curry powder
4 tablespoons butter
1 pint stock or coconut milk
1 handful of raisins
1 clove garlic, chopped
1 large apple, peeled and chopped
½ teaspoon black pepper
½ teaspoon ginger
Salt
Juice of ½ lemon

Saute' the onion and curry in butter. Add the stock or coconut milk, raisins, garlic, apple, seasonings and lemon juice. Cook slowly for 10 minutes.

Add meat to the sauce and simmer. Smooth, blend and correct the seasonings. Serve over rice with a few of these side dishes:

Side Dishes:
Major Grey's Chutney
Green onions, chopped
Coconut
Bananas, chopped
Hard-boiled eggs, chopped
Bacon, chopped
Tomatoes, chopped
Ripe olives, chopped
Raisins
Peanuts, chopped

This can be made ahead and reheated. Serves 4 to 6.

Note: This recipe may be doubled.

Chicken and Sausage Jambalaya

½ to 1 pound Italian sausage, sliced
3 chicken breasts, cooked, boned and cut in bite size pieces
1 onion, chopped
½ green pepper, chopped
3 tablespoons butter
1 cup rice
8 ounces stewed tomatoes
10½ ounces beef consomme'
5 ounces A-1 sauce (½ bottle)
¼ cup Pickapeppa sauce (optional)
¼ teaspoon garlic juice
1 teaspoon seasoned salt
1 bay leaf

Saute' onion and green pepper in butter until tender. Add rice and mix just until the rice is coated in butter. Remove from heat and set aside. Drain liquid from tomatoes in a large saucepan. Add to liquid, consomme', A-1 sauce, Pickapeppa sauce, garlic juice and enough water to make 2½ cups liquid. Mix well and add tomatoes, rice mixture, sausage, chicken and bay leaf. Bring to boil, cover and cook 20 to 25 minutes or until liquid is absorbed. Serves 6.

Chicken A'Dele

4 cups chicken, cooked and diced
2 cups soft bread, diced
2 cups chicken broth
2 raw eggs
Small onion, chopped
½ small green pepper, chopped
Cornflakes, crushed
Pats of butter
1 can cream of mushroom soup
1 can cream of chicken soup

Preheat oven to 350 degrees. Add the bread, broth, eggs, onion and green pepper to the chicken and pour this into a buttered pyrex loaf pan. Top with crushed cornflakes and dot with pats of butter. Put loaf pan in a larger pan of hot water. Bake for 45 minutes. Serve with sauce of undiluted cream of mushroom soup and undiluted cream of chicken soup which has been heated.

Chicken in Spicy Sauce

3½ pound chicken, cut-up
Water
½ cup flour
1 teaspoon salt
⅛ teaspoon pepper
¼ cup oil
1 cup celery, chopped
½ cup onion, chopped
1 clove garlic, minced
16 ounces stewed tomatoes
8 ounces tomato sauce
1 tablespoon brown sugar
2 teaspoons Worcestershire sauce
½ teaspoon marjoram leaves
2 drops Tabasco sauce
¼ cup water
Rice, hot cooked

Moisten chicken with water. Shake in bag of flour, salt and pepper. Brown chicken in oil in Dutch oven type skillet. Remove browned chicken from skillet. Add celery, onion and garlic and saute'. Add stewed tomatoes, tomato sauce, brown sugar, Worcestershire sauce, marjoram, Tabasco sauce and water. Place chicken back in sauce. Reduce heat to simmer. Cover for 50 minutes. Serve over rice. Serves 4.

Chicken and Broccoli

8 chicken breasts or one whole chicken, cut up
20 ounces frozen broccoli spears, cooked according to directions

Velvet sauce:
4 teaspoons butter
2 tablespoons flour
½ cup milk
2/3 teaspoon salt
Dash pepper
Dash paprika
1 can cream of mushroom soup
½ pound Cheddar cheese, grated
½ cup sour cream

Preheat oven to 350 degrees. For the sauce: Melt the butter and flour together. Gradually stir in the milk until it comes to a boil. Season and add the soup and 2/3 of the cheese. Stir until the cheese is melted. Remove and cool slightly. Stir in the sour cream. Layer the chicken and broccoli. Pour the sauce over this and put the cheese on top. Bake for 30 minutes until thoroughly heated. Serves 6 to 8.

Nashville Tetrazzini

1 hen or 4 whole chicken breasts
6 ribs celery, chopped
2 medium onions, chopped
3 tablespoons butter
1 tablespoon Worcestershire sauce
Salt and pepper to taste
1 pint chicken stock
10¾ ounces cream of mushroom soup
½ pound sharp cheese, grated
½ pound spaghetti, cooked
1 cup pecans, broken
1 small bottle stuffed olives, sliced
1 cup Parmesan cheese, grated

Cook hen, reserve stock. Cut meat from hen into small pieces. Saute' celery and onion in butter. Add Worcestershire sauce, salt and pepper. Add stock and simmer 15 minutes. Add soup slowly, then cheese. Add spaghetti and let stand 1 hour. Add chicken, olives and pecans. Place in 9 X 13 inch pyrex dish. Sprinkle top with Parmesan cheese. Bake at 300 degrees until hot and bubbly.

Note: This can be prepared ahead of time and frozen.

Chicken Espagnal

2 (4 to 5 pound) roasting chickens, cooked, boned and cut-up
¼ cup olive oil
1 clove garlic, minced
1 large onion, chopped
1 green pepper, cut into 1 inch pieces
Salt and pepper to taste
8 ounces pimiento, drained and chopped
16 ounces tomato soup
8 ounces black pitted olives, drained
1 large can mushrooms, drained or ½ pound fresh mushrooms, sautéed
½ cup red wine

Heat oil in pan. Saute' garlic, onion, green pepper, salt, pepper and pimiento for 5 minutes. Add soup and olives. Place chicken in sauce. Cover and bring to boil. Simmer ½ hour. Add mushrooms and wine and cook for 15 minutes more. Very good served over rice or place in Pepperidge Farm pattie shells. Can be frozen.

Curried Chicken and Rice

1 whole chicken
2 packages Lipton Onion Soup
1 package Uncle Ben's long grain and wild rice
1 can cream of mushroom soup
1 pint sour cream
1 tablespoon curry powder
1 tablespoon sherry
2 tablespoons parsley, chopped
1 can fried onions

Boil chicken in water with 1 package onion soup for 1 hour or until done. Debone and skin. Preheat oven to 325 degrees. Cook rice according to package instructions. Combine chicken, rice, soup, sour cream, other package of onion soup, curry powder, sherry and parsley. Put in casserole and top with fried onions. Heat thoroughly. Serves 8.

Note: Makes a nice luncheon dish served with green salad and crescent rolls.

Quick Chicken Pilaf

12 ounces canned chicken
¼ cup butter or margarine
1 1/3 cups minute rice, uncooked
3 or 4 ounces canned mushrooms, sliced
1 tablespoon instant onion
3 tablespoons raisins
2 teaspoons curry powder
¼ teaspoon ginger
1 teaspoon salt

Melt butter in saucepan or skillet. Add rice and saute' over medium heat. Stir constantly until light brown. Drain mushrooms. Add enough water to mushroom liquid to make 1½ cups. Add liquid, mushrooms, onion, chicken, raisins, curry, ginger, salt to rice. Stir with fork. Bring to boil, cover and remove from heat. Let stand 5 minutes. 4 to 6 servings.

Poultry

Chicken, Snow Peas and Cashews

2 pounds boneless chicken
  breasts, sliced and cubed
2 tablespoons oil, divided
10 ounces frozen pea pods
1 cup fresh mushrooms, sliced
1 cup cashews
2 tablespoons soy sauce

In a wok or large skillet, quickly cook chicken pieces in 1 tablespoon of oil. Remove chicken and set aside. Add 1 more tablespoon of oil to wok, cook peas and mushrooms. Add chicken to vegetables, as well as cashews. Add soy sauce and cook 2 minutes until well mixed and heated thoroughly. Serves 4.

Chicken Carolina

3 pound broiler-fryer chicken,
  cut into serving size pieces
1/3 cup flour
1 teaspoon salt
¼ teaspoon pepper
¼ cup shortening, melted
1 cup onion, chopped
1 cup green pepper, chopped
1 clove garlic, minced
1/3 cup catsup
1 cup water
¼ cup steak sauce
1/3 cup seedless raisins
3 cups rice, hot cooked

Combine flour, salt and pepper; dredge chicken pieces in flour mixture. Brown in heated shortening in electric skillet. Remove chicken and saute' onion, green pepper and garlic. Stir in catsup, water, steak sauce and raisins. Return chicken to skillet. Cover and simmer at 250 degrees for 30 to 40 minutes, or until tender, basting occasionally. Serve with rice. 4 to 6 servings.

Raspberry Chicken

3 pound chicken, cut up
Cooking oil
Pepper
10 ounces frozen red raspberries, quick thaw
2 tablespoons corn starch
¼ teaspoon ground cinnamon
1 tablespoon butter
1 teaspoon lemon juice
¼ cup almonds, sliced

Brush chicken with oil; season with pepper. Place chicken, skin side down, on broiler rack. Broil 5 to 6 inches from heat for 20 minutes or until browned. Turn. Broil 5 to 10 minutes or until browned.

Meanwhile, thaw raspberries; drain, reserving syrup. In a saucepan, blend the syrup into the corn starch; stir in the cinnamon. Cook and stir until bubbly. Add butter and lemon juice. Gently stir in the raspberries. Pour over the chicken and cook 10 minutes longer. The sauce can be doubled easily if more chicken is used.

Chicken-Shrimp Supreme

3 cups cooked seasoned chicken, cut in large pieces
1 or 2 pounds boiled, shucked shrimp, cut in pieces (or 1 to 2 pounds frozen small, pre-cooked shrimp)
1 box Uncle Ben's long grain and wild rice, cooked according to package directions
1 can cream of celery soup
1 large jar pimientos, sliced
20 ounces frozen French style green beans, cooked according to directions
1 cup mayonnaise
2 cups water chestnuts, thinly sliced
Salt and pepper to taste
Buttered bread crumbs

Preheat oven to 350 degrees. Mix all ingredients together and add buttered bread crumbs to top. Bake uncovered for 25 to 30 minutes. Serves 10 to 12.

Poultry

Chicken with Sour Cream and Wine Gravy

8 halves chicken breasts, deboned
4 tablespoons sweet butter
2¾ ounces slivered almonds
4 tablespoons flour
29 ounces chicken broth
½ cup water
¼ cup white wine
8 ounces mushrooms, sliced
8 ounces sour cream
2 scallions, chopped

Melt butter in large skillet. Brown chicken and remove from pan. Brown almonds in remaining butter. Add flour and stir to blend. Add chicken broth, water and wine (last), stirring constantly. Bring to a boil while stirring. Add chicken and mushrooms, cover and simmer 30 minutes. At this point you can freeze or refrigerate in 8 X 12 inch (2 quart) casserole. When ready to serve, bring to room temperature. Bake in 350 degree oven for 30 minutes, covered. Remove cover, stir in sour cream and garnish with scallions. Return to oven uncovered for 10 minutes. Serve with yellow rice.

Lemon Chicken

2 to 3 pound fryer, cut up
½ cup flour
1 teaspoon salt
2 teaspoons paprika
¼ teaspoon pepper
½ cup margarine, melted

Sauce:
1 tablespoon soy sauce
½ teaspoon salt
¼ cup vegetable oil
½ cup lemon juice
2 tablespoons lemon peel, grated
1 clove garlic, crushed

For sauce, combine the above ingredients and refrigerate 1 hour before using.

Preheat the oven to 400 degrees. Combine flour, salt, paprika and pepper and coat the chicken pieces. Arrange skin side down in a shallow pan. Brush well with margarine. Bake 30 minutes, then turn the chicken and remove fat from the pan. Pour sauce over the chicken and bake 30 minutes longer. Serves 4 to 6.

Chicken with Grapes

12 pieces of chicken (breasts, thighs, etc.)
Salt and pepper to taste
Flour
8 tablespoons butter, divided
¼ cup onion, minced
¼ cup chicken broth
¾ cup dry white wine
½ pound fresh mushrooms, sliced
2 cups muscat grapes, seeded, or seedless grapes

Preheat oven to 375 degrees. Sprinkle chicken pieces with salt and pepper and coat lightly with flour. Heat 5 tablespoons butter in a frying pan and quickly brown the chicken on all sides. Arrange the pieces closely together in a single layer in a large shallow baking pan. Add onion to butter in frying pan; cook until soft. Add chicken broth and wine; bring to a boil, then pour over the chicken. Bake, covered, for 40 minutes. Meanwhile, saute' mushrooms in 3 tablespoons butter. When chicken has cooked 40 minutes, add mushrooms and grapes; continue baking, covered, for 8 minutes more or until the grapes are just heated. Serves 6 to 8.

Marinated Chicken

8 chicken breasts or whole cut-up chicken
2 to 3 cloves of garlic, mashed in bowl
8 heaping teaspoons salt
1 teaspoon celery salt
1 teaspoon black pepper
2 heaping teaspoons dry mustard
½ teaspoon poultry seasoning
¾ cup Sauterne wine
1 cup red wine vinegar
¼ cup corn oil

Place chicken pieces in flat container with lid. Mix all above ingredients except corn oil in bowl and pour over chicken pieces. Marinate in refrigerator at least 5 to 6 hours, best overnight. Remove chicken and cook on barbecue grill using ¾ cup of the marinade juice with ¼ cup corn oil for basting. Cook until chicken is tender, but done. Fire should not be too hot or chicken will be charred. Turn chicken often on grill. 6 to 8 servings.

Lime Chicken with Cantaloupe

3 pound broiler-fryer chicken, cut up
1 teaspoon salt
¼ teaspoon tarragon
⅛ teaspoon pepper
2 tablespoons salad oil
1 cup onion, chopped
3 cups chicken broth
1/3 cup fresh lime juice
1 tablespoon sugar
1 medium cantaloupe, peeled, seeded, and cut into wedges
1 teaspoon lime peel, grated for garnish

Remove any visible fat from the chicken and discard it. Rub the chicken with salt, tarragon and pepper. In a Dutch oven over medium heat, heat the oil. Add the chicken and saute' until well browned on all sides. Add onion and saute' 5 minutes more or until onions are tender. Add the chicken broth. Cook, covered, 35 to 40 minutes or until tender. Remove chicken to large platter and keep warm. Remove and discard fat from the broth in the Dutch oven. To the remaining broth in the Dutch oven add lime juice and sugar. Boil the sauce rapidly until it is reduced to 1 cup. Add cantaloupe wedges and continue cooking just until heated through. Arrange cantaloupe around chicken on platter. Pour sauce over chicken and fruit. Garnish with grated lime peel. Serves 4. Only 320 calories per serving.

Winter Park Chicken

3 cups cooked chicken, cut in small pieces
½ onion, chopped
1 cup celery, diced
½ cup mayonnaise
½ cup cracker crumbs
2 hard-boiled eggs, diced
2 cans cream of chicken soup
2 tablespoons Worcestershire sauce
½ cup slivered almonds
1 can water chestnuts, drained and sliced
1 cup potato chips, crushed

Preheat oven to 350 degrees. Mix all ingredients except the potato chips. Place in 9X13X2 inch pan or other shallow casserole. Top with potato chips. Bake 30 to 40 minutes. Serves 6. Nice for luncheons.

Swiss Chicken-Ham Bake

2 cups chicken, cooked and cubed
1 cup ham, cooked and cubed
½ cup onion, chopped
2 tablespoons butter
3 tablespoons flour
½ teaspoon salt
¼ teaspoon pepper
3 ounces mushrooms, undrained and sliced
1 cup light cream
2 tablespoons dry sherry
7 ounces water chestnuts, sliced and drained
4 ounces Swiss cheese, grated
1 cup soft bread crumbs
3 tablespoons butter, melted

Preheat oven to 400 degrees. In a skillet cook onion in butter until tender, not brown. Blend in flour, salt and pepper. Add mushrooms, cream and dry sherry. Cook and stir mixture until thick and bubbly. Add chicken, ham and water chestnuts. Pour into 1½ quart casserole and top with Swiss cheese. Mix bread crumbs with melted butter. Sprinkle around edges. Bake for 25 minutes until lightly browned. Serves 6. May do ahead and freeze.

Chicken San Jose

2 to 2½ pounds choice chicken pieces
1½ teaspoons garlic salt
1½ teaspoons celery salt
1½ teaspoons paprika
⅛ teaspoon red pepper
1 cup rice, uncooked
½ cup onion, chopped
½ cup celery, chopped
1 can tomatoes, well-drained and quartered
1½ cups chicken broth, boiling
3 tablespoons parsley, chopped
¼ cup pitted ripe olives, sliced

Preheat oven to 450 degrees. Blend seasonings and sprinkle on each side of chicken pieces. Arrange skin side up in a lightly greased 2½ quart casserole. Brown for 30 minutes. Remove from oven; push chicken to one side and add rice, onion, celery, tomatoes and broth. Stir well. Cover and continue baking 25 minutes or until rice and chicken are tender and liquid is absorbed. Sprinkle with parsley and olives. 6 servings.

Poultry

Babe's Chicken

1 chicken, cooked and deboned
1 small onion, chopped
1 cup celery, sliced
1 tablespoon butter
1 can cream of celery soup
1 heaping tablespoon mayonnaise
¾ cup buttermilk
3 cups cooked rice, cooked in broth from the chicken
Paprika

Preheat oven to 350 degrees. Saute' onion and celery in butter. Add celery soup, mayonnaise and buttermilk. Mix well. Place the rice in a greased baking dish with chicken on top. Pour soup mixture over all. Sprinkle with paprika. Bake for 30 minutes. Serves 4 to 6.

Barbecued Chicken

3 pounds chicken, cut-up
1 tablespoon lemon juice
2 tablespoons vinegar
2 tablespoons Worcestershire sauce
2 tablespoons butter
3 tablespoons catsup
3 tablespoons brown sugar
1 teaspoon salt
1 teaspoon mustard (prepared or dried)
1 teaspoon paprika
1 teaspoon chili powder
½ teaspoon cayenne or black pepper
4 tablespoons water

Preheat oven to 500 degrees. Combine all ingredients except chicken in saucepan. Heat. Salt and pepper chicken, then dip into sauce and place in roasting pan. Pour remaining sauce over chicken. Cover pan and bake 15 minutes at 500 degrees, then lower oven to 350 degrees and cook 1¼ hours. Good served with rice. Serves 4 to 6.

Chicken L'Orange

2 pounds chicken breasts, skinned and deboned
2 teaspoons salt
4 tablespoons frozen orange juice concentrate, thawed and undiluted
4 teaspoons soy sauce
1 teaspoon powdered ginger

Preheat the oven to 350 degrees. Rinse chicken. Combine salt, orange juice, soy sauce and ginger. Place chicken in a shallow baking dish and brush with orange sauce. Bake for 35 minutes, basting frequently. Serves 4.

Note: Serve with rice made with 2 tablespoons of orange juice concentrate and 2 tablespoons of raisins. This recipe can be frozen.

Chicken Verona

3 pounds chicken, cut up in pieces
1 cup fine dry bread crumbs
1/3 cup grated Parmesan cheese
¼ cup parsley, minced
2 teaspoons salt
¼ teaspoon pepper
Pinch of mustard
¾ cup butter, melted
1 clove garlic (optional)

Preheat oven to 350 degrees. Mix bread crumbs, cheese, parsley, salt, pepper and mustard. Mix butter and garlic in separate pan and melt butter. Dip chicken pieces in butter, then dredge in crumb mix and arrange in single layer in a baking dish. Sprinkle remaining butter over top. Bake for 45 minutes. Serves 4 to 6.

Chicken Breasts Wellington

6 whole chicken breasts, boned and split
Seasoned salt and pepper
6 ounce package long-grain and wild rice
¼ cup orange peel, grated
2 eggs, separated
3 (8 ounce) cans refrigerated crescent dinner rolls
1 tablespoon water
20 ounces red currant jelly
1 tablespoon prepared mustard
3 tablespoons port wine
¼ cup lemon juice

Preheat oven to 375 degrees. Pound chicken with meat mallet; sprinkle with salt and pepper. Cook rice according to package directions for drier rice; add orange peel. Cool. Beat egg whites until soft peaks form; fold into rice mixture. On floured surface, roll 2 triangular pieces of dinner roll dough into a circle. Repeat with remaining rolls until you have 12 circles. Place a chicken breast in the center of each circle. Spoon about ¼ cup rice mixture over chicken; bring dough up over stuffed breast, moisten edges of dough with water, and press together to seal. Place seam side down on large baking sheet. Beat egg yolks lightly with water; brush over dough. Bake uncovered for 45 to 50 minutes or until breasts are tender. If dough browns too fast, cover loosely with foil. Heat currant jelly in saucepan; gradually stir in mustard, wine and lemon juice. Serve warm with chicken. Serves 12.

Orange Glazed Chicken Breasts

4 whole chicken breasts, halved
½ teaspoon salt
¼ cup butter
2 tablespoons flour
¼ teaspoon dry mustard
¼ teaspoon cinnamon
1/16 teaspoon ginger
2 tablespoons sugar
1½ cups orange juice
3 cups hot cooked rice

Sprinkle halved chicken breasts with salt and brown in butter. Remove breasts from skillet. Combine flour, spices, sugar and stir into drippings, forming a smooth paste. Gradually add orange juice. Cook, stirring constantly, until boiling and thick. Add chicken breasts. Cover and cook until done, approximately 1 hour. Serve over rice with sauce. Serves 6.

Chicken Chinoise

3 to 4 raw chicken breasts, deboned
2 tablespoons soy sauce
2 tablespoons shrimp cocktail sauce
2 tablespoons dry white wine
2 tablespoons salad oil
Dash of Tabasco sauce
2 tablespoons onion, chopped
2 green peppers, cut in 1 inch squares
1 red pepper, cut in 1 inch squares
16 small button mushrooms
4 green onions, cut into 1 inch squares
Oil for frying
Boiled rice

Slice each chicken breast in two lengthwise, then cut each section into 1 inch wide squares. Combine soy sauce, cocktail sauce, wine and salad oil in a bowl. Season with a dash of Tabasco sauce. Add diced chicken and chopped onion and toss well in mixture. Marinate chicken and onions for at least 2 hours. Place 3 tablespoons oil in a large wok or skillet and heat over a high heat; add half the marinated chicken pieces and quickly stir fry chicken in oil until brown on all sides. Remove pieces from wok, reserving the cooking liquid, and keep warm. Add remaining chicken pieces and repeat procedure. Add 2 tablespoons oil to wok; add pepper squares and toss until vegetables begin to lose their hard edges. Add button mushrooms and cook a minute more. Return chicken pieces to pan with green onions and toss until heated through. Check seasoning, adding more soy sauce, cocktail sauce or Tabasco sauce, if desired. Serve immediately, accompanied by boiled rice. Serves 4.

Poultry

Chicken Kiev

8 chicken breast halves, skinned boned and pounded to ¼ inch
½ cup lemon juice
Salt
White pepper
4 egg yolks
½ cup flour
1 cup fine breadcrumbs
Vegetable oil

Herbed butter:
1 cup lightly salted butter, softened
1 tablespoon lemon juice
1 clove crushed garlic
1 tablespoon chives, chopped
1 tablespoon parsley, chopped
1 teaspoon dried tarragon
1 teaspoon salt
½ teaspoon leaf rosemary, crumbled
¼ teaspoon pepper

Lay the chicken breasts, smooth side down, on a flat surface and sprinkle with lemon juice. Let stand, then season lightly with salt and pepper.

Mix butter, lemon juice, garlic and herbs together and put on a piece of waxed paper, shaping into a thick roll. Cover and place in freezer to harden. When herbed butter is hard, cut 1 tablespoon of it and place it on the end of a chicken breast. With the end of a small knife, place the meat over it and roll up the breast around the butter, tucking the sides in carefully. Secure with wooden toothpicks. Repeat with remaining chicken breasts.

In a shallow dish, lightly beat egg yolks. Arrange two separate mounds of flour and breadcrumbs. Dip the rolled up chicken breasts into the flour and gently shake off the excess. Now dip a soft pastry brush into the egg yolk and paint the chicken breasts thickly with it, being careful to fill all the cracks. Then roll in breadcrumbs, making sure that every crack is covered. Cover with waxed paper and keep in refrigerator for at least two hours. (You can prepare the dish up to this point a day ahead.)

Preheat oven to 250 degrees. In a deep fryer or electric skillet, heat oil to 370 degrees. Cook chicken breasts in oil two at a time for about 4 minutes. Lay several sheets of paper towels on a pan and place the fried chicken breasts on this, then place in 250 degree oven for 15 minutes. Serve immediately. Serves 8.

Note: Goes well with white and wild rice mixture. For hearty appetities, add 2 to 4 additional breast halves. You will have plenty of butter to stuff them, but you will need an extra egg yolk.

Chicken Breasts Dijon

4 large chicken breasts, halved
¼ cup flour
1 teaspoon salt
¼ teaspoon pepper
2 tablespoons oil
3 tablespoons butter
3 tablespoons flour
3 or 4 tablespoons Dijon mustard
1½ cups milk
¾ cup white wine
1 teaspoon salt
½ teaspoon tarragon leaves

Preheat oven to 350 degrees. Combine flour, salt and pepper and dredge chicken breasts. Saute' breasts in oil for about 10 minutes over medium heat. Put in baking dish. Melt butter in sauce pan and whisk in flour and mustard. Add milk, wine, salt and tarragon leaves. Cook until thick. Pour over chicken breasts. Bake covered until tender, about 25 to 30 minutes. Serves 6 to 8. Delicious. Can be made ahead and refrigerated until baking time.

Kentucky Chicken Breasts

6 to 8 chicken breasts
Flour, enough to coat chicken
Seasoned salt to taste
Pepper to taste
Paprika to taste
Stick of butter

Preheat oven to 325 degrees. Shake chicken, salt, pepper and paprika in bag. Melt butter and dip each breast in it. Place chicken in baking dish and dribble remaining butter on top. Cover with foil and bake for 90 minutes. Uncover the last 15 minutes to brown.

Sauce:
½ onion, finely chopped
½ pound fresh mushrooms
1 stick butter or margarine
1 tablespoon flour
½ pint whipping cream
½ pint sour cream
Salt to taste

Saute' onions and mushrooms in butter. Add flour to thicken slightly. Add creams, salt and heat to almost boiling. Pour over chicken and serve immediately. Serves 6 to 8.

Poultry

Hot Chicken or Turkey Salad

2 cups chicken or turkey, cooked and diced
1½ cups celery, diced
½ cup slivered almonds, toasted
1 tablespoon onion, grated
1 tablespoon lemon juice
½ to 1 teaspoon salt
⅛ teaspoon black pepper
Few dashes of Tabasco sauce
½ cup mayonnaise
2½ ounces water chestnuts, sliced
½ cup Cheddar cheese or Velveeta cheese, grated

Preheat oven to 375 degrees. Toss together all ingredients except cheese in greased baking dish. Top with cheese. Bake for 25 minutes or until cheese bubbles. Serves 4 to 6.

Optional: Top with 1 cup crushed potato chips before baking.

Note: May be mixed several hours ahead and refrigerated. Bring to room temperature before baking.

Chicken Salad Polynesian

2 cups cooked chicken, chopped
1½ cups celery, diced
¼ cup carrots, shredded
½ cup almonds, toasted
½ cup mayonnaise
¼ cup sour cream
1 teaspoon lemon juice
1 teaspoon curry powder
½ teaspoon salt
1½ cups canned pineapple, diced

Combine chicken, celery, carrots and almonds. Blend mayonnaise with sour cream and seasonings. Pour over chicken mixture and toss lightly. Chill thoroughly. Just before serving, add the pineapple. Arrange on lettuce leaves. 4 large servings.

Cranberry Chicken

8 chicken breasts
2 cups whole cranberry sauce
½ cup red wine

Dressing:
2 cups Pepperidge Farm herb dressing
¼ cup nuts, chopped
¼ cup golden raisins, chopped
¼ teaspoon sage
¼ cup chicken broth
¼ cup butter, melted
Salt and pepper to taste

Mix the above ingredients together. Place the dressing in the bottom of a greased casserole dish. Place the chicken breasts on top of the dressing. Mix the cranberry sauce and the wine together. Pour over the chicken. Bake uncovered for 1¼ hours. Serves 8.

Note: The dressing may also be used to stuff a chicken or turkey.

Vintage Chicken

4 or 5 large chicken breast halves
2 tablespoon flour
1 teaspoon garlic salt
¼ teaspoon pepper
½ teaspoon dried rosemary
8 tablespoons butter, divided
¾ cup white wine (Sauterne, Chablis, etc.)
¼ cup green onion, sliced
1 cup fresh mushrooms, sliced
2 tablespoons parsley, chopped

Dust chicken with mixture of flour, garlic salt, seasoned pepper and rosemary. Heat 6 tablespoons butter in heavy skillet until bubbling. Add chicken and brown well to a rich deep golden color on all sides, turning frequently. Add wine, turn heat low, cover pan tightly and cook 15 to 20 minutes. Meanwhile, saute' green onion and mushrooms in 2 tablespoons butter until soft. Add to chicken, cover and continue cooking until tender about 10 to 15 minutes more. Only a very small amount of rich pan gravy will remain. Sprinkle parsley over chicken and serve hot. Serves 4 to 5.

Poultry

Golden Chicken

8 chicken breasts, deboned
Flour
1 can cream of mushroom soup
Salt
¼ teaspoon pepper
½ pint sour cream
1 cup sharp Cheddar cheese, grated
½ teaspoon paprika
½ cup cream
½ cup almonds, slivered and toasted

Preheat oven to 350 degrees. Season chicken, flour and brown in hot oil. Drain on paper towel. Place chicken in greased casserole. Mix all other ingredients except almonds together and pour over chicken. Bake for 30 minutes, then add ½ cup slivered and toasted almonds and continue baking for 15 minutes. Serves 6.

Note: May be served with wild rice and spinach salad.

The Very Best Chicken Salad

2 hens
Water and Rhine wine or Sauterne
Celery stalks
2 onions
Bay leaf
Garlic clove
¾ cup celery, thinly sliced
2 cups green seedless grapes or red seedless grapes
Italian dressing
1 package slivered almonds, toasted
½ cup mayonnaise
½ cup sour cream

Cook hens in equal parts water and wine, celery stalks with leaves, onion, bay leaf and clove of garlic until tender. Let cool and then cut into bite size chunks, large enough so that you know you are eating chicken. Mix with celery and grapes. Marinate overnight in Italian dressing. Just before serving, drain and add slivered almonds and toss with mayonnaise and sour cream. Heap on a bed of lettuce and sprinkle with paprika and surround with curried deviled eggs decorated with sliced stuffed olives and pimiento. Serve with potato chips, cheese straws and black olives. Fresh chopped parsley can be used as a garnish. The more color, the prettier.

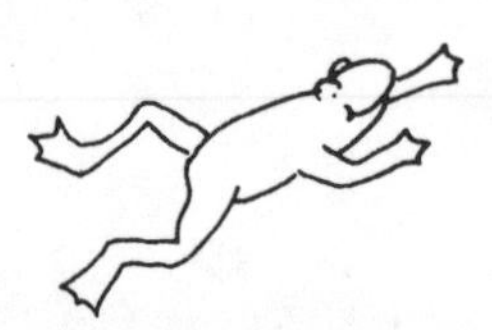

Kissimmee Casserole

2 fryers, cooked and cut-up
6 ounces taco flavored Doritos
1 cup onion, chopped
2 green peppers, chopped
1 tablespoon chili powder
Garlic salt, salt and pepper to taste
2 cans cream of chicken soup
1 can chicken broth
1 can green chilies and tomatoes
10 ounces Cheddar cheese, grated

Preheat oven to 400 degrees. Lightly butter 9 X 13 inch pan. Place Doritos in bottom and sides of pan. Place chicken on top of Doritos. Then add onion and peppers. Chili powder, garlic salt, salt, pepper, soup and broth are next mixed together and poured over peppers and onion. Add tomatoes and green chilies, then cheese. Bake for 30 to 40 minutes. Serves 8 to 10.

Frosted Sandwich Special

1 loaf sandwich bread
10 ounces canned boned chicken or two chicken breasts, cooked and diced
4 hard-boiled eggs, chopped
½ cup ripe olives, chopped
2/3 cup mayonnaise
10 ounces Old English Cheese Spread (in jars)
1 egg
½ cup soft butter or margarine

Cut large rounds from bread slices, using large cookie cutter. Combine chicken, eggs, olives and mayonnaise. Mix well. Spread filling on one bread, top with another and spread again with filling. Close the sandwich with the third bread round. Combine the cheese spread, egg and butter; beat until fluffy. Frost top and sides of sandwiches with cheese mixture. Let sandwiches stand in the refrigerator at least 24 hours. When ready to serve, bake at 375 degrees for 15 minutes. Serve hot. Serves 6. Do not freeze.

Poultry

Cornish Curry

2 Rock Cornish game hens
4 tablespoons butter
6 ounce package curry rice

Preheat oven to 350 degrees. If hens are frozen, thaw and remove giblets. Split hens. Place in 9 X 13 inch baking pan, skin side up. Brush with butter. Bake for 1 to 1¼ hours, basting occasionally with remaining butter, until fork tender. While hens are baking, bake rice in a 1½ quart covered casserole, according to package directions.

Sauce:
17 ounce can whole apricots
4 tablespoons butter
½ cup onion, sliced
½ cup celery, sliced
2 tablespoons flour
1 teaspoon curry powder
1 cup water
½ cup apricot syrup
2 chicken bouillon cubes
¼ cup medium size pitted ripe olives
Parsley

Drain apricots, reserving syrup. In saucepan melt butter. Saute' onion and celery until almost tender. Stir in flour and curry. Remove from heat. Gradually stir in water and reserved syrup; add bouillon cubes. Cook, stirring constantly, until mixture thickens and cubes melt. Cook 2 additional minutes. Add drained apricots and olives. Heat to serving temperature. To serve: On heated platter, arrange rice, Cornish hens, apricots and olives. Spoon some sauce over poultry and fruit. Garnish with parsley. Accompany with remaining sauce. Serves 4.

Cornish Hens Piquant

4 Rock Cornish game hens (¾ pound each), cut in half
½ teaspoon salt
⅛ teaspoon pepper
2 tablespoons salad oil
1 cup onion, chopped
1 cup dry white wine
2 tablespoons tomato paste
2 teaspoons sugar
¾ teaspoon ground cinnamon
4 whole cloves
3 nectarines, unpeeled, each cut into 8 wedges

Remove and discard any visible fat from hens. Rub hens with salt and pepper. In large skillet over medium high heat, heat salad oil. Add hens and cook until well browned on all sides. Add onion and saute' for 10 minutes more and, with a slotted spoon, remove hens and onion . Wipe out skillet with paper towels to discard all oil. In skillet, combine wine, tomato paste, sugar, cinnamon and cloves and heat on low temperature. Add hens and onion, cover and simmer 30 to 40 minutes or until fork tender, stirring occasionally. Remove hens to warm platter; keep warm. Add nectarines to skillet and cook until they are heated through and sauce has thickened slightly. Arrange nectarines around hens on platter. Spoon sauce over and around hens. Serves 4.

Italian Stuffed Capon

1 capon (3 to 4 pounds)
8 ounces yellow rice, cooked
2 ounces white raisins
1 pound Italian sausage
½ cup mushrooms, fresh or canned
2 ounces Galliano liqueur
Salad oil or butter

Preheat oven to 425 degrees. Cover rice and raisins with 1 inch of water. Boil 3 minutes; turn off heat. Cover pan and let stand 20 minutes. Brown sausage, add mushrooms, pour off fat and add to rice mixture. Stuff cavity of capon with this mixture. Pour 2 ounces of Galliano into the cavity and let seep down through the rice. Seal cavity and rub outer side with salad oil. Place in baking dish, breast side down. Add ¼ inch of water to pan and bake 40 minutes. Baste with pan drippings every 20 minutes. Lower heat to 325 degrees. Turn capon over and bake another hour. Let stand 15 minutes before serving. 2 servings.

Poultry

Quail Supreme

20 quail
½ stick butter
Bacon strips
3 cups heavy cream
4 tablespoons flour
1 cup sour cream
1 teaspoon lemon juice

Preheat oven to 375 degrees. Melt butter and brown birds on all sides. Place a bacon strip on each bird and put aside in a covered casserole. Bring heavy cream to a boil. Pour over the birds. Place birds in oven in a covered casserole and cook for 30 minutes. Add flour to butter in skillet and then add cream gradually from casserole containing the birds. Add salt and pepper to taste. Fold in sour cream with the lemon juice. Pour cream mixture back over birds and place back in the oven uncovered for 20 minutes more. Serves 8 to 10.

Florida Quail

8 quail
Salt and pepper to taste
Flour
¼ cup melted butter
1 clove garlic
1 medium onion, thinly sliced
1 pound fresh mushrooms
1 cup chicken broth
½ teaspoon each of thyme and parsley, chopped
1 bay leaf
1 tablespoon of white wine for each bird

Split quail down the back. Season with salt and pepper, dust with flour and brown in butter. Remove birds, add garlic, onion and mushrooms and saute' in the butter until mushrooms are cooked. Add chicken broth, seasonings and wine. Blend well. Put birds in a roasting pan, pour the sauce over them and cover tightly. Cook in a 350 degree oven for about 1½ hours or until quail are tender. Allow 2 quail per person. Serves 4.

This may be completely cooked and frozen. Just defrost and heat.

Note: You may freeze 4 to 5 quail in a ½ gallon milk carton filled with water to stockpile for a festive party.

Fried Quail with Sawmill Gravy

8 ready-to-cook quail
2/3 cup flour
1½ teaspoons salt
¼ teaspoon pepper
Shortening or lard for frying
¾ cup milk
¾ cup water

In a paper or plastic bag combine 1/3 cup of the flour, 1½ teaspoons salt and ⅛ teaspoon pepper. Add quail, two at a time; shake well to coat. In a deep 12 inch skillet heat ½ inch fat to 375 degrees. Add quail. Fry uncovered in hot fat on one side about 4 minutes or until browned. Turn pieces. Cover skillet; cook 3 to 4 minutes or until second side is browned. Uncover and turn once more. Cook about 2 to 3 minutes more until pieces are crisp. Remove pieces to platter; keep warm. Drain fat, reserving ¼ cup. Return reserved fat to skillet; stir in remaining flour, salt and pepper. Cook and stir flour/fat mixture over medium heat about 8 minutes or until mixture has a rich dark brown color. Combine milk and water; add all at once to the flour mixture. Cook and stir quickly until thickened and bubbly. Season to taste with salt and pepper. Add quail, cover and steep for approximately 20 minutes on very low heat. If you prefer the quail crispy, just serve the gravy on the side and don't add the bird to the cream mixture for the extra 20 minutes of cooking. They seem to be more tender though with the addtional cooking and immersed in the gravy. Serves 4.

Pheasants

12 pheasant breast halves
2 cans cream of mushroom soup
2 cans cream of chicken soup
1 cup sherry
Salt and pepper

Brown the breasts. They can be frozen at this point. When ready to prepare, lay the breasts overlapping in a casserole. Add the undiluted soups, the sherry, and the salt and pepper. Cover tightly with foil. Bake 1½ hour. Uncover and bake 1/2 hour in a 350 degree oven. Serves 10.

Baked Wild Goose

1 goose (6 to 10 pounds)
1 medium onion, whole and peeled
½ stick butter or margarine
Salt and pepper
1 medium apple, peeled and sliced
1 medium onion, peeled and sliced
1 small potato, peeled and sliced
1 large stalk celery, cut in 1½ inch strips
1 small orange, whole and peeled

Preheat oven to 450 degrees. Parboil goose in large pan of lightly salted water with a whole onion added for 5 to 10 minutes. Drain and pat dry. Rub cavity and outside of goose with butter; salt and pepper inside and out. Stuff the cavity with apple, onion, potato and celery, having placed an orange in the center. Place on rack in roasting pan; cover with foil and place in oven. Immediately reduce heat to 350 degrees. Bake 25 minutes per pound. When half done, rub with butter again. Prick skin in several places to let grease out. Replace foil and continue cooking. Remove foil for the last 30 minutes. Allow 20 minutes cooling time before slicing. Discard stuffing. Serve with pepper jelly or glaze.

Optional: To glaze, melt pepper jelly or currant jelly with cranberry juice, and brush on the goose the last 10 minutes of cooking.

Big Boy Barbecue Sauce

1½ cups brown sugar, firmly packed
1 tablespoon dry mustard
3½ cups catsup
1½ cups chili sauce
1/3 cup prepared mustard
2 tablespoons black pepper
1½ cups wine vinegar
1 cup fresh lemon juice
½ cup bottled thick steak sauce
¼ cup Worcestershire sauce
1 tablespoon soy sauce
2 tablespoons salad oil
1 can beer
Tabasco sauce to taste

Combine sugar and dry mustard first so mustard will not lump. Then add all other ingredients and mix well. Do not cook. Package in pint jars. This will keep for weeks in the refrigerator and can also be frozen. Makes about 5 pints.

Salads

NOW TOSS!

Herbed French Dressing

1 teaspoon salt
⅛ teaspoon freshly ground pepper
1 teaspoon oregano
1 teaspoon basil
1 teaspoon tarragon
2 teaspoons onion, finely chopped
½ teaspoon sugar
1 small clove garlic, crushed
½ teaspoon dry mustard
1 cup salad oil
¼ cup cider vinegar
½ cup lemon juice

Combine all ingredients except vinegar and lemon juice. Allow to stand at least one hour. Pour into tightly covered jar. Add vinegar and lemon juice and cap. Shake vigorously or blend in blender. Makes 1½ cups.

Note: Excellent served over salad of lettuce leaves, sliced oranges and avocado and thinly sliced red onion.

Poppy Seed Dressing

1½ cups sugar
2 teaspoons salt
2/3 cup vinegar
2 teaspoons dry mustard
1 tablespoon onion juice
2 cups salad oil
3 tablespoons poppy seeds

Mix sugar, salt, vinegar and mustard together and mix well. Add onion juice. Add oil slowly, beating constantly until thick. Add poppy seeds and mix well. Store in an air-tight container in the refrigerator. If the consistency seems thick or slightly separated after being stored, just stir well. Serve over fruit. Serves 30.

Note: This can be stored in the refrigerator for several weeks. A blender can be used for blending oil, using slow speed.

Dressings

Tarragon Salad Dressing

1 cup salad oil
½ cup tarragon vinegar
1 teaspoon tarragon leaves
¼ teaspoon salt
⅛ teaspoon pepper
1 tablespoon or more sugar
½ teaspoon Dijon mustard

Mix well all the ingredients. Good on spinach and other greens.

Lemon Salad Dressing

3 cups salad oil
1 cup lemon juice
½ cup Dijon mustard
½ cup red wine vinegar
1 teaspoon garlic, chopped
1 teaspoon Worcestershire sauce
1 tablespoon sugar
Salt and pepper to taste

Blend ingredients with wire whisk. Season with salt and pepper. Serve on greens or spinach. Makes a large quantity!

Garlic-Cheese Dressing

2 garlic cloves, quartered
¼ cup salad oil
¼ cup Parmesan cheese, grated
¼ cup bleu cheese, crumbled
½ cup salad oil
1 tablespoon Worcestershire sauce
¾ teaspoon salt
¼ teaspoon pepper
1 raw egg
Juice of two lemons **or** ½ cup vinegar

Soak garlic cloves in ¼ cup oil. Set aside and later add to the rest of the ingredients which have been combined well.

Note: This is excellent on romaine lettuce. It is similar to a Caesar salad dressing.

Roll lemons, oranges and grapefruit on counter before cutting to soften. You will get more juice.

Curried Caesar Salad Dressing

1 pint mayonnaise
3 eggs
½ package dried onion soup
1 teaspoon garlic salt or powder
½ to 1 teaspoon curry powder
3 ounce can Parmesan cheese
1 to 2 inches of anchovy paste
(or 2 to 3 anchovy filets)

Mix thoroughly in blender and refrigerate. (Empty mayonnaise jar is perfect for storage.) Serve over romaine leaves with croutons (good only on romaine). Stores for several weeks.

Egg Salad Dressing

3 green onions, chopped
Small cucumber, diced
1 green pepper, chopped
2 celery sticks, chopped
5 hard-boiled eggs, diced
1½ cups Kraft Miracle Whip
Salt and pepper to taste

Combine ingredients. Make 2 days in advance. Serve over iceberg lettuce wedges. Serves 8.

Bavarian Salad Dressing

½ cup ham, diced
1/3 cup onion, chopped
1 teaspoon prepared mustard
1/3 cup red tarragon vinegar
1 teaspoon parsley, chopped
Salt to taste
Pepper to taste
½ cup oil
Lettuce, romaine or spinach

Saute' ham and onion in a small amount of oil. Mix together mustard, vinegar, parsley, salt, pepper and oil. Add chopped lettuce, romaine and/or spinach to this dressing mixture. Toss. Add hot ham and onion on top of greens.

Dressings

Blue Cheese Dressing

1 cup mayonnaise
¾ cup buttermilk
6 ounces blue cheese, crumbled
1 teaspoon steak sauce
7 drops hot sauce
1 tablespoon Italian seasoning
1 tablespoon parsley flakes
1 clove garlic, pressed

Combine all ingredients in a medium bowl and stir well. Chill thoroughly in a covered container. Serve on tossed salad or with assorted raw vegetables. Makes 2½ cups.

Cole Slaw Dressing

1 cup sugar
1 cup white vinegar
1 cup mayonnaise
1 cup salad oil
1 teaspoon dry mustard
Dash of Tabasco sauce
1 teaspoon salt
Yellow food coloring

Blend in mixer for 5 minutes. Keeps in refrigerator for 6 weeks.

Spiced Oranges

4 whole navel oranges, unpeeled
½ teaspoon soda
Soda water
2 cups sugar
1½ cups water
½ cup vinegar
3 pieces stick cinnamon
10 whole cloves

Cover oranges with soda water and boil 20 to 30 minutes or until easily pierced with a fork. Drain and cut each orange into eight wedges. Combine sugar, 1½ cups water, vinegar and spices. Stir over low heat until sugar is dissolved, then boil 5 minutes. Add oranges and simmer 25 minutes. Cool, cover and refrigerate. Serves 6 to 8.

Note: May serve with pork, ham, duck, poultry or corned beef and cabbage.

Cheese Fruit Salad

1 20-ounce can mandarin oranges
1 20-ounce can pineapple tidbits
1 cup sugar
½ cup corn starch and enough water to make a thick paste
1 egg yolk
1 cup sharp Cheddar cheese, grated
1 cup pecans, chopped
Small container Cool Whip

Drain first two ingredients well and retain juice. Mix together the juice, sugar, corn starch mixture and egg yolk and slowly bring to a boil. Stir constantly. Must be very thick. Cool mixture (put in freezer a few minutes). Mix together in a large serving bowl the fruit, cheese and nuts. Pour the cooled sugar mixture over the fruit mixture. Toss. Fold in the Cool Whip. Chill for 10 to 12 hours for best results. Serves 12.

"Cool" Cottage Cheese

12 ounces cottage cheese (Sealtest best)
4½ ounces Cool Whip
8¼ ounces canned crushed pineapple, drained
½ cup nuts
½ (3 ounce) package lime Jello

Combine all ingredients and mix well. Best when allowed to set for at least 30 minutes. Serves 6.

Salads

Blueberry Heaven

6 ounces blackberry Jello
1 cup boiling water
1 cup pineapple juice (cold water added to make 1 cup)
16 ounces crushed pineapple (drain and reserve juice for above)
1 can blueberry pie filling

Topping:
8 ounce package cream cheese
12 ounce container Cool Whip

Dissolve Jello in boiling water. Add 1 cup pineapple juice drained from pineapple. Stir, then add crushed pineapple and blueberry pie filling. Stir and pour into a 9X13 inch dish, refrigerate until firm. When congealed, make topping and spread on top of blueberry mixture. Refrigerate again for 30 minutes, then serve. Serves 10 to 12.

Topping: Let cream cheese soften, then beat together Cool Whip and cream cheese. Spread on Jello like icing. Can also be used as a dessert.

Best Ever Fruit Salad

3 cups orange juice
1 cup pineapple juice, reserved from chunks
1 cup sugar
3 apples, diced
32 ounces pineapple chunks, drained
3 small cans mandarin oranges, drained
1 cup mini-marshmallows
1 cup pecans, chopped
2 bananas, sliced

Mix the orange juice, pineapple juice and sugar together in a saucepan. Cook at low temperature until the sugar is dissolved. Cool the mixture. Place apples in the bottom of serving dish. Add the pineapple chunks and the oranges. Add the marshmallows and the pecans. Cover with the juice. Keep refrigerated. Add the sliced bananas when ready to serve.

Fresh pineapple does not ripen further after it is picked. Choose one that is firm. Use within 5 days.

Frozen Lime-Mint Salad

28¼ ounces crushed pineapple, undrained
3 ounce package lime-flavored gelatin
3½ cups miniature marshmallows
1 cup butter mints, crushed
9 ounces Cool Whip, thawed
Lettuce leaves
Fresh mint sprigs (optional)

Combine pineapple, gelatin, marshmallows and crushed mints. Mix well. Cover and chill 1 to 2 hours. Fold in Cool Whip. Spoon into a 13 X 9 X 2 inch dish or 16 paper baking cups placed in muffin tins. Cover and freeze. Cut into squares or remove from papper cups. Serves 15 to 16.

Serve salad on lettuce leaves; garnish with mint sprigs, if desired.

Holland Rusk Shrimp Salad

Shrimp, cooked and cleaned, about 7 to 10 per serving
Holland Rusks
Cream cheese, seasoned with lemon juice, onion juice, salt and pepper
Tomato slices
Shredded lettuce

Sauce:
¾ cup salad oil
½ cup chili sauce
½ cup sugar
¼ cup white vinegar
½ cup water
1 teaspoon salt
1 teaspoon paprika
Juice of one grated onion

Mix the above ingredients for the sauce. This may be kept in the refrigerator for a couple of weeks.

When you are ready to serve, spread the Holland Rusks with cream cheese mixture. Cover this with a tomato slice, then shredded lettuce, then shrimp. Pour sauce over this. Do not prepare ahead of time. For a luncheon, serve one Holland Rusk per person.

Sprinkle freshly cut avocados, bananas, apples and peaches with lemon juice to prevent darkening.

Baked Hot Fruit

Coconut macaroons, crumbled
3 large cans mixed fruit, drained
1 can pineapple tidbits, drained
Jar of cherries
1 stick margarine
1 cup brown sugar
1 cup sherry
Bananas, sliced
Almonds, slivered

Put crumbled macaroons on bottom of pyrex dish. On top of this, add the mixed fruit, pineapple tidbits and the cherries. Melt the margarine with the brown sugar. Add the sherry and pour over the fruit. Add the sliced bananas and almonds last. Bake at 325 degrees for 30 minutes. Wait until the last minute to slice the bananas or else put lemon juice on the slices.

Curried Fruit

1 large can peach halves
1 large can pears
1 large can apricots
1 large can pineapple chunks
Small jar cherries
1 cup butter
2 teaspoons curry
½ cup brown sugar

Drain all fruit and alternate layers, except cherries (which are on top), in a large casserole dish. Melt 1 cup butter, add 2 teaspoons curry powder and brown sugar in a saucepan. Pour over fruit and cover. Bake at 350 degrees for 1 hour the day before serving. Refrigerate. Then bake at 350 degrees for ½ hour the second day.

Conch Salad

2 cups raw conch meat, minced
½ cup celery, chopped
½ cup onion, chopped
½ cup green pepper, chopped
1 cup cucumber, chopped
1½ cups fresh tomatoes, chopped
½ cup lemon juice
Tabasco sauce to taste
Salt to taste
Optional: ½ to ¾ cup salad dressing or mayonnaise

Combine all ingredients and mix thoroughly. Cover the bowl and refrigerate for 30 minutes. Mix well before serving. Serves 4.

Shrimp Salad Mold

1 pound shrimp, cooked, cooled and chopped
1 can tomato soup, undiluted
9 ounces cream cheese
1½ tablespoons unflavored gelatin
½ cup cold water
1 cup celery, chopped
Small onion, chopped
1 cup mayonnaise

Heat soup. Add cream cheese, stir until smooth. Add gelatin which has been soaked in ½ cup cold water. When cool, add other ingredients and pour into ring mold or small molds as desired. The center of ring may be filled with marinated vegetables. Also may be used as an appetizer with crackers.

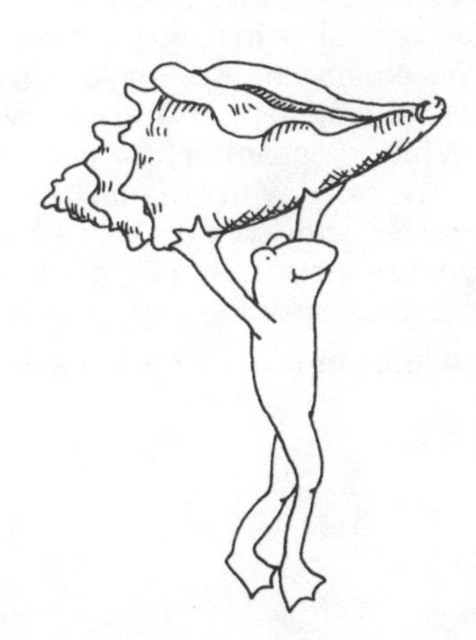

Oriental Salad

10 ounces frozen peas, cooked
4½ ounces precooked rice
9 ounces canned shrimp
1½ cups celery, sliced
¼ cup onion, chopped
½ cup salad oil
½ teaspoon sugar
2 tablespoons cider vinegar
1 tablespoon soy sauce
2 teaspoons curry powder
1 teaspoon salt
½ teaspoon Accent
½ teaspoon celery seed
¼ cup slivered almonds, toasted

Combine and chill cooked peas, rice, shrimp, celery and onion. Combine the other ingredients except almonds. Pour dressing over pea mixture. Refrigerate. Toss in almonds just before serving.

Artichoke Fantasy

8 ounces fresh mushrooms
1 small or medium onion
1 clove garlic
1 tablespoon butter
24 ounces artichoke hearts
8 ounces cream cheese
1 cup mayonnaise
3 tablespoons lemon juice
3 tablespoons Worcestershire sauce
1½ teaspoons Tabasco sauce
½ teaspoon pepper
1 teaspoon celery salt
2 envelopes gelatin
1 can beef consomme'
1½ teaspoons paprika

Grate mushrooms and onion in food processor. Chop garlic finely and saute' with mushrooms and onion in butter. Drain excess liquid. Drain artichoke hearts and slice in food processor. In a large bowl with an electric mixer, combine cream cheese, mayonnaise, lemon juice, Worcestershire sauce, Tabasco sauce, pepper and celery salt. Heat consomme' in small sauce pan. While consomme' is heating, add gelatin and stir. Pour consomme' in the bowl with cream cheese and mayonnaise. Blend slowly with electric mixer until cream cheese has melted. Stir in artichokes and mushroom mixture. Pour into a lightly mayonnaised mold and refrigerate at least 3 hours. May sprinkle with paprika and serve on lettuce.

Hint: To remove from mold wipe outside with hot towel to loosen.

Avocado — Cucumber Mold

3 ounces lemon flavored gelatin
2 tablespoons cold water
½ cup boiling water
1 cup sour cream
¾ teaspoon salt
2 tablespoons lemon juice, freshly squeezed
½ cup unpeeled cucumber, minced or coarsely grated
1 cup avocado, diced
2 tablespoons chives or onion, minced

Soften gelatin in cold water for 5 minutes. Dissolve in hot water. Blend into sour cream, beating until smooth. Add all other ingredients and pour into mold. Chill until set. Serves 4.

Note: For a cocktail supper for about 20, make 4 times the recipe. To lend added firmness to a very large heavy mold, add 1 package of plain unflavored gelatin to the four packages of lemon flavored gelatin.

Bean and Pea Salad

1½ cup salad dressing (Miracle Whip)
1 medium onion, chopped
1 teaspoon prepared mustard
1 teaspoon Worcestershire sauce
4 teaspoons salad oil
Dash Tabasco sauce
3 hard-boiled eggs, chopped
1 package frozen baby limas, cooked
1 can green beans
1 can green peas

Mix salad dressing, onion, mustard, Worcestershire sauce, salad oil, Tabasco sauce and eggs. Toss with beans and peas. Refrigerate at least one day. Serve cold. Serves 8 to 12.

Salads

Asparagus Mold

14½ ounces cut green asparagus spears
Liquid from asparagus with water added to make 1 cup
1 packet unflavored gelatin
½ cup mayonnaise
½ cup cream, whipped (or sour cream)
1 teaspoon salt
2 tablespoons lemon juice
1 cup blanched almonds, finely chopped

Heat the liquid and pour over the gelatin which has been dissolved in cold water. Refrigerate until partially set, then fold in mayonnaise, sour cream, salt and lemon juice. Add asparagus and almonds, then pour the mixture into a mold and congeal. Serve with mayonnaise mixed with a little lemon juice. Serves 8.

Avocado — Shrimp Salad

1 pound medium shrimp, boiled, peeled and chunked
½ cup celery, chopped
2 medium ripe avocados
1 tablespoon Dijon style mustard
Dash of Tabasco sauce
1½ teaspoons Worcestershire sauce
1/3 cup mayonnaise
1 tablespoon fresh lemon juice
Seafood seasoning to taste
Garnish: cherry tomatoes, sliced, and parsley

Scoop out the meat of the avocados and reserve the skins to serve the salad in. Mix the ingredients lightly yet thoroughly. Place the mixture back in the avocado shells. Chill. Garnish. Serves 4.

Note: This is great for luncheons!

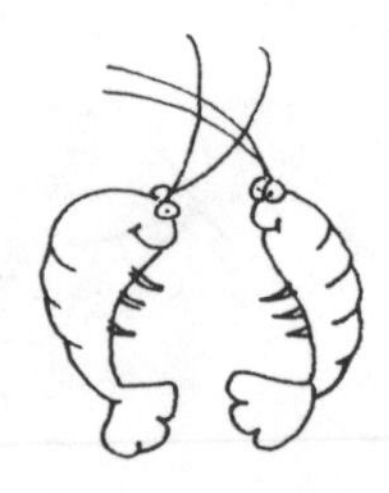

Bean Salad with Sour Cream

32 ounces of green beans, drained
1 cup sour cream
2 tablespoons lemon juice
½ teaspoon salt
½ teaspoon celery salt
1 teaspoon Worcestershire sauce
2 cloves of garlic, minced

Mix all ingredients together, cover and refrigerate overnight. Serves 6 to 8.

Broccoli Salad

1 bunch fresh, raw broccoli, chopped by hand (tenderest stems only)
½ cup stuffed olives, chopped
½ cup green onion, chopped
2 hard-boiled eggs, chopped
¾ cup mayonnaise

Blend ingredients together. Refrigerate for 30 to 45 minutes. Stir again and serve. May garnish with celery or fresh mushrooms. Serves 6. Very good as a luncheon side dish.

Mixed Cauliflower Salad

1 head cauliflower
¼ cup vinegar
½ cup salad oil
1 tablespoon tarragon
1 ounce anchovies, chopped
1 teaspoon salt
1½ teaspoons pepper
1 teaspoon sugar
1 teaspoon garlic powder (or small minced garlic clove)
1 pimiento (or more), diced
½ cup fresh mushrooms (or more), sliced
¾ cup onion, sliced

Soak head of cauliflower in cold salt water for 15 minutes. Slice cauliflower in small pieces. Mix remaining ingredients. Add to drained cauliflower. Toss and chill at least 3 hours. Serves 4.

Green Bean Salad

Dressing:
1 small clove garlic, halved
¼ teaspoon salt or more, to taste
½ teaspoon sugar
⅛ teaspoon dry mustard
⅛ teaspoon paprika
⅛ teaspoon whole oregano

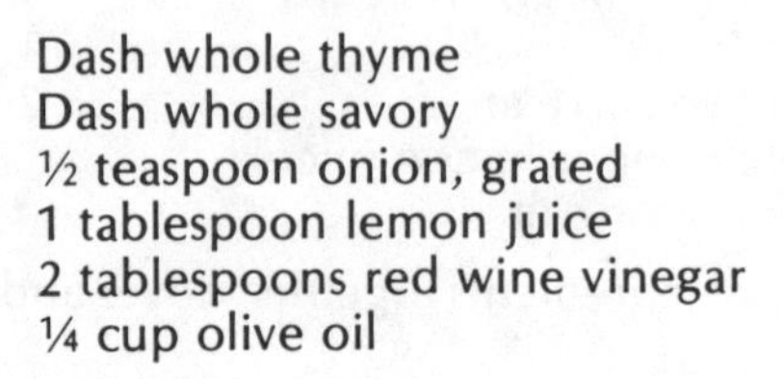
Dash whole thyme
Dash whole savory
½ teaspoon onion, grated
1 tablespoon lemon juice
2 tablespoons red wine vinegar
¼ cup olive oil

Salad:
1 pound green beans
2 tablespoons green onion, finely chopped
2 or 3 tomatoes, sliced
1½ tablespoons bleu cheese, crumbled
Lettuce leaves

Garnish:
2 hard-boiled eggs, peeled and sliced
2 ounces sliced pimientos, drained
12 ripe olives

Prepare the dressing at least an hour or two before using to allow the flavors to blend. Put all the ingredients, except the oil, in a small jar. Shake to dissolve the salt, sugar and mustard. Shake again with the oil. Remove the garlic and shake again before using.

Nip the ends off the beans and cut in 1 inch pieces. Drop the beans, a handful at a time, into a 4 quart pot of rapidly boiling salted water, letting the water come back to a simmer before dropping the next handful. Boil, uncovered, just until the beans are tender-crisp, about 5 to 7 minutes from the time the water comes back to a full boil. Drain in a colander and run cold water over the beans to stop the cooking. Drain and dry on paper towels. Toss with the chopped green onion, bleu cheese and the prepared dressing. Cover and refrigerate 3 to 4 hours.

To assemble: Line 6 salad plates with lettuce leaves. Top these with a circle of overlapping thin tomato slices. Spoon the bean salad in mounds on the tomatoes, using a slotted spoon. Garnish with egg slices, pimiento strips and ripe olives. Serves 6.

Cauliflower Surprise

1 head cauliflower, broken in small pieces
1 small onion, diced
8 strips bacon, cooked and crumbled

Sauce:
1 cup mayonnaise
¼ cup sugar
1 tablespoon Parmesan cheese
Salt and pepper

Layer cauliflower, onion and bacon in that order to make three layers.

Combine mayonnaise, sugar, Parmesan cheese and a couple of dashes each of salt and pepper. Spread mixture over layers and marinate at least 24 hours. Just before serving toss mixture. Serves 6.

Cauliflower Salad

1 head lettuce, torn
1 small head cauliflower, divided in flowerets
½ to 1 pound bacon, cooked and crumbled
8 ounces fresh Parmesan cheese, grated
1 cup mayonnaise

Layer the above ingredients in order. Chill overnight. Do **not** mix. Before serving, toss well. Serves 10 to 12.

Caulibroc Salad

1 head cauliflower
2 cups broccoli (tops)
Green and red onion to taste, sliced
2 tablespoons vinegar
2 tablespoons sugar
2 tablespoons sesame seeds
1 cup mayonnaise

Wash and trim raw vegetables. Mix together. Combine vinegar, sugar, sesame seeds and mayonnaise. Mix with vegetables. Refrigerate overnight. Stir occasionally. Serves 8.

Note: Using red onions makes this a pretty Christmas salad.

Chicken-Rice-Artichoke Salad

1 cup cooked chicken, bite size pieces
1 package chicken-flavored rice mix
2 green onions, thinly sliced
¼ green pepper, seeded and chopped
8 pimiento stuffed olives, sliced
6 ounce jar marinated artichoke hearts
½ teaspoon curry powder (or more to taste)
1/3 cup mayonnaise

Cook rice according to package directions. Cool. Add chicken pieces, green onions, green peppers and olives. Drain artichokes, reserving liquid. Chop artichokes into bite size pieces. Combine ½ of the marinade with curry powder and mayonnaise. (Discard rest of marinade.) Toss all together. Chill. Perfect for a summer luncheon with muffins and fresh fruit. Serves 6 to 8.

Cold Curried Rice Salad

2 cups rice, cooked with 2 tablespoons butter
10 ounces frozen peas and celery
1/3 cup mayonnaise
½ to 1 teaspoon curry powder
1/3 cup Hidden Valley Ranch dressing (mixed according to directions on package)
48 ounces artichoke hearts, halved
6 green onions, chopped (including tops)
2 cans water chestnuts, sliced
16 ounces mushroom buttons

Cover cooked rice and refrigerate until chilled. Cook celery and peas and chill. Combine mayonnaise, curry powder and Hidden Valley Ranch dressing. Mix well chilled rice and vegetables. Stir in dressing mixture and chill thoroughly. Serves 12 to 14. (May add more dressing mixture if desired).

Note: This is best if made 24 hours in advance. A perfect dish for a picnic or a large crowd. Shrimp or chicken may be added for a main dish. (about 1 cup bite size pieces)

Cleopatra Salad

Croutons:
1 cup small bread cubes
1 tablespoon butter, melted
1 tablespoon Parmesan cheese

Toss bread cubes with butter and Parmesan cheese in skillet. Toast over moderate heat, stirring frequently until golden brown. Cool.

Salad:
½ head each romaine & iceberg lettuce
3 cups seedless grapes, sliced in half
½ cup blue cheese, crumbled
3 tablespoons Parmesan cheese

Tear romaine and iceberg lettuce in large pieces. Arrange greens, grapes, croutons and blue cheese in large salad bowl. Pour dressing over salad. Sprinkle with remaining Parmesan cheese. Toss lightly before serving.

Dressing:
1 egg
1/3 cup olive oil
¼ cup lemon juice
1 teaspoon Worcestershire sauce
1 clove garlic, crushed
¾ teaspoon salt
¼ teaspoon pepper

Beat egg in small bowl. Add olive oil, lemon juice, Worcestershire sauce, garlic salt and pepper; beat until blended. Serves 6.

Salads

Day-Ahead Layered Salad

½ head iceberg lettuce, shredded
6 hard-boiled eggs, sliced
1 large sweet onion, thinly sliced
½ package fresh spinach
¾ pound bacon, cooked and crumbled
10 ounces frozen green peas, defrosted
10 to 12 ounces Swiss cheese, grated
1 cup mayonnaise
1 cup Miracle Whip salad dressing (or sour cream)

In large serving dish layer all ingredients (except mayonnaise and salad dressing) in order listed, beginning with lettuce. Mix mayonnaise and salad dressing and spread on top of the salad, bringing it to the edges of the dish to seal it. Cover with plastic wrap and refrigerate overnight. Serves 10 to 12.

Gourmet Potato Salad

French dressing:
1/3 cup vinegar
2/3 cup olive oil or salad oil
3 tablespoons sugar
1 teaspoon salt
2 cloves garlic, crushed

Make French dressing by combining all ingredients, mix well, cover and refrigerate. The dressing should be made a day or more ahead of time. (Only about ¼ of the dressing will be used for the potato salad.)

2 pounds new potatoes
Salt
Celery salt
3 hard-boiled eggs, diced
1 cup candied pickle, chopped
½ green pepper, diced
½ cup radishes, diced
½ cup mayonnaise
¼ cup pickle juice
1 small onion, chopped

Cook the potatoes in the skins, cool slightly, peel and cut into cubes while still warm. Toss with about ¼ of French dressing, adding salt and celery salt to taste. Combine remaining ingredients and add to potato mixture.

Pappa's Greek Salad

Potato Salad:
6 boiling potatoes
2 medium onions or 4 green onions
¼ cup parsley, finely chopped
½ cup green pepper, thinly sliced
½ cup salad dressing

Salad ingredients:
1 large head lettuce
3 cups potato salad
12 roka leaves (Greek vegetable) or 12 sprigs watercress
2 tomatoes, each cut into 6 wedges
1 cucumber, peeled and cut into 8 fingers, lengthwise
12 black olives
12 medium hot Salonika peppers (can be bought in a bottle)
4 radishes, cut in rosettes
4 whole green onions
1 avocado, peeled and cut into wedges
1 green pepper, cut into 8 rings
4 cooked canned beets, sliced
4 cooked shrimp, peeled and cleaned
4 anchovy filets
Oregano
8 ounces Feta cheese, crumbled
½ cup white vinegar
¼ cup each of olive oil and salad oil, blended

To make potato salad: Boil the potatoes in their jackets for about 30 minutes, until tender but not soft when tested. Drain and peel when cold. Cut into slices in a bowl. Cut onions and peppers into thin slices and add with chopped parsley to the potatoes. Sprinkle lightly with salt. Fold in the salad dressing using more if necessary to hold the salad together lightly.

To make the salad: Line a large platter with the outside lettuce leaves and place 3 cups of the potato salad in a mound in the center of the platter. Cover with the remaining lettuce, which has been shredded. Arrange the roka or watercress on top of this. Place the tomato wedges around the outer edge of salad and place the cucumber wedges in between the tomatoes. Arrange olives, peppers, radishes, green onions and avocado in the center of the salad. Place green pepper slices over all on very top, then add sliced beets with a shrimp on each beet slice and an anchovy filet on the shrimp. Sprinkle oregano and Feta cheese over all. Entire salad is then sprinkled with vinegar and then the blended oils. Serve with garlic toasted Greek bread. This salad makes a meal for 4.

For better flavor, do not refrigerate tomatoes.

Freshen wilted lettuce by letting it stand about 10 minutes in cold water to which a few drops of lemon juice have been added. Store in zip lock bags.

German Slaw

4 pounds cabbage, shredded
1 onion
2 green peppers
4 carrots (may use more)
1 cup vinegar
1½ cups sugar
1 cup oil
1 teaspoon celery seed
Salt and pepper to taste

Shred cabbage, chop onion and green pepper and slice carrots thinly. Combine in large container and set aside. Heat vinegar and sugar until dissolved. Cool. Add oil, celery seed, salt and pepper to vinegar mixture. Blend together and toss over vegetables. Will keep indefinitely in refrigerator. Drain before serving. Serves 12 to 16. Very quickly made in food processor.

Shakespeare Salad

1 head lettuce, torn
1 large clove garlic, chopped and soaked in 1 tablespoon lemon juice
2 carrots, sliced
1 teaspoon celery salt
2 green onions, sliced
½ green pepper, sliced
1/3 cup Cheddar cheese, shredded
½ cup pecans, toasted
1 avocado, sliced
1 tablespoon soy sauce
1 teaspoon lemon juice
¼ teaspoon pepper
2 heaping tablespoons sour cream
2 heaping tablespoons mayonnaise
¼ cup Parmesan cheese

Place torn lettuce in bowl, add garlic with lemon juice, carrots, celery salt, onions, pepper, Cheddar cheese, pecans and avocado. Sprinkle with soy sauce and lemon juice. Add pepper. Top with sour cream and mayonnaise. Sprinkle Parmesan cheese over all and toss and serve. Serves. 4.

Spinach Salad

2 packages frozen chopped spinach
½ cup celery, finely chopped
1/3 cup onion, finely chopped
1 cup Cheddar cheese, grated
3 hard-boiled eggs, chopped
6 slices bacon, cooked and crumbled
1 cup mayonnaise
½ teaspoon salt
1½ teaspoons lemon juice
½ teaspoon Tabasco sauce
2 heaping teaspoons horseradish

Thaw spinach and squeeze out all excess water. In large bowl mix spinach, celery, onion, cheese and eggs. In another bowl, mix remaining ingredients except bacon. Add mayonnaise mixture to spinach mixture and stir lightly to combine. Refrigerate. Just before serving, top with bacon bits. Serves 8.

Spinach and Apple Salad

1½ to 2 bags fresh spinach, cleaned and torn in bite size pieces

Dressing:
½ cup mayonnaise
½ cup sour cream
1 wedge blue cheese, crumbled
3 apples, peeled and diced
2 hard-boiled eggs, diced
1 onion, finely chopped

Mix dressing ingredients together. Before serving, toss with spinach. Serves 8.

Salads

Spinach Salad (Still Another Way)

1 pound fresh spinach, cleaned and torn
2 Temple oranges or 1 can mandarin orange sections
1 small red onion

Dressing:
1½ teaspoons Dijon mustard
1 tablespoon white wine
5 tablespoons salad oil

Wash and dry greens. Cut oranges into bite size pieces. Slice onion paper thin. Toss with dressing. Serves 6.

Sunsational Caesar Salad

2 bunches romaine lettuce
½ cup GOOD olive oil
3 dashes garlic wine vinegar
Juice of ½ lemon
2 teaspoons Worcestershire sauce
¼ teaspoon freshly ground pepper
½ teaspoon salt
½ teaspoon dry mustard
½ teaspoon ground oregano
¼ teaspoon dill weed, crushed,
3 cloves (good size) garlic, crushed
1 tablespoon anchovy paste
1 egg
½ cup seasoned croutons
½ cup Parmesan cheese

Wash lettuce and tear into pieces. (Use the Salad Spinner to get the moisture off.) Wrap in a towel and refrigerate until ready to toss. Put rest of the ingredients, except croutons and Parmesan cheese, in a blender and blend until well mixed. Store in jar until ready to toss. Pour into bottom of wooden bowl. Add romaine lettuce. Put seasoned croutons and ¼ to ½ cup Parmesan cheese on top. Toss and serve immediately. More garlic and anchovy paste may be used, depending on taste. (Can double or triple the recipe and keep in the refrigerator to use "on call".) This is super on fresh spinach also.

To slice firm fresh mushrooms, use an egg slicer.

Tomato Aspic

24 ounces V-8 juice
6 ounces lemon Jello
1 cup water

Boil 12 ounces of the V-8 juice. Add to Jello. Stir well. Add the remaining V-8 juice and water. Stir well. Put in mold and chill. Serves 8.

Note: A dash of horseradish may be added if desired. Lemon Deserta may be substituted for Jello to make a low calorie dish.

Summer Salad

4 tablespoons Dijon mustard
4 tablespoons red wine vinegar
3 to 4 cloves garlic, crushed
4 tablespoons vegetable oil
4 tablespoons olive oil

In a jar or dressing bottle, combine mustard, wine vinegar and garlic. Shake until well blended. Add oils and shake again. Serve over salad.

Salad:
Boston lettuce leaves for 4 to 6 people
Purple onions, thinly sliced
Mandarin orange slices
Sunflower seeds

Watercress Salad and Vinaigrette Dressing

4 bunches watercress or 1 head romaine or escarole lettuce, torn
4 ounces slivered almonds
3 stalks or 1 can hearts of palm
Sliced mushrooms

Dressing:
1 cup salad oil
½ cup cider vinegar
2 tablespoons sugar
1 hard-boiled egg, cooled
1 tablespoon salt
1 tablespoon capers
2 tablespoons onion, grated
½ tablespoon dried parsley

Combine dressing ingredients in blender for 1 minute. Refrigerate for 1 hour and serve on salad of combined watercress or other greens, almonds and hearts of palm.

Desserts
Jeni

Chocolate Swirl Cheesecake

6 ounces chocolate chips
½ cup sugar
1¼ cups graham cracker crumbs
2 tablespoons sugar
¼ cup butter, melted
16 ounces cream cheese, softened
¾ cup sugar
½ cup sour cream
1 teaspoon vanilla
4 eggs

Preheat oven to 325 degrees. Combine over hot (not boiling) water the chocolate chips and ½ cup sugar; heat until the chocolate melts and the mixture is smooth. Remove from heat; set aside. In small bowl, combine graham cracker crumbs, 2 tablespoons sugar and melted butter and mix well. Pat firmly into 9 inch springform pan, covering bottom and 1½ inches up the sides. Set aside. In large bowl, beat cream cheese until light and creamy. Gradually beat in ¾ cup sugar. Mix in sour cream and vanilla. Add eggs, one at a time, beating well after each addition. Divide batter in half. Stir melted chocolate mixture into first half. Pour into crumb lined pan; cover with plain batter. With a knife, swirl plain batter with chocolate batter to marbleize. Bake for 50 minutes or until only a 2 to 3 inch circle in center will shake. Cool at room temperature; refrigerate until ready to serve. Makes one 9 inch cheesecake.

Pecan Praline Cake

Cake:
½ cup margarine
1 cup buttermilk
2 cups light brown sugar
2 eggs
2 cups all purpose flour
1 teaspoon soda
1 teaspoon vanilla

Preheat oven to 325 degrees. Grease and flour a 9 X 14 inch pan. Warm together margarine and buttermilk. Add sugar and eggs. Beat thoroughly. Sift dry ingredients. Add to mixture and mix well. Add vanilla and mix. This batter will be thin. Pour into pan and bake 25 minutes.

Topping:
¼ pound margarine, softened
1 cup light brown sugar
1/3 cup evaporated milk
1 cup pecans, chopped

With a mixer combine and beat all ingredients. Spread on cake while it is warm. Put in the oven and broil until the topping bubbles and is slightly browned. Cool.

Mardi Gras Party Cake

2/3 cup butterscotch chips
¼ cup water
½ cup butter
2½ cups sugar
3 eggs
2 cups flour
1 teaspoon salt
1 teaspoon baking powder
1 teaspoon baking soda
1 cup buttermilk

Preheat oven to 375 degrees. Melt the chips in the top of a double boiler or in a heavy iron pan on very low heat. Cream the butter and add the sugar gradually. Add one egg at a time. Mix in the melted chips and the dry ingredients which have been sifted together, alternating with the buttermilk. Bake in three greased 8 or 9 inch cake pans for about 15 minutes.

Filling:
½ cup sugar
½ cup evaporated milk
1 tablespoon corn starch
1/3 cup water
1/3 cup butterscotch chips
1 egg yolk
2 tablespoons butter
1 cup coconut
1 cup pecans, chopped

Combine the sugar, milk, corn starch, water, butterscotch chips and egg yolk. Cook over low to medium heat, stirring until thick enough to spread. If this doesn't thicken in 15 minutes or so, set the mixture in a sink of cold water and stir. Remove from the heat and add the butter, coconut and pecans. Spread this between the layers and on top of the cake.

Icing:
4 ounces cream cheese
2 ounces butter
½ box confectioners' sugar
1 tablespoon evaporated milk

Mix the above ingredients and apply this to the sides of the cake.

Chocolate Covered Strawberries

1 large Hershey candy bar
1 to 1½ tablespoons paraffin
1 quart fresh, ripe strawberries, washed and drained

Melt the candy bar and paraffin slowly in a double boiler. Stir constantly. Hold the whole berry by the stem and dip it in the slightly cooled chocolate. Let dry on wax paper. Refrigerate. Use these as a garnish.

Cake in a Cloud

2/3 cup graham cracker crumbs
1/3 cup margarine or butter, melted
½ cup walnuts, chopped
2/3 cup chocolate chips
½ cup butter
1½ cups sugar
2 eggs
½ cup chocolate chips, melted
1 teaspoon vanilla
2 cups flour
1 teaspoon baking soda
1 teaspoon salt
1¼ cups buttermilk

Topping:
1½ pints whipping cream, whipped with 12 tablespoons sugar

Preheat oven to 375 degrees. Combine the crumbs and melted butter. Stir in the nuts and 2/3 cup chocolate chips. Set this aside. Cream the ½ cup butter and add the sugar. Cream until fluffy. Add the eggs one at a time. Blend in the melted chocolate and vanilla. At low speed, add the combined dry ingredients; alternate with buttermilk. Mix well. Pour into two 9 inch round pans that have been greased and floured. Sprinkle evenly with the crumb mixture and bake. (You may prefer to bake the cake about 10 minutes before adding the crumbs. They will remain on top of each layer better.) Bake the layers for 30 to 40 minutes totally. Cool thoroughly and frost the top of each layer with mounds of sweetened whipped cream.

Chocolate Almond Mousse Cake

16 ounces Bakers German Sweet Chocolate
½ cup water
1 1/3 cup sweetened condensed milk
4 cups heavy cream
1 teaspoon vanilla
1 cup slivered almonds, toasted
2 packages ladyfingers, cut in half lengthwise

Combine chocolate and water in pan. Stir over very low heat until blended and smooth. Cool. Combine cooled chocolate, milk, cream and vanilla in a large mixing bowl and chill. Then whip until soft peaks form. Fold in almonds. Place ladyfingers in the bottom and around the sides of a springform pan; cut side of the ladyfinger towards the inside. Pour in the mousse and freeze. Serve with topping. Serves 10 to 12.

Topping: Whipped cream with chocolate curls and almond pieces.

Waldorf — Astoria Cake

½ cup butter
2 cups sugar
3 squares bitter chocolate, melted
2 eggs
1½ cups milk
2 cups flour
1 teaspoon salt
2 teaspoons baking powder
2 teaspoons vanilla
1½ cups pecans, chopped

Preheat oven to 375 degrees. Beginning with the butter, mix each ingredient one at a time, mixing thoroughly. Bake in three 9 inch cake pans, baking for 35 minutes. Cool completely before frosting.

Frosting:
3 sticks butter
2 squares bitter chocolate
1½ pounds confectioners' sugar
2 tablespoons lemon juice
2 eggs, beaten
1 teaspoon vanilla
1½ cups pecans, chopped

Melt the butter and chocolate; remove from heat and mix by hand with confectioners' sugar, lemon juice, eggs, vanilla and pecans.

Halve the 3 layers, frost between each layer (6 layers) and then the top. Freeze. When frozen you can wrap in foil or keep in the freezer in a container.

No-Fault Sour Cream Pound Cake

2 sticks butter, softened
3 cups sugar
6 eggs
3 cups cake flour
¼ teaspoon baking powder
½ pint sour cream
1 teaspoon almond extract
1 teaspoon vanilla

Preheat oven to 300 degrees. Grease and flour a tube or bundt pan. Cream butter and sugar. Add eggs, two at a time, beating thoroughly after each. Sift together cake flour and baking powder; add to batter alternately with sour cream. Blend in almond and vanilla. Bake 1¼ to 1½ hours.

Note: This can be frozen.

Choco-Kahlua Pound Cake

1 box (pudding recipe) devil's food cake mix
½ cup sugar
1/3 cup oil
3 eggs
¾ cup water
¼ cup bourbon
½ cup Kahlua
¾ cup black coffee, double strength
2 teaspoons cocoa

Preheat oven to 350 degrees. Mix all the ingredients and beat for 4 minutes. Bake in a greased bundt pan for 50 minutes. Let cool for 10 minutes, then ice.

Icing:
1 stick butter
1 cup sugar
1/3 cup evaporated milk
1½ cups chocolate chips

Heat the butter, sugar and milk; boil for 2 minutes, stirring constantly. Take off the heat and rapidly stir in the chocolate chips and pour over the cake immediately.

Oatmeal Chocolate Cake

1 cup oatmeal
1 stick margarine
1¼ cups boiling water
1 cup brown sugar, packed
1 cup sugar
2 eggs
1¼ cups flour
1 teaspoon soda
3 tablespoons cocoa

Preheat oven to 350 degrees. Pour water over oatmeal and margarine, let stand 20 minutes. Add both sugars, eggs, and then dry ingredients. Mix well, pour into greased 9 X 13 inch pan. Bake for 25 to 30 minutes. Mix icing and pour over cake while hot.

Icing:
½ cup Pet milk
1 cup sugar
1 stick margarine
1 teaspoon vanilla

Bring all ingredients to a boil (approximately 2 minutes) over medium heat stirring constantly.

Cakes

Banana Chocolate Cake

2½ cups cake flour, sifted
1 teaspoon baking powder
¾ teaspoon baking soda
1 teaspoon salt
1½ sticks butter
1½ cups sugar
2 eggs
2 ounces unsweetened chocolate, melted
1 teaspoon vanilla
1 cup ripe bananas, mashed
½ cup buttermilk

Preheat oven to 350 degrees. Sift flour, baking powder, soda and salt together. Cream shortening with sugar until fluffy. Add eggs one at a time, beating thoroughly after each. Add melted chocolate and mix thoroughly. Stir in vanilla. Add sifted dry ingredients alternately with bananas and milk. Begin and end with flour. Turn into two 8 inch greased pans and bake for 30 to 35 minutes.

Frosting:
3 ounces cream cheese
¼ cup milk
3 cups confectioners' sugar, sifted
⅛ teaspoon salt
1 teaspoon vanilla
3 squares unsweetened chocolate, melted

Blend cream cheese with milk. Add sugar and vanilla; beat in chocolate. Frost the cake.

St. Louis Cake

1¾ cup chocolate chips
3 tablespoons sugar
2 tablespoons water
4 egg yolks, beaten
4 egg whites, room temperature
Prepared yellow cake or pound cake
½ pint heavy cream, whipped and sweetened

Put chocolate chips in top of double boiler with the sugar, water and beaten egg yolks. Stir over heat until thick and melted. Take off the heat and cool slightly. Beat egg whites until stiff but soft peaks form. Gently fold egg whites into chocolate mixture. Line a 9x5 inch pan with wax paper. Line this with thin slices of cake. Pour a layer of chocolate mixture over the cake. Alternate layers of cake and chocolate. Leave in refrigerator overnight. Turn out of the pan and cover with whipped cream before serving.

Italian Cream Cake

1 stick margarine
½ cup vegetable shortening
2 cups sugar
5 eggs, separated; whites stiffly beaten
2 cups flour
1 teaspoon baking soda
1 cup buttermilk
1 teaspoon vanilla
4 ounces coconut
1 cup pecans, chopped

Preheat oven to 350 degrees. Cream margarine and shortening; add sugar and beat until smooth. Add egg yolks and beat. Sift together the flour and soda and add the other mixture alternating with buttermilk. Mix in vanilla, coconut and nuts. Fold in egg whites. Pour into three 8 inch pans that have been greased and floured. Bake for 25 minutes.

Frosting:
8 ounces cream cheese, softened
½ cup margarine
1 box confectioners' sugar, sifted
1 teaspoon vanilla
Chopped pecans for garnish

Beat the cheese and margarine until smooth. Add sugar, mixing well. Blend in vanilla. Frost cake and top with pecans. Refrigerate for a few hours until icing hardens.

Rum Angel Cake

1 angel food cake
1 stick margarine
1½ cups confectioners' sugar
5 egg yolks, beaten
4 tablespoons rum
¾ cup slivered almonds, divided
½ pint whipping cream, whipped

Cream margarine and sugar. Add egg yolks, rum and ½ cup almonds. Chill mixture before layering. Slice angel cake horizontally into 4 layers (Use serrated knife.) Place filling on each layer and restack the layers. Ice with whipped cream and garnish with ¼ cup almonds. Chill overnight. Serves 8 to 12.

To keep dried fruit from falling to the bottom of a cake, coat them lightly with flour.

Cakes

Sour Cream Walnut Coffee Cake

¾ cup butter, softened
1½ cups sugar
3 eggs
2 teaspoons vanilla extract
3 cups all purpose flour
1½ teaspoons baking powder
1½ teaspoons soda
½ teaspoon salt
1 pint sour cream
¾ cup light brown sugar
2 teaspoons cinnamon
1 cup walnuts, chopped

Preheat oven to 350 degrees. Combine butter and sugar, creaming until light and fluffy. Add eggs, one at a time, beating well after each addition. Stir in vanilla. Combine flour, baking powder, soda and salt; add to creamed mixture alternating with sour cream, mixing well after each addition. Combine brown sugar, cinnamon and walnuts; mix well. Spoon about 1/3 of the batter into a greased and floured 10 inch tube pan or bundt pan. Sprinkle with 1/3 of nut mixture. Repeat layers twice. Bake for 1 hour or until done. Let stand 5 minutes before removing from pan. Place on serving dish and drizzle with glaze.

Glaze:
1½ cups confectioners' sugar
½ teaspoon vanilla extract
2 tablespoons water

Combine the confectioners' sugar, vanilla and water. Mix well.

Note: To freeze, let cool completely and wrap in freezer paper.

Chess Squares

1 stick of butter, melted
1 box yellow cake mix
1 egg
8 ounces cream cheese
1 box confectioners' sugar
3 eggs
Pecan halves for garnish

Preheat oven to 300 degrees. Mix the first 3 ingredients together and press into the bottom of a 9 X 13 inch aluminum pan. Mix thoroughly the remaining ingredients and pour over above mixture. Add pecan halves to the top. Bake for 45 minutes to one hour. Better after it sets for awhile.

Orange Sour Cream Cake

Cake:

½ cup shortening
1 teaspoon salt
1 tablespoon orange rind, grated
1 cup sugar
2 eggs
2 cups flour
1 teaspoon baking powder
1 teaspoon soda
8 ounces sour cream
1/3 cup orange juice
1 cup nuts, finely chopped

Preheat oven to 350 degrees. Blend shortening, salt and 1 tablespoon orange rind together. Gradually cream in sugar and then add eggs one at a time, beating well after each. Sift dry ingredients into creamed mixture alternating with sour cream and orange juice, mixing until smooth after each addition. Add chopped nuts. Pour into a greased and floured bundt cake pan. Bake 45 to 50 minutes. Cool 10 minutes and remove from pan.

Topping:

2 tablespoons honey
½ cup orange juice
1 tablespoon orange rind
2 tablespoons lemon juice

Heat honey, orange juice, orange rind and lemon juice. Using pastry brush spread warm honey mixture on top of warm cake.

Peanut Butter Candy

½ pound butter, softened
1 pound peanut butter, smooth or crunchy
1½ pounds confectioners' sugar, sifted
24 ounces chocolate chips

Mix butter and peanut butter until smooth. Add sugar slowly. When blended, roll into balls. Place on greased foil and freeze until hard. At least two hours later, melt chocolate chips in top of double boiler. Dip balls in melted chocolate. Refrigerate or may be frozen. Makes 100 balls.

All purpose flour can be substituted for cake flour: one cup minus 2 tablespoons of all purpose flour equals 1 cup cake flour.

Candies

5-Minute Chocolate Whiskey Truffles

1 tablespoon lightly salted butter
¼ cup cocoa
½ cup confectioners' sugar
1 tablespoon whiskey

In a small saucepan melt the butter; remove from heat and stir in the remaining ingredients. Mixture will be very stiff. If it seems too dry, add a few additional drops of whiskey. When well mixed, take one tablespoon at a time and roll into a small ball. Sprinkle with additional confectioners' sugar when serving. Store in airtight container. Makes 12 small truffles.

Mints

¼ teaspoon peppermint extract
Pinch of salt
3 ounces cream cheese, softened
Food coloring (a few drops)
16 ounces confectioners' sugar

Add extract and salt to the cream cheese and blend until creamy using a wooden spoon. Add coloring to secure the shade desired. Add sugar, a little at a time, working in until the dough becomes very stiff. The last few ounces of sugar may need to be kneaded in with your hands. When mixture is ready, press the mixture into mold, turn rubber mold over, press with thumbs, dropping mint on waxed paper. Leave them on the waxed paper until you have finished all of them. The mints can be frozen in an airtight container. Yield: 8 dozen.

Two Minute Fudge

16 ounces confectioners' sugar
½ cup cocoa
¼ teaspoon salt
¼ cup milk
1 tablespoon vanilla extract
½ cup butter
1 cup nuts, chopped

In a 1½ quart casserole stir in the sugar, cocoa, salt, milk and vanilla until partially blended. Put butter over top in center of dish. Microwave on HIGH for 2 minutes. Stir vigorously until smooth. If all the butter has not melted in cooking, it will as the mixture is stirred. Blend in the nuts. Pour into an 8 X 8 X 2 inch plate and place in refrigerator for 1 hour or freezer for 20 minutes. Cut into squares.

Apricot Coconut Balls

1½ cups dried apricots, ground
2 cups coconut
14 ounces sweetened condensed milk
Confectioners' sugar

Combine apricots and coconut. Add condensed milk and mix well. Shape into small balls. Roll in confectioners' sugar.

Kookie Brittle

1 cup butter, softened
1 teaspoon salt
1 teaspoon vanilla
1 cup sugar
2 cups flour, unsifted
6 ounces chocolate chips
1 cup pecans, chopped

Preheat oven to 375 degrees. Grease a 15½ X 10 X 1 inch jelly roll pan. (May use a cookie sheet and shorten it with a strip of foil.) In a large bowl cream butter with electric mixer. Add salt and vanilla. Beat in sugar until light and fluffy. Add flour and mix well. Stir in chocolate and pecans. Pat dough with hands into prepared pan. Bake 20 to 25 minutes or until lightly brown at edges. Cool in pan on wire rack. When cool, break with hands into pieces (like peanut brittle). Makes 5 dozen.

Cinnamon Nut Syrup

2 cups sugar
1 cup water
¾ cup dark corn syrup
2 teaspoons cinnamon
1 cup pecans or walnuts, chopped

Heat all ingredients except nuts in 9 inch heavy skillet over medium heat to boiling, without stirring, approximately 15 minutes. Be sure to watch carefully as this burns easily. Stir in nuts. Cool slightly and pour over ice cream.

Glazed Bar Chews

2 cups brown sugar, divided
2 cups flour, sifted
¾ cup butter or margarine, softened
1 teaspoon vanilla
2 eggs, well beaten
2 tablespoons flour
1/3 teaspoon salt
½ teaspoon baking powder
1 cup walnuts, chopped
1½ cups coconut, shredded

Lemon Frosting:
2 tablespoons butter
½ cup or more confectioners' sugar
1 tablespoon orange juice
1 tablespoon lemon juice

Preheat oven to 325 degrees. Mix 1 cup brown sugar, flour and butter together well. Pack into a greased 9 X 13 inch pan and bake for 15 minutes. While baking, mix together other cup of brown sugar, vanilla, eggs, flour, salt, baking powder, nuts and coconut. Spread this mixture over the cookie base as soon as it is baked. Return to the oven and bake for 25 minutes more. Cool. Frost with lemon frosting.

For lemon frosting, beat together butter, confectioners' sugar, orange juice and lemon juice. Add a little more sugar if necessary to make frosting of spreading consistency. Makes 24 bars.

Chocolate Fudgies

½ stick butter
12 ounces chocolate chips
1 teaspoon vanilla
15 ounces condensed milk
1 cup flour
8 ounces pecans, broken

Preheat oven to 350 degrees. Melt in top of double boiler the butter and chocolate. Add vanilla and remove from heat. Stir in milk and flour and add nuts. Using an iced teaspoon, spoon small amount onto greased cookie sheet and bake 7 minutes ONLY. Will be soft until cool. Makes Approximately 100 cookies.

"Almost Pecan Pie" Cookies

Crust:
2 sticks butter, melted
2 cups flour
1 cup light brown sugar

Filling:
4 eggs, slightly beaten
¼ cup flour
3 cups dark brown sugar
1 can coconut
2 cups pecans, chopped
1 teaspoon salt
½ teaspoon vanilla
Confectioners' sugar

Preheat oven to 350 degrees. Mix the butter, 2 cups flour and the light brown sugar. Spread this mixture evenly over a 9 X 13 inch pan. Bake for 15 minutes. Remove from oven and cool.

Lower the oven temperature to 325 degrees. Mix the filling ingredients except the confectioners' sugar. Spread this over the baked layer. Bake for 40 minutes — until the mixture is firm. Sprinkle the top with confectioners' sugar while it is still warm. Cool. Cut into 48 squares. This can be frozen.

Date and Nut Crescents

2 pie crusts, mix or sticks

Roll the pie crusts to the thickness of ⅛ inch. Cut into 2½ inch rounds. Place on wax paper and chill while making filling.

Filling:
½ cup dates, chopped
½ cup walnuts, chopped
1 cup sugar
1 egg, well beaten
Juice of 1 lemon

Preheat oven to 400 degrees. Combine all ingredients in a bowl and mix well. Spoon mixture onto center of pastry rounds. Brush edges with water and fold over into crescents. Press the edge closed with a fork. Prick the tops of the pastries before baking. Bake until golden brown, about 8 to 10 minutes. Makes 3 dozen.

Cookies

Butter Pecan Turtle Cookies

Crust:
2 cups flour
½ cup brown sugar
½ cup butter, softened
1 cup whole pecan halves

Caramel layer:
½ cup brown sugar
2/3 cup butter
1 cup milk chocolate chips

Preheat oven to 350 degrees. For the crust, combine the flour, ½ cup brown sugar and ½ cup butter. Mix at medium speed 2 to 3 minutes, until the particles are fine. Pat firmly into an ungreased 9 X 13 X 2 inch pan. Sprinkle pecan halves over the unbaked crust.

Combine the ½ cup brown sugar and the butter in a 1 quart saucepan. Cook over medium heat, stirring constantly until the mixture begins to boil. Boil ½ to 1 minute, stirring constantly. Pour the caramel over the pecans and crust. Bake for 18 to 22 minutes or until caramel layer is bubbly and the crust is light brown. Remove from the oven. Sprinkle with chocolate chips. Swirl the chips as they melt. Do **NOT** spread the chips. Cool. Cut into 3 to 4 dozen bars.

Half Way Cookies

1 cup butter
½ cup sugar
½ cup light brown sugar
2 egg yolks
1 tablespoon cold water
1 teaspoon vanilla
2 cups flour, sifted
¼ teaspoon salt
1½ teaspoons baking powder
12 ounces chocolate chips
½ cup nuts, chopped
2 egg whites
1 cup light brown sugar

Preheat oven to 375 degrees. Cream butter. Add sugar and ½ cup brown sugar. Add egg yolks, cold water and vanilla. Sift flour, salt and baking powder and add to creamed mixture. Spread in greased 9 X 13 inch pan. On top sprinkle chocolate chips and nuts. Beat egg whites until stiff. Add 1 cup brown sugar. Spread on top. Bake for 25 minutes. Cool and cut into bite size pieces.

World's Best Cookie

1 cup butter or margarine
1 cup sugar
1 cup brown sugar
1 cup crunchy peanut butter
2 eggs
1 teaspoon baking soda
2 cups flour, sifted
6 ounces chocolate chips

Preheat oven to 325 degrees. Mix the butter, sugars, peanut butter and eggs. Add the baking soda and sifted flour. Then add the chips. Drop on cookie sheet. Bake for 10 to 12 minutes. Makes 5½ dozen.

Pool Side Cookies

24 graham crackers
½ pound butter or margarine
1 cup light brown sugar
½ cup pecans, finely chopped

Preheat oven to 350 degrees. Put the crackers on an ungreased cookie sheet. In a saucepan, melt the butter and sugar; bring to a boil and stir constantly for 5 minutes. Pour the caramelized mixture evenly over the crackers. Sprinkle with nuts. Bake for 10 minutes. Cool 10 minutes and cut into bars. Makes 48 bars.

Pecan Meltaways

1 cup butter, softened
2 cups flour
2/3 cup brown sugar
Generous pinch of salt
2 cups pecans, ground
Confectioners' sugar

Preheat oven to 350 degrees. Mix thoroughly all ingredients. Mixture will be dry and crumbly. Using hands, roll into balls approximately 1 teaspoon each. Place on greased cookie sheet. Bake about 20 minutes or until lightly browned. While hot, roll cookies in confectioners' sugar. Cool, then roll again in confectioners' sugar. Makes 4 to 5 dozen.

Cookies

Marvelous Brownies

2 cups sugar
4 tablespoons cocoa
4 eggs, beaten
2 sticks butter, melted
1½ cups flour
½ teaspoon salt
½ teaspoon baking powder
2 teaspoons vanilla
1 cup nuts, chopped
Mini-marshmallows

Preheat oven to 350 degrees. Sift together the sugar and cocoa. Mix the eggs, butter, flour, salt, baking powder, vanilla and nuts, in that order. Mix well. Pour into three 8 X 8 inch pans that have been greased and floured lightly. Use about 1 cup of batter for each pan. Bake 20 minutes. Remove and, while hot, pour mini-marshmallows over top, covering it. Cool and then frost.

Frosting:
2/3 cup butter
1 cup dark brown sugar, packed
2 dashes salt
6 tablespoons milk
3 cups confectioners' sugar
2 tablespoons cocoa

In saucepan, melt the butter; add the brown sugar and salt. Mix well and cook for 2 minutes. Add the milk and cook, stirring constantly until boiling. Remove from heat. Cool 10 minutes. Gradually beat in the confectioners' sugar and cocoa. Spread while warm, ½ cup per pan. Serves 48.

Note: Throw away aluminum pans can be used for baking. These brownies can be prepared ahead and frozen.

Italian Chews

¼ cup butter
1 cup sugar
2 eggs
2 tablespoons milk
1 teaspoon vanilla
1 cup flour
1 teaspoon baking powder
1 cup dates, chopped
1 cup nuts, chopped
Confectioners' sugar

Preheat oven to 375 degrees. Cream together butter, sugar, eggs, milk and vanilla. Sift together flour and baking powder and add to creamed mixture. Add dates and nuts. Bake for ½ hour in a 8 X 8 inch pan. When cool, cut in strips and sprinkle with confectioners' sugar. Makes 24. Can freeze.

Fruited Oat Bars

Filling:
8½ ounces crushed pineapple
½ cup sugar
12 ounces thick apricot preserves
1/3 cup corn starch
¼ teaspoon salt

Crust:
1½ cups flour, sifted
1 teaspoon baking powder
½ teaspoon salt
1 cup brown sugar
½ teaspoon nutmeg
¾ cup butter or margarine
2 cups oatmeal

Preheat oven to 375 degrees. Combine the pineapple, sugar, preserves, corn starch and ¼ teaspoon salt. Cook, stirring constantly, until very thick and clear. Cool.

Mix the flour, baking powder, ½ teaspoon salt, brown sugar and nutmeg. Cut the butter into this until crumbly. Stir in the oatmeal.

Reserve 2½ cups crumb mixture for the top. Pack the remaining crumbs over the bottom of a greased 9 X 13 inch baking pan. Spread evenly, then spread the preserve filling over it. Sprinkle the remaining crumbs over the filling and press slightly. Bake about 30 minutes. Cool and cut into bars.

Butterscotch Sticks

1 stick butter
1 pound dark brown sugar
2 eggs
2 cups flour
2 teaspoons baking powder
2 teaspoons vanilla
1 cup nuts
Pinch salt
Confectioners' sugar

Preheat oven to 350 degrees. Melt butter, add sugar and stir until well blended. Cool. Add eggs, flour, baking powder, vanilla, nuts and salt. Beat well. Bake in greased and floured 9 X 13 inch pan for 20 minutes. Sprinkle with confectioners' sugar. Cut in strips.

Desserts

Napoleon Creams

Crust:
½ cup margarine
¼ cup cocoa
¼ cup sugar
1 teaspoon vanilla
1 egg, slightly beaten
2 cups graham cracker crumbs
1 cup coconut, flaked

Cook first four ingredients in double boiler until butter melts. Stir in egg and cook three minutes. Add graham cracker crumbs and coconut and mix well. Press in 9X9 inch pan.

Filling:
½ cup butter
3 tablespoons milk
4 ounces vanilla instant pudding
1 to 1½ cups confectioners' sugar

Cream butter in mixer. Add milk and pudding. Beat until fluffy. Beat in confectioners' sugar. When well mixed spread evenly over crust.

Topping:
6 ounces chocolate chips
2 tablespoons butter

Melt chocolate chips and butter slowly in double boiler. Spread over filling. Chill in refrigerator. Cut into small squares because it is very rich. Serves 16.

Date Nut Pudding

3 eggs, beaten
1 cup sugar
¼ cup flour
1 teaspoon baking powder
1 teaspoon salt
1 cup dates, chopped
1 cup walnuts, chopped
Whipped cream or ice cream

Heat oven to 350 degrees. Grease 8X8X2 inch pan. Combine eggs and sugar and beat until light and fluffy. Add flour, which has been sifted with baking powder and salt. Mix well. Add dates and nuts. Pour into greased pan. Place in pan of water. Bake 1 hour. (Be sure to place pan on bottom shelf of oven or the crust will be too brown.) Serve with whipped cream or spoonful of ice cream. Serves 6.

Garden Party Dessert

Crust:
1 cup flour
¼ cup brown sugar
½ cup walnuts or pecans, chopped
½ cup butter, melted

Preheat oven to 350 degrees. Mix all ingredients and spread 2/3 of mixture on bottom of 9 X 12 inch pan. Bake for 20 minutes, stirring occasionally. Set aside.

Filling:
2 egg whites
2 cups strawberries, fresh or frozen, chopped
2 tablespoons lemon juice
1 cup sugar
1 cup heavy cream, whipped

Beat egg whites until stiff; add strawberries, lemon juice and sugar. Beat until stiff again. Fold in whipped cream. Pour mixture into pie crust. Top with remaining nut mixture. Freeze. Thaw slightly before serving. Serves 12.

Note: Can be done one week ahead.

Coffee-Rum Dessert

1 stick butter
1¼ cups confectioners' sugar, sifted
4 egg yolks, beaten
¼ cup coffee, double strength
6 lady fingers, split
Rum
Slivered salted almonds, for garnish

Cream together the butter and sugar until light. Add egg yolks and beat well with electric mixer. Add coffee very slowly, continuing to beat well. Line a small loaf pan with wax paper. Put one third of the lady fingers on bottom of pan and sprinkle with rum. Top with one half of the creamed mixture. Continue layers, ending with lady fingers sprinkled with rum. Refrigerate overnight or for 24 hours. At serving time, turn out of pan onto an attractive silver or glass serving plate. Sprinkle with slivered salted almonds. Slice and serve. Serves 4.

Press plastic wrap directly on surface of custards, puddings, or white sauce right after cooking to prevent a skin from forming.

Amaretto Souffle'

1 tablespoon gelatin
¾ cup warm water
4 eggs, separated
1 cup sugar
2 tablespoons Amaretto liqueur
½ teaspoon vanilla
2 cups heavy cream, whipped
Slivered almonds for garnish

Chill dessert dishes. Soften the gelatin in the warm water in a saucepan for 5 minutes. Heat the gelatin until white foam starts to appear on top, then cool over ice until noticeably cooler than body temperature. Set aside. Beat the egg yolks and sugar together until light. Add Amaretto and vanilla and blend thoroughly. Set aside. Beat egg whites until peaks form. With a hand whip, mix the gelatin quickly and thoroughly into egg-sugar mixture. Fold in the whipped cream by hand. Fold in egg whites only until mixture is smooth. Ladle into chilled dessert dishes. Garnish with slivered almonds. Refrigerate for at least 1 hour. Makes six 1 cup servings.

Luscious Florida Lime Souffle'

2 envelopes unflavored gelatin
½ cup cold water
8 eggs, separated
1 cup Florida lime juice
1 teaspoon salt
2 cups sugar, divided
2 teaspoons Florida lime peel, grated
2 cups heavy cream, whipped

Sprinkle gelatin over cold water to soften. In top of double boiler, combine egg yolks, lime juice, salt and 1 cup sugar. Cook over boiling water, stirring constantly, until mixture coats back of spoon. Stir in dissolved gelatin and lime peel. Turn into 3 quart bowl; refrigerate until slightly thickened, stirring occasionally. Beat egg whites until they hold their shape. Gradually beat in 1 cup sugar; continue to beat until mixture holds peaks. On top of lime mixture, pile stiffly beaten egg whites and whipped cream. Gently fold mixture together. Pour into 6 cup souffle' dish. Refrigerate 3 hours or until firm. Makes 12 to 14 servings.

Strawberry Torte

¼ cup butter, softened
½ cup granulated sugar
4 egg yolks, beaten
1 teaspoon vanilla
1 cup flour
¼ teaspoon salt
2 teaspoons baking powder
¼ cup milk
4 egg whites
¾ cup sugar
¼ cup nuts, chopped
16 ounces frozen strawberries, thawed, or 1 pint fresh strawberries, sliced and sprinkled with sugar
½ pint heavy cream, whipped and sweetened

Preheat oven to 350 degrees. Cream butter and sugar well. Add egg yolks and vanilla. Mix well. Mix the flour, salt and baking powder together. Add flour mixture alternately with the milk to the creamed mixture. Pour the batter into two well greased springform pans. (Layer pans may be used.) Beat egg whites with sugar for meringue. Spread on top of both layers. Sprinkle nuts on top of one layer of meringue. Bake in preheated oven for 20 to 25 minutes. Cool. Remove from pans. Place plain layer on cake plate, meringue side down. Put strawberries and whipped cream on top. Place the other layer on top, nut and meringue side up. Refrigerate.

Note: Tastes best when made 6 to 24 hours ahead. Do not make on a rainy day!

Chocolate Pompadour

6 ounces semi-sweet chocolate chips
3 eggs, separated
2/3 cup heavy cream, whipped
4 to 6 tablespoons crème de menthe and/or crème de cacao

Melt chocolate over very low heat. Put in mixing bowl, add egg yolks slowly, beating well as you mix. Mixture will be quite thick. Fold in whipped cream. Add liqueur to taste. Fold in stiffly beaten egg whites. Place in individual dishes and chill at least an hour. Makes 6 small servings.

Note: This recipe can be doubled or tripled with ease. This is a very elegant dessert and very easy.

Windermere Delight

2 to 3 pints fresh strawberries, washed and hulled
3 to 4 oranges, peeled and sectioned

Sauce:
3 cups Burgundy wine
2 inch piece lemon peel
1 cinnamon stick
3 whole cloves
5 tablespoons Grand Marnier

Garnish:
Toasted almonds, slivered
Toasted coconut

In a glass serving bowl, combine strawberries and oranges. In a heavy saucepan, combine all sauce ingredients except Grand Marnier. Bring to a boil, cook until reduced by half. Strain, cool completely. Add Grand Marnier and serve over or with fruit. Garnish with toasted almonds or toasted coconut. Serves 6 to 8.

Filled Orange Cups

4 oranges
2 cups strawberries
1 cup confectioners' sugar
2 teaspoons maraschino syrup
Whole strawberries for garnish
Mint sprigs for garnish, optional

Halve oranges. Scoop out meat and pulp. Remove seeds. Mix oranges with coarsely crushed strawberries. Add confectioners' sugar and maraschino syrup and refill orange cups. Top with whole strawberries and garnish with mint sprig. Serve chilled. Serves 8.

Kahlua Mousse

1 cup sugar
1 cup water
12 ounces chocolate chips
4 eggs
Dash of salt
1/3 cup Kahlua
¼ cup Cognac
3 cups heavy cream, whipped

Combine sugar and water in saucepan. Heat slowly until sugar is completely melted (about five minutes). Place chocolate chips in blender with eggs and salt. Turn on slowest speed and add syrup in a slow, steady stream. Blend until smooth. Add Kahlua and Cognac and mix well. Fold in whipped cream. Spoon into individual serving dishes or a quart mold. Chill several hours. At serving time, top with whipped cream. Serves 10 to 12.

Chocolate Fondue

12 ounces milk chocolate, semi-sweet or sweet
¾ cup light cream
1 to 2 tablespoons Kirsch, Cointreau or Brandy

In a heavy saucepan melt the chocolate and cream over low heat, stirring until smooth. Remove from heat, stir in liqueur. Pour into fondue pot or chafing dish to keep warm. Serves 6 to 8.

Dippers:
Apple wedges
Angel food cake, cut into cubes
Pound cake, cut into cubes
Bananas
Mandarin oranges
Cherries
Marshmallows
Pineapple chunks
Fresh strawberries

Desserts

Frozen Chocolate Frango

1 cup butter (not margarine)
2 cups confectioners' sugar, sifted
4 squares unsweetened chocolate, melted and cooled
4 eggs
1 teaspoon vanilla
3 tablespoons crème de menthe
1 cup or more vanilla wafers, crushed
Whipped cream
Cherries

Beat butter and sugar until fluffy; add chocolate and eggs. Beat in vanilla and crème de menthe. Do not stop beating at any time as you add the mixtures. Put ½ of vanilla wafers in bottom of 16 to 18 paper cups in muffin tins. Spoon in mixture. Fill cups full, nice and rounded, and then sprinkle top with the rest of the vanilla wafer crumbs. Put in freezer. When serving, remove from paper cups, top with whipped cream and cherries. These do not freeze solidly and can be taken out of the freezer and served immediately. Serves 16 to 18.

Apricot Ice Cream

3 ounce package lemon Jello
1 cup sugar
2 cups water
2½ cups canned apricots, puréed
1 cup syrup from apricots
1 cup heavy cream, whipped

Bring water to a boil and add Jello. Cool and add sugar, juice, apricots and whipped cream. Fold together and freeze in loaf or square pan.

Note: Light and delicate — perfect for summer or after a heavy meal.

Substitute for buttermilk: put 1 tablespoon of vinegar or lemon juice in a measuring cup with milk. Let stand 5 minutes.

Substitute light brown sugar for white in most recipes. It adds delicious flavor.

Fruit Ice Dessert

3 cups water
2 cups sugar
3 bananas, crushed
1 small can crushed pineapple
Juice of 3 lemons
Juice of 3 oranges

Heat water. Add sugar and dissolve. Cool and mix remainder of ingredients with the sugar water. Freeze. Stir a couple of times while freezing. Thaw to mush before serving. Makes 3 quarts.

Note: Perfect after a Mexican dinner.

Ice Cream Delight

Crust:
1 cup saltine or Ritz crumbs
1 cup graham cracker crumbs
¼ cup butter, melted

Preheat oven to 350 degrees. Combine cracker crumbs and butter. Press into a 13 X 9 X 2 inch baking pan. Bake for 8 minutes and set aside.

Filling:
1 quart butter pecan ice cream
2 packages (3⅝ ounces) instant vanilla or butter pecan pudding mix
2 cups milk
12 ounces whipped topping
Chocolate covered toffee bars, chopped, or butter brickle chips

Combine ice cream, pudding mix and milk. Add half of whipped topping. Pour over crust and freeze until set. Spread remaining topping over ice cream and sprinkle with candy. Allow to thaw at room temperature about 15 minutes before serving. Serves 12 to 15.

Mocha Parfait

6 ounces chocolate chips
1/3 cup water
1 tablespoon light corn syrup
Dash salt
2 egg whites
¼ cup sugar
1 cup heavy cream
1 tablespoon instant coffee
¼ cup light brown sugar, packed
⅛ teaspoon almond extract

Combine and melt in double boiler the chocolate chips, water, corn syrup and salt. Let cool approximately 10 minutes. Beat the egg whites until stiff but not dry. Add the sugar gradually and beat until glossy. Fold into chocolate mixture. Combine cream, coffee, sugar and almond extract and beat until stiff. Alternate layers of chocolate mixture and coffee mixture in parfait or sherbert glasses. Serves 8.

Cappucino Parfait

½ cup butter
1½ cup light brown sugar
⅛ teaspoon salt
2 tablespoons corn syrup
(light or dark)
½ cup heavy cream
½ teaspoon cinnamon
1 teaspoon orange rind, grated
½ cup walnuts, chopped
Coffee ice cream
Whipped topping garnish,
optional
Grated orange rind garnish,
optional

Melt butter in saucepan. Add brown sugar, salt and corn syrup. Bring to a boil and cook, stirring until sugar is dissolved. Gradually add heavy cream, stirring constantly. Bring to boiling point again. Remove from heat and cool. After it is cooled, stir in walnuts. Add cinnamon and orange rind. (This makes 1½ cups butterscotch sauce.) Alternate coffee ice cream with sauce in parfait glasses. Top with whipped topping and sprinkle with grated orange rind, if desired.

Note: Can keep the sauce in the freezer or refrigerator. Delicious!

Apple Waldorf Pie

Crust:

- 2 cups flour
- ¼ teaspoon salt
- 1 tablespoon baking powder
- 2 sticks butter, softened
- ¼ teaspoon baking soda
- 1 cup buttermilk

Sift flour, salt and baking powder together in a bowl. Add butter and thoroughly work into mixture. Mix baking soda with buttermilk and add this to the flour mixture. Blend lightly and toss on floured pastry board, kneading until soft and spongy. Grease freely with margarine a deep 10 inch pie pan. Line the pan with the crust, bringing dough up around the edge to flute.

Filling:

- 6 cups fresh apples, pared and sliced
- ½ cup tart apple jelly, melted to syrup over low heat
- ½ lemon, juiced and rind grated
- 1 cup brown sugar
- ¾ cup flour
- ½ cup margarine
- ½ cup walnuts, finely chopped

Preheat oven to 350 degrees. Fill crust with sliced apples. This should make a heaping mound. Pour apple jelly over the top. Add lemon juice and grated rind. Mix the brown sugar and flour together with the margarine. Pack this over the top, covering the apples completely. Sprinkle nuts over this and press slightly into the apples. Bake at 350 degrees until apples are tender and topping is crisp and brown. Allow pie to cool.

Topping:

- 1 cup plain yogurt or sour cream
- 1 cup cottage cheese
- ½ cup tart apple jelly
- 1 cup fresh apples, pared and diced

Whip together until thick the yogurt, cottage cheese, jelly and apples.

Cut the pie and serve with generous amount of topping.

Note: This won first place in an apple pie contest out of over 250 entries.

Orange Delicious Apple Pie

Crust:
2 cups flour, sifted
1½ teaspoons salt
½ cup oil
¼ cup low pulp orange juice

Mix together the flour and salt. Measure in the same cup the oil and orange juice. Pour liquid without stirring into the flour mixture. Stir briefly and divide into halves. While second half is in the refrigerator, roll out the first half between two sheets of wax paper. When large enough for a 9 inch pie plate, remove top sheet of paper and fit into pan by turning it over while the bottom half of paper is still attached to the dough. Remove the paper. If the dough breaks, it can easily be pressed together. Trim off dough. Secret of this pastry is not to handle too much — work quickly.

Filling:
6 to 7 cups slightly tart
  Delicious apples, peeled
  and sliced about ¼ inch
  (about 2 pounds apples)
1 to 2 teaspoons orange juice
2/3 to ¾ cup sugar
¼ teaspoon nutmeg
⅛ teaspoon salt
½ teaspoon orange peel, grated
½ teaspoon cinnamon
1 tablespoon butter or margarine

Preheat oven to 425 degrees. Mix all ingredients and fill the pie shell. Roll out the second half of the dough and fit on top. Trim and flute the edges to seal. Make several slits in the top of the crust to allow steam to escape. If you prefer, make a round hole in the center of the crust and stick in a small funnel made of aluminum foil so that the liquid will not spill onto the crust. Bake approximately 40 minutes or until the apples are tender when tested with a toothpick and the crust is golden brown. Serve warm with cheese, hard sauce, vanilla ice cream or your favorite topping. Caution: If apples are too ripe, you need to substitute lemon juice for orange juice in the filling.

Note: This took second place in an apple pie contest.

Apple Rum Custard Pie

9 inch deep dish pie crust

Filling:

7 to 8 medium apples, peeled, cored and sliced
1½ tablespoons flour
1½ tablespoons cinnamon
½ teaspoon nutmeg, freshly grated
¼ cup sugar
2 tablespoons lemon juice
2 tablespoons butter or maragraine

Preheat oven to 400 degrees. Place ingredients one at a time in the pie shell starting with the apples and going on through the butter. Set aside.

Crumb topping:

¼ cup butter or margarine, firm
¼ cup plus 1 tablespoon flour
1/3 cup brown sugar
1/3 cup old-fashioned oats
¼ teaspoon cinnamon

Mix all ingredients together with fingers to coarse consistency. Sprinkle around the outer perimeter of the pie leaving approximately a 2 inch opening in the center of the pie. Bake for 15 minutes.

Rum Custard:

¾ cup light cream
1 egg
1/3 cup amber rum (not Myers)

While the pie is baking, pour cream in a saucepan and scald. In a bowl combine the egg and rum and beat together. Gradually add the scalded cream to the egg mixture. After the 15 minutes baking period, remove the pie from the oven and pour the custard in the center opening of the pie. Reduce oven heat to 350 degrees and continue baking the pie for 20 to 25 minutes.

This pie is delicious served warm out of the oven, at room temperature or refrigerated.

To prevent a soggy crust in custard pies, brush egg white on the uncooked pie shell.

Meringue Aux Pommes

6 to 8 medium apples, firm
Cinnamon
Sugar
Pastry shell, baked
Marmalade
Coconut macaroons, crushed

Preheat oven to 400 degrees. Peel and core apples and place in baking dish. Sprinkle liberally with cinnamon and sugar. Bake, covered, for 25 to 30 minutes or until tender. Cool. Arrange apples in a baked pie shell and fill each center with marmalade and macaroons.

Meringue:
3 egg whites
6 tablespoons sugar
Slivered almonds

Beat egg whites with sugar. Cover entire top of the pie with meringue. Make a swirled peak on each apple to guide you later when you serve the pie. Bake in hot oven (500 degrees) until the meringue is delicately browned. Scatter with slivered almonds to give it a festive touch.

Note: This a prize winning recipe.

Variation: Baked Alaska Apple Pie

Use the same recipe but instead of the marmalade in the centers use ice cream and spoon ice cream between spaces around apples. Top with meringue and bake.

Hawaiian Macadamia Pie

1 quart vanilla ice cream
6 ounces Cool Whip
8 ounces crushed pineapple
½ cup macadamia nuts, finely chopped
9 or 10 inch prepared graham cracker crust
¼ cup flaked coconut, toasted, if desired

Soften 1 quart vanilla ice cream. Reserve ½ cup whipped topping. Blend together ice cream and container of whipped topping. Fold in drained pineapple and nuts. Pour into prepared graham cracker crust. Cover and freeze until solid. Then frost pie with reserved whipped topping. Sprinkle with coconut and additional chopped nuts. Recover pie and return to freezer until needed. To enhance flavor, remove from freezer 15 minutes prior to serving.

Hot Pepper Jelly Pie

9 inch pie crust
1/3 cup hot pepper jelly
1 tablespoon water
1½ cups sugar
12 ounces cream cheese
4 egg yolks
1/3 cup lemon juice

Preheat oven to 450 degrees. Melt the pepper jelly with water in a saucepan over low heat. Spread the mixture on the bottom of the pie crust and set aside. In the bowl of an electric mixer or food processor, cream the sugar and cream cheese together until light and fluffy. Beat in one egg yolk at a time, mixing well after each addition. Add lemon juice and blend for about one minute. Spread this mixture over the pepper jelly. Bake for 5 minutes. Reduce oven temperature to 375 degrees and bake an additional 20 minutes. Remove and top with meringue.

Meringue:
4 egg whites
1 tablespoon vanilla
1/3 cup sugar

Return oven heat to 450 degrees. Beat egg whites until peaks form. Gradually add vanilla and sugar, beating until glossy. Bake in hot oven until golden brown. You can serve it warm after allowing the pie to set before cutting. Chill if serving later.

Kentucky Bourbon Pie

3 egg yolks
½ cup sugar
½ package unflavored gelatin
2½ tablespoons water
½ square bitter chocolate, grated
2 tablespoons bourbon
½ cup pecans, chopped
1 teaspoon vanilla
½ pint whipping cream, whipped
1 graham cracker crust

Beat egg yolks and sugar together. Add gelatin to water, then dissolve over hot water. Add dissolved gelatin to sugar mixture. Add grated chocolate. Fold into whipped cream. Add bourbon, vanilla and nuts. Pour into crust and freeze until ready to serve.

Pies

Key Lime Tarts

Crust:

3 egg whites, room temperature
1 cup sugar
1 teaspoon vinegar
1 teaspoon vanilla

Preheat oven to 275 degrees. Cover cookie sheet with wax paper. Draw 3 to 3½ inch circles on wax paper and set aside. Place egg whites in small mixer bowl and beat at high speed to soft peak stage. Reduce speed slightly and gradually add 1/3 cup of sugar, 1 tablespoon at a time. Add vinegar, then gradually add 1/3 cup more sugar. Add vanilla and last 1/3 cup sugar gradually by tablespoons and continue to beat until very stiff. Using a spoon and spatula, or pastry tube, shape meringue into shells within circles on wax paper. Bake for one hour. When done, lift shells off wax paper immediately. (Use spatula to lift off.)

Filling:

3 egg yolks
15 ounces condensed milk
½ cup key lime juice

After tarts are cooled, combine egg yolks and condensed milk. Mix well. Add lime juice and blend well. Fill tart shells with this mixture and refrigerate. May garnish with whipped cream.

This filling may be used to fill one baked pie crust. Top with meringue.

Brownie Pecan Pie

2/3 cup sugar
⅛ teaspoon salt
1 cup light corn syrup
4 ounces sweet chocolate, broken in pieces
3 tablespoons butter
3 eggs, slightly beaten
1 teaspoon vanilla
1 cup pecans, coarsely chopped
Whipped cream
9 inch pie crust, unbaked

Preheat oven to 350 degrees. Combine sugar, salt and corn syrup in a small saucepan. Bring to a boil over medium heat, stirring until sugar is dissolved. Boil 2 minutes. Remove from heat and add chocolate and butter, stirring until chocolate is melted and mixture is smooth. Cool. Gradually pour chocolate mixture over eggs, stirring constantly. Add vanilla and pecans. Mix well. Pour into pastry shell. Bake for 50 to 55 minutes. Cool. Top with whipped cream. Serves 6.

Date Nut Tarts

Crust:
1 cup flour
1 stick butter, softened
3 ounces cream cheese, softened

Mix all ingredients together until creamy and refrigerate until ready to use.

Filling:
1 stick butter
1 cup sugar
2 eggs, separated
1 teaspoon vanilla
1 cup dates, chopped
1 cup nuts, chopped

Preheat oven to 325 degrees. Cream butter and sugar. Add egg yolks and vanilla. Mix well. Add dates and nuts. In separate bowl beat egg whites until stiff. Fold into date mixture. Make crust into marbles. Press into mini-cupcake tins. Fill with date mixture. Bake for 20 to 30 minutes. Makes 30 to 36.

Orange Meringue Pie

9 inch pie shell, baked
1 cup sugar, divided
¼ cup corn starch
¼ teaspoon salt
1½ cups water
6 ounces frozen concentrated orange juice, thawed and undiluted
4 eggs, separated
1 cup plain yogurt

Preheat oven to 400 degrees. Prepare pie shell. Set aside. In medium saucepan combine ½ cup sugar, corn starch and salt. Blend in water, orange juice concentrate and lightly beaten egg yolks. Cook over medium heat, stirring constantly, until mixture begins to boil; cook 2 to 3 minutes longer. Stir in yogurt; cool slightly. Pour into prepared pie shell. In large bowl beat egg whites with electric mixer until stiff, but not dry. Gradually beat in remaining ½ cup sugar. Continue beating until meringue forms stiff, glossy peaks. Make sure filling is cool before spreading meringue. Spread meringue so that it touches crust all the way around to prevent shrinkage. Bake 8 to 10 minutes or until meringue is tipped with brown.

Pies

Amaretto Pie

Crust:

¼ cup sugar
1 cup graham cracker crumbs
½ stick butter, softened

Grease the bottom of a 10 inch springform pan. Combine the sugar, crumbs and butter. Press evenly on bottom of pan to form crust. Set aside.

Filling:

1¼ cups sweetened coconut, shredded
1 cup sugar
4 eggs
2 tablespoons unflavored gelatin
1/3 cup cold water
½ cup Amaretto
⅛ teaspoon almond extract
1 quart whipping cream
Fresh strawberries for garnish

Preheat oven to 300 degrees. Evenly distribute the coconut on baking sheet. Toast in oven until golden brown, about 15 minutes, stirring frequently. Set aside. Using an electric mixer at medium speed, beat the sugar and eggs in a large bowl until fluffy. Sprinkle gelatin over the cold water in a heat-proof measuring cup or bowl and let stand about 5 minutes to soften. Set cup in small pan of hot water over direct heat until gelatin is completely dissolved. Fold the gelatin, Amaretto and almond extract into the egg mixture. Let stand until slightly thickened. Beat whipping cream until soft peaks form. Fold coconut (reserving small amount for garnish) into thickened egg mixture. Fold in whipped cream and blend thoroughly. Pour into springform pan and chill. Just before serving, remove sides of springform pan and sprinkle the top of the pie with reserved coconut. Garnish with strawberries.

Lemon Ribbon Pie

9 inch pastry crust, baked

Lemon butter sauce:
6 tablespoons butter
Grated peel of 1 lemon
1/3 cup lemon juice
⅛ teaspoon salt
1 cup sugar
2 eggs
2 egg yolks

Melt butter; add lemon peel, lemon juice, salt and sugar. Slightly beat whole eggs with egg yolks; combine with the other mixture and cook over boiling water, beating constantly with a whisk until thick and smooth. Cool.

Filling:
1 quart vanilla ice cream
3 egg whites
6 tablespoons sugar

Preheat oven to 475 degrees. Smooth half of the ice cream into pastry shell; freeze. Spread over it half the cooled lemon butter; freeze. Cover with the other half of the ice cream; freeze. Top with remaining lemon butter; freeze. Beat egg whites until stiff, gradually beat in the 6 tablespoons sugar. Spread meringue on pie. Place on a board in hot oven and bake until lightly browned on top. Serve immediately or freeze. Serves 6 to 8.

Rum Cream Pie

3 egg yolks
½ cup sugar
1½ teaspoons gelatin
½ cup cold water
1 cup heavy cream, whipped
¼ cup dark rum
9 inch baked pie crust
Bittersweet chocolate, shaved

Beat the egg yolks until lemon colored. Add the sugar while still beating. Soften the gelatin in the water. Put the gelatin mixture over low heat and, stirring constantly, let it come to a boil. Pour this over the egg mixture, stirring briskly. Fold in the whipped cream. Add rum. Cool, but do not let it set. When cool, pour into the pie shell and chill. When filling has set, sprinkle top of pie generously with shaved chocolate. Serves 6.

Pies

Pineapple Millionaire Pie

1 cup crushed pineapple
2 cups confectioners' sugar
1 stick margarine, softened
1 large egg
¼ teaspoon salt
¼ teaspoon vanilla
2 (8 inch) pie crusts, baked pastry or graham cracker
1 cup heavy cream
½ cup nuts, chopped

Cream together sugar and margarine. Add eggs, salt and vanilla. Mix until light and fluffy. Spoon evenly into pie crusts. Chill. Whip cream until stiff. Blend in drained pineapple and nuts. Spoon on top of egg mixture and chill thoroughly. Makes two pies. Rich!

Grapefruit Custard Pie

1 graham cracker crust

Filling:
1 cup sugar
½ cup flour
½ teaspoon salt
¼ teaspoon nutmeg
3 egg yolks
½ teaspoon vanilla
1¼ cups evaporated milk
½ cup fresh grapefruit juice,

Sift sugar, flour, salt and nutmeg into a bowl. Slightly beat egg yolks with vanilla; blend into sugar mixture. In the top of double boiler, scald milk. Stir ½ the milk into the sugar mixture and mix well. Return the mixture into remaining milk and cook until thick, stirring constantly. Add grapefruit juice and cook 5 minutes longer, stirring with wire whisk. Pour into graham cracker crust.

Topping:
1/3 brown sugar
½ cup flour
1 tablespoon butter, softened
½ cup nuts, chopped
1 grapefruit, sectioned

Mix brown sugar, flour, butter and nuts with fingers until coarse, then sprinkle on top of pie. Garnish with grapefruit sections. Broil pie in oven until topping bubbles. Remove and let pie cool completely in order for it to set before serving. Serves 6 to 8.

Note: Extra egg whites can be frozen for later use.

Amelia Island Mud Pie

Crust: 1½ cups Oreo cookies, crushed
2 tablespoons butter, melted

Combine and press the mixture into a pie plate and freeze.

Filling:
1 pint chocolate ice cream, softened
1 tablespoon Sanka, liquid
2 tablespoons Brandy
2 tablespoons Kahlua
2 tablespoons whipped cream
Kraft fudge topping

Whip ice cream with coffee, Brandy and Kahlua. Fold in whipped cream. Place in pie shell. Freeze. Top with fudge topping and freeze again.

Topping:
Serve with whipped cream and a cherry.

Chocolate-Mallow Pie

3 squares unsweetened chocolate
1 envelope unflavored gelatin
1/3 cup water, cold
½ cup sugar
2/3 cup Karo white corn syrup
1 teaspoon vanilla
½ pint whipping cream, whipped
9 inch pie crust, baked

Melt chocolate over low heat in double boiler; set aside until cool. Soften gelatin in cold water in a saucepan. Place over hot water and stir until dissolved. Add sugar until it also is dissolved. Remove from heat. Pour Karo syrup into large bowl of electric mixer; add vanilla and gelatin mixture. After blending on medium speed, beat 8 to 10 minutes on high or until mixture is of soft marshmallow consistency. Fold in cooled chocolate and cream which has been whipped. Put into pie shell and chill at least 4 hours.

Note: May be served with whipped cream and either shaved chocolate or peppermint on top. Absolutely melts in your mouth! Extremely rich and calorific so serve small pieces!

Marshmallows do not dry out if stored in the freezer. Cut while frozen.

Blueberry Cassis Pie

Meringue:

¼ teaspoon salt
1 teaspoon vanilla
4 egg whites
1 cup sugar
1 teaspoon baking powder
1 cup graham cracker crumbs
½ cup coconut, shredded
½ cup filberts or hazelnuts, chopped

Preheat oven to 350 degrees. To make the crust, add salt and vanilla to egg whites and beat until foamy. Add sugar in a slow stream and continue beating until egg whites form shiny peaks. Combine the baking powder, crumbs, coconut and the nuts and fold the mixture into the beaten egg whites. Spread in a well greased and floured 9 inch pie pan, making the rim slightly higher than the center. Bake for 30 minutes. Cool.

Filling:

3 cups fresh or frozen blueberries
1 cup sugar
3 tablespoons flour (or more if the berries are juicy)
¼ teaspoon salt
1 tablespoon lemon juice
2 tablespoons crème de cassis
3 egg yolks, beaten

If you are using fresh blueberries, pick through them to remove any stems. Place berries, sugar, flour, salt, lemon juice, crème de cassis and beaten egg yolks in the top of a double boiler and cook over simmering water until mixture thickens (about 10 minutes). Pour the berry mixture into the cooled pie shell and chill at least 6 hours.

Topping:

1 cup heavy cream
1 to 3 teaspoons sifted confectioners' sugar
1 tablespoon crème de cassis
Candied violets (optional)

When ready to serve, whip the cream and fold in the sugar to taste and 1 tablespoon crème de cassis. Using a decorative tip and pastry bag, mound the cream on top of the pie and decorate with candied violets if desired.6 servings.

Note: A can of whipped cream may be substituted for the recipe topping.

Mock Date Pie

14 chocolate ice box cookies crushed (Nabisco or similar cookie)
1 cup sugar
½ cup nuts, chopped
1 teaspoon vanilla
3 egg whites, stiffly beaten

Preheat oven to 325 degrees. Crush cookies and add sugar, nuts and vanilla. Fold in the beaten egg whites. Mix all together well. Pour into a greased pie plate (preferably glass) and cook for ½ hour. Cool before serving. Top with topping mixture. Serves 6 to 8.

Topping:
½ pint whipping cream
¼ cup sugar
Whip the cream and sugar together. Serve on top of the pie.

Marbled Chocolate Rum Pie

1 envelope unflavored gelatin
1 cup sugar, divided
2 eggs, separated
1 cup milk
1/3 cup rum
12 ounces semi-sweet chocolate chips
1 cup heavy cream
1 teaspoon vanilla
10 inch pie crust

In a saucepan, combine the gelatin and ¼ cup sugar. Beat in egg yolks, milk and rum. Cook over low heat until slightly thickened. Remove from heat and stir in chocolate until well blended. Chill until thickened but not set. Beat egg whites until foamy; gradually add ½ cup sugar and beat until very stiff. Fold into chocolate mixture. Whip cream with remaining sugar and vanilla. Alternate the two mixtures in the pie shell. Swirl with a spoon. Chill until firm.

For attractive pastry crusts, brush the top with milk or lightly beaten egg white before baking.

Pies

Brandy Alexander Pie

1 envelope unflavored gelatin
½ cup water, cold
2/3 cup sugar
⅛ teaspoon salt
3 eggs, separated
¼ cup cognac
¼ cup crème de cacao
2 cups heavy cream, whipped
9 inch graham cracker crust
Chocolate curls for garnish

Sprinkle the gelatin over the cold water in a saucepan. Add 1/3 cup of the sugar, the salt and egg yolks. Stir to blend. Heat over low heat while stirring until gelatin dissolves and mixture thickens. Do not boil. Remove from heat and stir in cognac and crème de cacao. Chill until mixture starts to mound slightly. Beat egg whites until stiff. Gradually beat in remaining sugar and fold into thickened mixture. Fold in half of the whipped cream. Turn into the crust. Chill several hours or overnight. Garnish with remaining cream and chocolate curls. Serves 6 to 8.

Mystery Pie

Crust:
3 egg whites
1 cup nuts, chopped
23 Ritz crackers, crushed
1 cup sugar
1 teaspoon vanilla

Preheat oven to 350 degrees. Beat egg whites until stiff. Gradually beat in sugar until well blended. Fold in remaining ingredients. Place mixture in buttered pie plate, shaping to sides and bottom of plate. Bake for 30 minutes. Cool.

Filling:
8 ounces whipping cream
2 tablespoons instant cocoa

Combine and whip until peaks form. Spoon into crust and chill. Serve cold. Serves 6 to 8.

Holiday
1983

Jeni

Holiday Gift Cake

1 cup pecans, finely chopped and divided
8 ounces cream cheese
1 cup butter
1½ cups sugar
1½ teaspoons vanilla
4 eggs
2¼ cups cake flour, sifted
1½ teaspoons baking powder
8 ounces maraschino cherries, well drained and chopped
2 tablespoons milk
1½ cups confectioners' sugar, sifted
Pecans halves and cherries, optional for garnish

Preheat oven to 325 degrees. Grease a 10 inch bundt or tube pan. Sprinkle ½ cup of the chopped pecans on sides and bottom of pan. Cream cheese, butter, sugar and vanilla together until light and fluffy. Beat in eggs, one at a time, beating well after each addition. Sift together 2 cups of the flour with the baking powder. Add to creamed mixture. Combine remaining flour with cherries and remaining ½ cup chopped nuts. Fold into batter. Pour batter into prepared pan. Bake 1 hour and 20 minutes. Cool 5 minutes, then remove from pan. Cool thoroughly. Combine milk and confectioners' sugar; blend well. Pour over top of cake and decorate with cherries and nuts, if desired.

Variations: 2 cups of batter may be poured into three greased 1 pound coffee cans and baked at 325 degrees for 60 minutes; or 1½ cups of batter may be poured into four greased 1 pound shortening cans and baked for 1 hour.

Sherry Cake

1 package yellow cake mix
4 eggs
3½ ounces instant vanilla pudding mix
¾ cup cream sherry
¾ cup oil
1 teaspoon nutmeg
Confectioners' sugar

Preheat oven to 350 degrees. Grease and lightly flour bundt cake pan. Place all ingredients in a large bowl. Beat together with electric mixer for 5 minutes, then pour into cake pan and bake 50 minutes. Cool 30 minutes. Invert onto serving plate. Glaze with confectioners' sugar mixed with sherry.

Holiday

Flower Garden Cake

1 large angel food cake
1½ cups sugar, divided
¾ cup lemon juice
6 eggs, divided
1½ teaspoons lemon rind, grated
1 envelope gelatin
¼ cup cold water
Orange or cherry juice (optional)
½ pint whipping cream, whipped
Coconut (optional)

In a double boiler, make a custard of ¾ cup sugar, lemon juice, egg yolks and lemon rind. Stir constantly until thickened. Meanwhile, melt the gelatin in the cold water. Add the gelatin to the custard while it is hot. Stir well and set aside to cool. Beat the egg whites until stiff. Add ¾ cup sugar gradually. Tear the angel food cake into small pieces. Sprinkle with orange or cherry juice if desired. Fold together the cake pieces, custard and egg white mixture. Place in a tube pan and refrigerate. When set, ice with whipped cream and sprinkle with coconut. Keep refrigerated. Serves 16 or more.

For holidays, add food coloring to the whipped cream - red or green for Christmas, red for Valentines Day, green for St. Patrick's Day, etc.

Breakfast Cake

1 stick butter
Zest of lemon
1 cup sugar
2 eggs
1 teaspoon vanilla
⅛ teaspoon salt
1 cup flour
1½ teaspoons baking powder
1½ cups fresh blueberries, peaches or apricots, diced
4 tablespoons brown sugar
2 tablespoons flour
1 tablespoon butter

Preheat oven to 350 degrees. Cream butter, lemon zest and sugar well in a food processor. Stop processor and add eggs, vanilla and salt. Turn on and off 3 times. Add 1 cup flour and baking powder and process until just blended. Pour into a well greased 9 inch cake pan. Add fruit to the top of the batter. In a small bowl combine brown sugar, flour and butter with pastry blender until crumbly. Sprinkle brown sugar mixture over cake. Bake for 30 to 35 minutes. Serves 6 to 8.

Fruitcake Cookies

9 tablespoons butter
1 cup brown sugar
4 eggs
2 tablespoons buttermilk
3 cups flour
1 teaspoon baking soda
½ teaspoon nutmeg
¼ teaspoon salt
½ to 1 cup wine or whiskey
1 teaspoon vanilla
1 pound raisins
1 pound nuts, chopped
1 pound candied pineapple
½ pound candied cherries

Preheat oven to 350 degrees. Cream butter and sugar. Add eggs and buttermilk. Sift in dry ingredients alternately with wine or whiskey. Add vanilla. Stir in raisins, nuts, pineapple and cherries. Drop by teaspoonfuls onto a cookie sheet. Bake for 10 minutes.

Wedding Cookies

½ pound butter
½ cup sugar
2 teaspoons vanilla
2 cups pecans, ground (measure before grinding)
2 cups flour
Confectioners' sugar

Preheat oven to 300 degrees. Grind pecans. Cream the butter and sugar. Add the vanilla, pecans and flour. Shape into small balls. Bake for 25 minutes. Roll in confectioners' sugar while hot. Store in a tight container. Makes approximately 7 to 8 dozen.

Caramel Brownies

1 bag caramels (50)
2/3 cup evaporated milk, divided
1 package German chocolate cake mix
2/3 cup butter, melted
1 cup nuts
12 ounces chocolate chips

Preheat oven to 350 degrees. Combine 1/3 cup milk and caramels and heat until melted. Combine cake mix, butter, milk and nuts. Put ½ of mixture in 9 X 13 inch pan. Bake 6 minutes. Remove from oven and sprinkle chocolate chips on top and press down. Pour caramel mixture over this and cover with the remaining cake mixture. Bake 18 minutes. Allow to set at least 6 hours, preferably overnight, before serving.

Scandinavian Apple Cake

4 large apples, peeled, cored and chopped
1 cup sugar
1 cup nuts, chopped
2/3 cup butter, melted
2 eggs, beaten
2 teaspoons vanilla
2 cups flour, sifted
2 teaspoons baking soda
2 teaspoons cinnamon
2 teaspoons allspice
1 teaspoon ginger

Preheat oven to 350 degrees. Grease two 8 or 9 inch square cake pans. Combine apples, sugar, nuts and butter in a large bowl. Stir in eggs and vanilla. Sift together dry ingredients and add the apple mixture, stirring **only** until blended. Divide batter between pans and bake 45 to 50 minutes. Serve at room temperature. Cut into bars. Also would be good frosted like a carrot cake. Great to serve with coffee. Can make a week ahead and refrigerate. Can freeze for 3 months. Makes 2 cakes, each serving 6 to 8.

Boo's Fruit Cake

1 cup butter or margarine
1 cup sugar
2 teaspoons baking soda
1½ cups applesauce
3 cups flour
1 teaspoon ginger
1 teaspoon cinnamon
1 teaspoon nutmeg
½ teaspoon ground cloves
2 cups pecans, chopped
1 cup raisins
1 cup candied pineapple, chopped
1 cup candied cherries, chopped
Wine or whiskey (about ½ cup)
Garnish: pecan halves and cherries

Preheat oven to 325 degrees. Cream the butter and sugar together. Mix the soda with the applesauce. Mix all the ingredients together except the wine or whiskey. Moisten the batter with the wine or whiskey. Pour into a tube pan lined with foil. Bake for 1½ to 2 hours. Garnish. May be wrapped in whiskey soaked cloth. You should make this cake ahead of time.

Black Bottom Cupcakes

8 ounces cream cheese, room temperature
1 egg
1/3 cup sugar
⅛ teaspoon salt
1 cup semi-sweet chocolate chips
¼ cup cocoa
1¼ cups all purpose flour
1 teaspoon baking soda
1 cup sugar
½ teaspoon salt
1 cup water
1/3 cup vegetable oil
1 tablespoon white vinegar
1 teaspoon vanilla

Preheat oven to 375 degrees. Line muffin pan with paper muffin cups. Using wooden spoon, blend cream cheese, egg, sugar and salt in bowl. Carefully fold in chocolate chips. Set aside. Combine the dry ingredients in another bowl and mix well. Add remaining ingredients and blend. Fill cupcake papers about 1/3 full. Drop one heaping teaspoon of cream cheese mixture into center of each. Bake 30 to 35 minutes until done. Makes 18.

Cheese Blintz

8 ounces cream cheese, softened
1 egg yolk
1 drop lemon extract
¾ loaf regular sliced white bread
1 cup margarine, melted
1½ cups cinnamon sugar

Cream cheese, egg yolk and extract. Cut crust off each slice of bread. Roll out flat with rolling pin. Spread 1 teaspoon cheese mixture on with knife. Roll as jelly roll and cut in half. Each slice makes 2 blintzes. Drop quickly in melted margarine and roll in cinnamon sugar. Place on cookie sheet and bake 15 minutes in a 375 degree oven or until light brown. Serve warm.

Note: To freeze, place on cookie sheet in freezer until blintzes harden, about 10 minutes. Put in an air-tight container and into freezer. When ready to use, put frozen blintzes onto cookie sheet and bake. These freeze great and will keep for months. These can be used for holiday coffees, parties or have on hand when friends drop in.

Christmas Holly Cookies

½ cup butter
30 large marshmallows
½ teaspoon green food coloring
½ teaspoon vanilla
3½ cups cornflakes
Red cinnamon candies

Melt the butter and marshmallows in top of a double boiler. Add the food coloring and vanilla. Stir until uniformly green in color. Remove from heat, and gently fold in the cornflakes. While still warm, drop from teaspoon on wax paper. Form into holly sprig. Trim with 3 candies before cookies harden. Cool in the refrigerator.

Chocolate Spiders

6 ounces chocolate morsels
1 can chow mein noodles
1 small can salted peanuts

Melt the chocolate. Add the noodles and peanuts. Toss. Drop by teaspoonfuls on wax paper. Chill to set.

Note: Butterscotch morsels can be substituted for chocolate.

Penuche Nuts

Pinch of salt
½ cup white sugar
½ cup light brown sugar
½ cup heavy cream
1 teaspoon vanilla
2½ cups pecan halves

Combine the salt, sugars and cream in a saucepan and simmer to soft ball stage - approximately 10 minutes. Remove and add vanilla. Beat until slightly thickened. Add nuts, stirring to coat. Pour on waxed paper and, when cool, separate the nuts.

Use these as an appetizer or put them in decorative jars and give them to friends during the holidays.

Bourbon Brownies

1 large package brownie mix
4 tablespoons bourbon
2 cups confectioners' sugar
1 stick butter
2 tablespoons crème de menthe
6 ounces chocolate chips
1 tablespoon Crisco

Bake the brownies according to package directions. While still hot, pour bourbon on top. Cool in the refrigerator. Combine sugar, butter and crème de menthe. Spread this on the cooled brownies. Refrigerate again. Melt the chocolate chips and the Crisco. Spread this on sugar topping. Refrigerate again. Cut into bite size pieces. Makes 60 small brownies.

Note: Crème de menthe can be replaced with rum and green food coloring.

Chocolate Mint Squares

2 ounces unsweetened chocolate
½ cup butter
2 eggs
1 cup sugar
1 teaspoon vanilla
½ cup flour
¼ teaspoon baking powder
¼ teaspoon salt
½ cup chopped nuts

Melt the chocolate and butter. Cool. Add eggs, sugar, vanilla, flour, baking powder and salt. Mix well. Add nuts and pour into a greased 9 X 13 inch pan. Bake at 350 degrees for 15 minutes. Cool and frost with Chocolate Mint Icing. Makes about 36 squares.

Icing:
3 tablespoons butter
1 tablespoon heavy cream
1 cup confectioners' sugar
¾ teaspoon peppermint extract
1 ounce unsweetened chocolate

Combine 2 tablespoons butter, cream, sugar and extract. Frost the cake after it has cooled. Chill until firm. Then melt the chocolate with 1 tablespoon butter and drizzle this over the white icing. Chill.

Holiday

Pumpkin Squares

Crust:

1 cup flour	½ cup brown sugar
½ cup oats	½ cup butter

Mix together and pat in bottom of 9 X 13 inch pan. Bake at 375 degrees for 12 to 15 minutes until golden.

Filling:

16 ounces pumpkin pie filling	1 teaspoon cinnamon
13 ounces evaporated milk	½ teaspoon ginger
2 eggs	½ teaspoon salt
¾ cup brown sugar	½ teaspoon cloves

Preheat oven to 375 degrees. Mix and pour in crust. Bake for 15 to 20 minutes or until firm.

Topping:

1 cup brown sugar	¼ cup butter
1 cup nuts, chopped (pecans or walnuts)	2 tablespoons flour

Mix together and sprinkle over pumpkin. Bake 10 to 15 minutes. Cool and cut into squares.

Walnut Shortbread

2 cups soft butter	2 teaspoons vanilla
1 cup sugar	¼ teaspoon salt
1 cup walnut pieces	4 cups sifted flour

Preheat oven to 325 degrees. Cream the butter and sugar until fluffy. Grind the walnuts to a coarse meal. Beat the nuts, vanilla, salt and flour into the butter-sugar mixture. Spoon the dough into a lightly greased jelly roll pan (15½ X 10½ X 1 inch) and smooth it out to fill the pan evenly. The dough won't change shape so level the top with a spatula to make it even. Bake this 40 to 45 minutes or until lightly browned. Cool in the pan. Cut into bars. Makes 75, 1 X 2 inch, bars. Keeps well for a few days in an airtight container.

Pumpkin Roll

3 eggs
1 cup sugar
2/3 cup canned pumpkin
1 teaspoon lemon juice
¾ cup flour
1 teaspoon baking powder
1 teaspoon cinnamon
½ teaspoon ginger
½ teaspoon nutmeg
½ teaspoon salt
1 cup pecans, chopped
Confectioners' sugar

Beat eggs on high speed for 5 minutes, gradually beat in sugar. Stir in pumpkin and lemon juice. Separately mix flour and remaining dry ingredients together. Fold into pumpkin mixture. Spread batter onto greased and floured jelly roll pan (15 X 10 X 1 inch). Top with the chopped nuts. Bake at 375 degrees for 15 minutes. Turn out on towel sprinkled with confectioners' sugar. Starting at narrow end, roll towel and cake together. Cool and unroll.

Beat together until smooth:

1 cup confectioners' sugar
8 ounces cream cheese, softened
4 tablespoons margarine
½ teaspoon vanilla

Spread over cake; roll. Chill. Sprinkle top with confectioners' sugar. Slice to serve. Freezes well.

Aunt Clara's Fudge

4 cups sugar
3 squares unsweetened chocolate or ½ cup cocoa
½ cup Karo syrup
1¼ cups evaporated milk
2 tablespoons butter (4 tablespoons butter if using cocoa)
2 teaspoons vanilla
1½ cup nuts, coarsely chopped

Combine the sugar, chocolate or cocoa, Karo syrup and milk in a heavy sauce pan over medium heat. Stir until soft ball stage is reached. Remove from heat and cool slightly. Beat in the butter and vanilla by hand. Add the nuts when the fudge begins to lose gloss and pour quickly into buttered 9 X 13 inch pan.

Holiday

Buckeye Candy

½ pound margarine or butter
18 ounces creamy peanut butter
1½ boxes confectioners' sugar
1 pound Hershey's chocolate
½ block paro wax (2½ X 2½ inch)

Mix the margarine and peanut butter together. Add the sugar and mix by hand. Roll into balls the size of a walnut. Melt the chocolate and wax in top of a double boiler. Put on olive holder or fondue fork and twirl in the chocolate just part way down on the ball. Put on wax paper and put in the freezer. When set, divide into small plastic bags and keep in the freezer. Makes about 82 pieces.

Southern Pralines

1½ cups brown sugar
1½ cups granulated sugar
3 tablespoons maple syrup
1 cup whipping cream
1 teaspoon vanilla
1½ cups pecans, halves or chopped

Combine sugar, syrup and cream in a heavy pan and cook to soft ball stage (234 degrees). Cool 10 minutes. Add vanilla and beat by hand about 2 minutes. Add pecans and beat until mixture loses gloss. Drop by spoonfuls on buttered foil or wax paper. Add hot water, a few drops at a time, if necessary to keep candy at the right stage for candy making.

Note: Brown sugar may be substituted for granulated sugar. Additional pecans can be used if desired.

French Chocolates

2 sticks butter
2 pounds confectioners' sugar, sifted
2/3 cup condensed milk
1 teaspoon vanilla
1 cup pecans, finely chopped
14 to 16 squares chocolate, unsweetened
2/3 cake paraffin

Cream butter, sugar, milk; add vanilla and nuts. Roll into balls. Chill. Melt chocolate and paraffin in top of double boiler. Dip chilled balls into mixture with a toothpick or spoon. Place on wax paper until set. Top with pecan halves if you like. Good for Christmas gifts.

Baked Caramel Corn

1 cup butter or margarine
2 cups brown sugar, firmly packed
½ cup corn syrup, light or dark
1 teaspoon salt
½ teaspoon baking soda
1 teaspoon vanilla
6 quarts popcorn, popped

Melt the butter. Stir in the sugar, syrup and salt. Bring to a boil, stirring constantly. Boil without stirring for 5 minutes. Remove the pan from the heat. Stir in soda and vanilla. Gradually pour over the popped popcorn, mixing well. Turn into 2 large shallow greased roasting pans. Bake in a 250 degree oven for 1 hour, stirring every 15 minutes. Remove from the oven. Cool completely. Break apart and store in tightly covered container. Makes 5 quarts caramel corn. You can do this ahead, but do not freeze it. This is so crisp and good, nobody will believe you made it!

Cracker Jill

10 cups popped corn
1½ cups unsalted peanuts
½ cup margarine
1 cup brown sugar, firmly packed
¼ cup dark corn syrup
¼ teaspoon salt
¼ teaspoon baking soda
½ teaspoon vanilla

Preheat the oven to 250 degrees. Mix the popped corn and peanuts in a very large bowl or roasting pan. Keep warm in the oven set at 250 degrees. Melt the margarine in a heavy pan. Stir in the brown sugar, corn syrup and salt and bring to a rolling boil, stirring constantly. Boil without stirring 5 minutes. Remove from heat. Stir in baking soda and vanilla. Quickly pour over warm popcorn mix. Stir until well coated. Bake in shallow pan or cookie sheet 45 minutes, stirring every 15 minutes. 2 quarts.

Mango Chutney

- 16 cups sliced mangoes (11 to 12 medium size)
- 12 cups sugar (5 pounds), either white or brown or part of each
- 3 cups vinegar
- 6 onions, finely chopped
- 2/3 cup ginger root, finely chopped
- 2 to 4 tablespoons garlic to taste, finely chopped
- 1 tablespoon salt
- 1½ cups seeded or seedless raisins, white preferably
- 1 tablespoon cloves
- 1 tablespoon cinnamon
- 1 tablespoon nutmeg
- 1 pound almonds, blanched and cut into slivers (any nuts can be used except peanuts)
- ¼ pound citron in small slices
- 1 dozen small hot red peppers, seeded and cut up (1 inch chili peppers)

Peel and slice the mangoes; put in large pot. A porcelain lined dishpan can be used. Add sugar, pour on vinegar. Let this stand 15 minutes to partly dissolve the sugar and form a liquid in the bottom of the pan. Put on low heat and heat slowly to avoid sticking, stirring often until the sugar is dissolved. Chop the onion, ginger root and garlic. Add all other ingredients to the mangoes. Cook on medium heat until the mixture is the consistency of thin applesauce, at least 1¼ hours, usually about 1½ hours. Do not cook too thick as mangoes contain starch and the chutney will thicken as it cools. Remove from heat, immediately place in jars and seal or cover with paraffin.

Note: If green ginger root is not available, 1 teaspoon of dry ginger powder and, if available, 2 tablespoons of preserved ginger cut very fine may be substituted. Citron is available at Christmas time and can be stored frozen. To speed things along, the mangoes can be sliced the evening before. Measure the sliced mangoes, put in a pot, sprinkle with salt and let stand overnight. Before preparing, pour off liquid but do not wash. The mangoes will shrink overnight but proceed with recipe as above.

Quick Chutney

28 ounces apple butter
28 ounces mincemeat
9¾ ounces sweet relish, drained
¼ cup onion, minced
¼ teaspoon Tabasco sauce

Combine all ingredients in a large kettle and mix well. Simmer, stirring occasionally, for approximately 1 hour. Spoon into sterilized jars. Store in a cool, dark place. Marvelous on cream cheese for an easy hors d'oeuvre.

Apricot - Apple Chutney

1 large package dried apricots
1 large package dried apples
1 pound white seedless raisins
1 large can pumpkin
1 large can crushed pineapple
1 pound crystallized ginger
2 pounds brown sugar
2 bottles white syrup
2 quarts white vinegar
½ teaspoon salt
½ teaspoon cayenne pepper
4 tangerines, quartered and seeded
1 small package pickling spices
1 small box mustard seed
4 sticks cinnamon
4 garlic buds, sliced
4 medium green peppers

Steam apricots and apples until tender. Cut into small pieces. Wash raisins. Put mixture into a large boiler. Add pumpkin, pineapple, ginger (sliced), sugar, syrup, vinegar, salt, cayenne pepper and tangerines. Put into a spice bag and tie securely: pickling spices, mustard seed, cinnamon, garlic and green pepper, sliced. Mix together and cook until thick, stirring occasionally. As this burns easily, cook slowly all day at 200 degrees. Remove the spice bag, squeezing juices into chutney. Let cool. Pour into hot, sterlized jars and seal immediately.

Sweet Cucumber Pickles

4 quarts cucumber, sliced
6 medium white onions, chopped
2 green peppers, chopped
3 cloves garlic, chopped
1/3 cup salt
Ice
3 cups vinegar
1½ teaspoons turmeric
2 tablespoons mustard seed
5 cups sugar
1½ teaspoons celery seed

In large pan mix cucumbers, onions, peppers, garlic and salt. Cover with ice cubes and let stand 3 hours. Drain. In separate bowl mix vinegar, turmeric, mustard seed, sugar and celery seed. Pour over drained cucumbers and heat to boiling point. Seal in sterile jars.

Green Tomato Pickles

⅛ bushel medium size green tomatoes
Garlic
Celery
Hot pepper
Dill
2 quarts water
1 quart vinegar
1 cup salt

Pack medium size tomatoes in quart jars either whole or cut in half. To each jar add 1 clove garlic, 1 stalk celery, 1 hot pepper and 1 teaspoon dill. Combine 2 quarts of water and 1 quart vinegar, 1 cup salt and cook 5 minutes. Fill jars within a half inch from top and seal.

Note: Jars should be hot when you fill with tomatoes as it assures the jars will seal properly.

Cranberry - Orange Relish with Burgundy

4 cups fresh cranberries, washed
2 large oranges, peeled, quartered and seeded
1 cup Burgundy
1 cup orange juice
1 cup white, seedless raisins
1 small onion, chopped
2 cups sugar
1 teaspoon cinnamon
½ teaspoon cloves
½ teaspoon orange peel/rind
1 box Sure-Jell

Remove any stems from washed cranberries. Put cranberries and oranges through coarse blade of a food processor, only to chop. Put into a large boiler. Add Burgundy, orange juice, raisins, onion, sugar, spices and Sure-Jell. Mix thoroughly. Cook about 30 minutes over a moderate heat. Pour into hot sterilized jars and seal. Refrigerate.

Note: Great condiment for Thanksgiving and Christmas season.

Brandy Baked Apples with Sherry Cream Sauce

10 baking apples, cored but not peeled
½ cup apple butter
½ cup raisins
1½ cups light brown sugar
¾ cup Brandy
4 tablespoons butter

Arrange apples in shallow baking pan. Mix raisins and apple butter together and fill centers of apples. Combine sugar, Brandy and butter in pot; bring to a boil and simmer 5 minutes. Pour over apples. Bake at 350 degrees for 45 to 60 minutes, spooning juice over apples every 15 minutes.

Sauce: (3 cups)
2 tablespoons corn starch
¼ cup brown sugar
1 cup cream sherry
2 cups whipping cream
2 teaspoons vanilla

Combine sauce ingredients in a pan and stir over low heat until sauce thickens. Serve over warm apples.

This is an elegant and delicious side dish or dessert, particularly for the holiday season!

Saint Nick's Salad

6 ounces red raspberry flavored gelatin
2 cups hot water
2 packages frozen red raspberries (partially defrosted)
12 large marshmallows
6 ounces cream cheese
1 cup whipping cream

Dissolve gelatin in the hot water. Add the raspberries and juice. Pour into an 8 inch square pan. Chill in the refrigerator until firm. Combine the marshmallows and cream cheese using an electric beater. Add the whipping cream. Whip until stiff. (This takes a very little amount of whipping.) Spread over gelatin mixture and chill thoroughly.

Serves 10 to 12.

Hot Fruit Compote

28 ounces canned peach halves
28 ounces canned peach slices
28 ounces canned pear halves
28 ounces canned pear slices
15 ounces canned pineapple chunks
16 ounce jar figs in light syrup
16 ounces canned pitted dark cherries
16 ounces slivered toasted almonds
4 bananas
Lemon juice
6 dozen almond or coconut macaroon cookies
Brown sugar
1/3 cup banana liqueur
Butter

Preheat oven to 300 degrees. Drain all canned fruits well. Slice bananas and sprinkle with lemon juice. Crumble macaroons. Mix all fruits together. In a 3 quart casserole dish, layer as follows: ½ of the fruit, ½ of the macaroons, dot with approximately 1 stick of butter, sprinkle with brown sugar, then ½ of the almonds. Repeat layers. Pour 1/3 cup banana liqueur over top (more if desired), and bake for 20 to 30 minutes. Serves 12.

Note: This an excellent dish for a brunch.

Restaurants & Menus

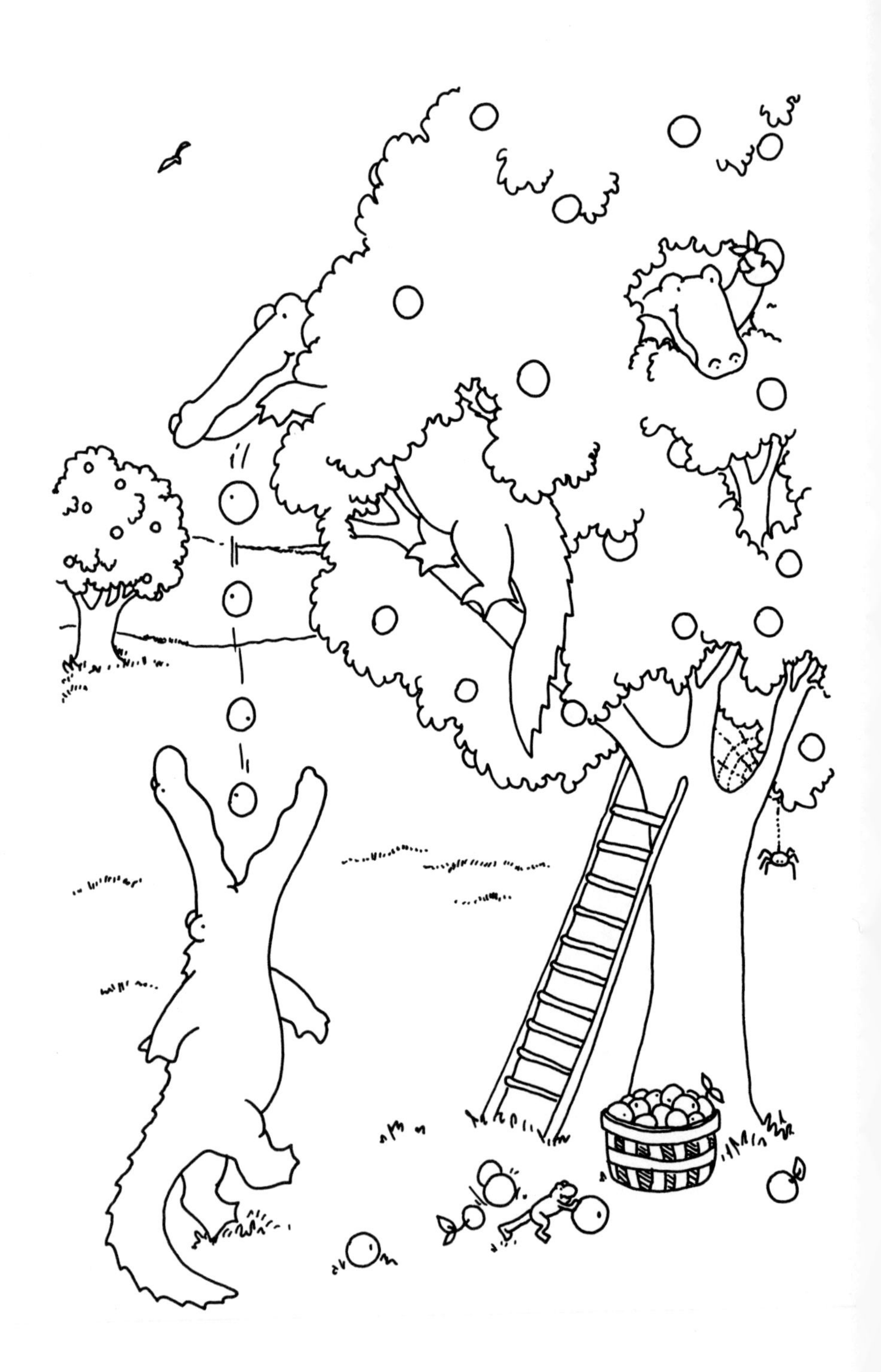

Italian Vegetables

Italian Republic at EPCOT

2 large ripe firm tomatoes
2 medium green peppers
2 medium red peppers
3 medium zucchini
2 large artichoke bottoms (can use canned)
2 tablespoons butter, melted
1 teaspoon fresh garlic, chopped
Salt
1 teaspoon fresh basil, chopped
Pepper

Peel, seed and squeeze tomatoes. Carefully cut green and red peppers in julienne strips. Bring salt water to boil. Blanch the vegetables one by one for about 20 to 30 seconds. Cool off quickly in ice water. Drain. Heat a skillet. Place butter in the pan. Heat well. Add garlic and saute' well. Place equal amounts of vegetables in the pan and saute' well. Season with salt, basil and pepper. Vegetables should be tasty and crisp. Serves 6 to 8.

Japanese Salad

Japan Pavilion at EPCOT

¾ pound firm, ripe tomatoes, peeled, seeded and diced
1 yellow heart of curly chicory, washed
1 avocado, sliced, brushed lightly with lemon juice
2 very large white mushroom caps, thinly sliced
Salt
Pepper, freshly ground
Optional: julienne strips of truffles

Vinaigrette Sauce:
1 tablespoon sake vinegar or red wine vinegar
½ teaspoon mustard
Pinch of coarse salt
Pepper, freshly ground
3 tablespoons olive oil
1 dash soy sauce

Divide the avocado slices between two plates, arranging the slices on one side of each plate, slightly overlapping. Place a few tufts of chicory in the center of each plate. Divide the tomatoes and the mushrooms into two parts, arranging them on the plates. If you wish, you can place truffle strips in the center of each plate. Sprinkle the salad lightly with salt and pepper and spoon the vinaigrette sauce over it. Serves 2.

To make the vinaigrette sauce, combine the vinegar with the mustard, salt and pepper in a small bowl. Then beat in the olive oil, one tablespoon at a time. Add the soy sauce.

Cheese Bread

The Land Pavilion at EPCOT

4 ounces Swiss cheese, grated
4 ounces Romano cheese, grated
4 ounces Gruyère cheese, grated
1 pint water
¾ ounce salt
1 ounce sugar
2 whole eggs
2 ounces vegetable oil
1 ounce dry malt
2 pounds high gluten flour
½ ounce dry yeast

Blend the cheeses. Set aside 2 ounces of the cheese mixture. Put the rest of the cheese mixture and the remaining ingredients into a mixing bowl and mix on medium speed for 8 to 10 minutes. Let rest for 20 minutes. Then portion into three pieces. Mold them round and cover. Let rest for 15 minutes. Make up into three loaves and put into small loaf pans. Let rise in pan three-quarters of the way to the top of the pan. Split on top and sprinkle extra cheese mixture into slit. Bake at 400 degrees for 18 to 20 minutes. Makes 3 loaves.

Raspberry Fool

United Kingdom at EPCOT

1 quart heavy cream
1 ounce confectioners' sugar
1 teaspoon vanilla
8 ounces raspberry pulp*
1 ounce Kirsch Wasser (Dettling)

Whip cream, confectioners' sugar and vanilla until firm. Combine the raspberry pulp and Kirsch Wasser. Then fold whipped cream into raspberry pulp mixture in small amounts. Do not whip.

*Raspberry Pulp:
16 ounces raspberries, fresh or frozen
4 ounces sugar

Combine the raspberries and sugar and simmer until the amount is reduced by half. Remove from the heat and cool. Serve with English Shortbread or other sweet biscuit.

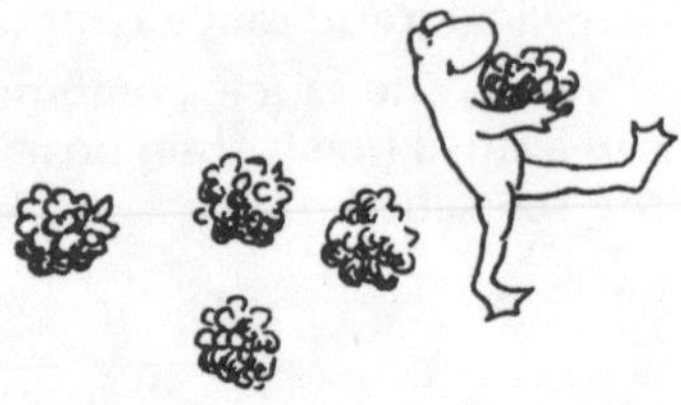

Guacamole and Chips

United Mexican States at EPCOT

2 ounces onion, finely chopped, separated
1 to 2 chilies serranoes
4 sprigs fresh coriander, finely chopped, separated
½ teaspoon salt
2 medium avocados
6 to 8 ounces tomato, skinned, seeded and chopped
Chips

Grind 1 ounce of the onion, the chilies, ½ of the coriander and the salt together to a smooth paste. Cut the avocado flesh into pieces. Mash the flesh roughly with the chili paste. Add the tomato, the rest of the onion and coriander to the avocado. Mix well. Serve with chips.

Walnut Bread

Liberty Tree Tavern at Walt Disney World

2/3 ounce dry yeast
2 ounces very warm water
14 ounces homogenized milk
4 teaspoons salt
8 teaspoons sugar
1½ ounces vegetable oil
26 2/3 ounces bread flour
12 ounces high gluten flour
3 whole fresh eggs
3 1/3 ounces walnuts, chopped

Dissolve the yeast in the warm water and let it stand for 5 minutes. Combine all the ingredients except the walnuts and mix for 15 minutes at medium speed. Let the dough rest for 10 to 12 minutes. Fold in the walnuts and section the dough into 13 (5-ounce) portions. Mold into bread loaves and let rise. Bake in a 375 degree oven for approximately 35 minutes. Since oven temperature readings vary greatly on home ovens, check after 25 minutes. When done, bread will have a medium brown crust. Bread can be frozen and reheated as needed. Makes 13 (5-ounce) loaves.

Note: Bread flour and high gluten flour are best measured by weight. Method of sifting, humidity and other factors will vary measurement if measured by volume or cup ounces.

Brandied Apple Cobbler

Liberty Tree Tavern at Walt Disney World

Short dough:
9 ounces shortening
¼ ounce salt
5 ounces sugar
3 whole fresh eggs
½ ounce lemon juice
18 ounces pastry flour
¼ ounce baking powder
½ cup milk

Cobbler:
6 ounces sugar
1 ounce cinnamon
½ gallon fresh apples, sliced
¾ ounce corn starch
1 ounce lemon juice
1 ounce butter

Vanilla topping:
2 cups homogenized milk
½ cup sugar
Pinch of salt
2 teaspoons vanilla
½ ounce corn starch
1 egg
3 teaspoons cold water
½ ounce Brandy (to taste)

Prepare the short dough first. Cream together lightly the shortening, salt and sugar. Then add slowly the eggs and lemon juice and mix for 3 minutes on low speed. Then add the flour and baking powder and begin mixing. Add the milk slowly and continue mixing until well blended. Roll out the dough to cover the baking pan.

To make the cobbler, blend the sugar and cinnamon together. Then mix with the apples and corn starch. Pour into a 6 X 9 X 1¾ inch baking pan. Sprinkle the lemon juice over the apples and flake the butter on top. Cover the apples with the short dough. Bake in a 400 degree oven for approximately 15 minutes or until golden brown. Let cool.

For the vanilla topping, combine the milk, sugar, salt and vanilla in a sauce pan and bring to a boil. Reduce heat. In a separate container, blend well the corn starch, egg and cold water. Gradually add this corn starch mixture to the ingredients in the sauce pan, stirring to maintain smoothness. Let simmer for about 5 minutes, then add Brandy. Blend and remove from heat. Add the topping to the cobbler after the cobbler has cooled.

Macadamia Nut Pie

Polynesian Village Resort at Walt Disney World

4 ounces butter
4 ounces brown sugar
1 knife point vanilla
1 knife point salt
8 ounces Karo syrup
3 fresh eggs
3 ounces macadamia nuts
1 unbaked pie shell

Cream together the butter, brown sugar, vanilla and salt. Add Karo syrup. Then add eggs slowly, stirring until ingredients are mixed. Fold macadamia nuts into the mix and fill pie shell. Bake in a 400 degree oven for 10 minutes. Then reduce the heat to 325 degrees and bake an additional 45 minutes.

Black Bean Soup

Empress Lilly's Steerman's Quarters - Lake Buena Vista

1 pound black beans, washed and soaked for 8 hours
2 medium onions, diced
2 cups celery, diced
1 cup bell pepper, diced
Bacon fat
1 gallon light chicken stock
3 ham hocks
1 cup rice, uncooked
Salt and pepper to taste
Cumin to taste
3 ounces vinegar or red wine
Onion, chopped, for topping

Saute' the onion, celery and bell pepper in bacon fat for 5 minutes. Add the black beans, chicken stock and ham hocks and cook until the beans are almost done. Add rice and cook until the rice is tender. Add the seasonings and vinegar or wine. Serve with chopped onion, if desired.

Roast Duck and Duck Sauce

Top of the World at the Contemporary Resort Hotel at Walt Disney World

5 pound self-basted duck
1 ounce cooking salt
1 ounce white pepper
Thyme
8 ounces water
Grand Marnier
Duck Sauce*

Season the duck with salt and pepper. Put thyme in the back end of the duck and place in a roasting pan. Add water to keep from sticking to the pan. Preheat the oven to 400 degrees. Cook the duck for 1 hour. Remove from the oven and split the duck and debone. Place on a small sheet pan. Roast duck in the oven at 250 degrees, basting it with Grand Marnier for approximately ½ hour. Remove from oven; turn oven to 350 degrees. Spread duck sauce over it. Put it back in the oven for 5 to 7 minutes to glaze.

*Duck Sauce
10 pounds duck bones
4 gallons water
1 stalk celery
1 large white onion
6 oranges
1½ cups roux (flour and butter)
1 tablespoon thyme
2 tablespoons salt
1 tablespoon white pepper
½ cup chicken base
3 pounds sugar
½ pound butter
1 quart orange juice
4 cinnamon sticks
Juice from 2 lemons
2 ounces Grand Marnier
⅛ ounce macadamia nuts, chopped

Brown duck bones. Place in a kettle and add the water. Bring to a hard boil. Add the celery, onion and oranges and reduce heat. Cook slowly for 1 hour.

Strain and put in a sauce pan and thicken with roux. Add salt, white pepper and chicken base. In a separate sauce pan, mix the sugar, butter, orange juice, cinnamon sticks and lemon juice. Caramelize. Add to the duck sauce. Simmer for 45 minutes. Before serving, add Grand Marnier and macadamia nuts. Makes 3 gallons of duck sauce.

Serve the duck with:
5 ounces nutty rice
1 sprig watercress
½ teaspoon currant jelly
2 ounces duck sauce (on the side)
4 ounces zucchini
½ orange crown
1 mint leaf

Contemporary Dressing

Contemporary Resort Hotel at Walt Disney World

20 whole eggs
4½ ounces anchovies, chopped
1½ ounces garlic, chopped
6 ounces onion, finely diced
4 ounces apple cider vinegar
3 tablespoons lemon juice
2 tablespoons Worcestershire sauce
⅛ teaspoon dry mustard
⅛ teaspoon pepper
10 cups oil
Salt to taste

Place eggs in the top of a double boiler. Whip until warm, being careful not to curdle the eggs. The eggs can not be cooked too long. Place the warm eggs in a bowl and, using an electric mixer, mix all ingredients except the oil and salt. When all ingredients are mixed, begin to add oil slowly while continuing to mix on medium speed. The oil must be added very slowly. After all the oil is added, let dressing mix until well blended. Check for taste and add salt if necessary.

French Fried Ice Cream

Golf Resort Hotel at Walt Disney World

Vanilla ice cream
Egg white
Almond paste
Graham cracker crumbs
Peach halves, drained
Vanilla sauce
Walnuts, chopped
Fresh mint sprigs

Scoop vanilla ice cream (or use any other flavor) into balls. Return to the freezer until the ice cream is very hard. Then roll each ball in egg white, followed by almond paste and graham cracker crumbs. Return the ice cream balls to the freezer until solidly frozen. You may do this much in advance and then store until needed. When ready to serve, deep fry each ice cream ball until it is golden brown. Drain; then place on a drained peach half in a Champagne glass. Top with vanilla sauce (from your favorite recipe), sprinkle with walnuts and add a sprig of fresh mint.

Thousand Island Dressing

Village Restaurant
Walt Disney World Village

2¼ cups mayonnaise
1 cup catsup
¾ cup celery, finely chopped
¾ cup onion, finely chopped
½ cup green pepper, finely chopped
1 cup sweet pickle relish
2 ounces granulated sugar
4 teaspoons Worcestershire sauce
3 teaspoons salt

Combine mayonnaise and catsup and blend. Add remaining ingredients and mix thoroughly. Store in refrigerator in covered container. Makes 1½ quarts.

Coq Au Vin Cordon Bleu

Le Cordon Bleu

3 pounds frying chicken, cut up
½ cup flour
½ teaspoon salt
¼ teaspoon pepper
¼ teaspoon thyme
¼ cup olive oil or vegetable oil
2 tablespoons bacon, diced
6 small white onions, diced
4 ounces canned sliced mushrooms, drained
1 bay leaf
1 clove garlic, minced
1 tablespoon fresh parsley, minced
2 cups Chianti wine
2 to 4 cups chicken broth or bouillon
4 teaspoons corn starch or roux thickener
4 tablespoons water

Dredge chicken in flour seasoned with salt, pepper and thyme. Pat off excess flour. Let stand a few minutes. In a skillet, heat the oil and brown the chicken until very brown. Transfer to a large pot so chicken isn't stacked. In the same skillet, saute' the bacon, onion, mushrooms, bay leaf, garlic and parsley until the onion is soft. Add to chicken. Cover the chicken with wine and cook until the wine is reduced by ½. Cover the chicken with chicken broth (bouillon). If needed add more salt and pepper. Simmer until chicken is tender. Thicken sauce with blend of corn starch and water or roux thickener. Serves 4.

Chocolate Mousse — Le Cordon Bleu

4 eggs
8 ounces sugar
2 ounces Brandy
4 ounces dark bittersweet chocolate, melted
1 quart whipping cream, whipped

Whip the eggs and sugar together. Add the Brandy and chocolate. Fold in the whipped cream.

Apple Annie's Banana Banshee — Church Street Station

1 whole banana, overripe
1 ounce light crème de cocoa
1 ounce cream of banana
2 scoops of vanilla ice cream
1 small scoop of ice
Garnish: banana slice

Blend the banana, crème de cocoa, cream of banana, ice cream and ice in a blender for 30 seconds. Garnish with a banana slice.

Rosie O'Grady's Hurricane — Church Street Station

3 ounces light rum
3½ ounces passion fruit mix
6 ounces sweet and sour mix
Garnish: orange slice
1 sugar cube
151 proof rum

Mix light rum, passion fruit mix and sweet and sour mix in a shaker glass. Fill one 24 ounce hurricane glass to the top with ice. Pour drink over ice. Garnish with orange slice. Dip one sugar cube in 151 proof rum. Set this on top of drink and light.

Scallops "Papillon"

Lili Marlene's at Church Street Station

3 pounds scallops (20 to 30 count)
Flour
8 ounces butter
1 teaspoon paprika
Salt and pepper to taste
3 cucumbers, peeled, cut 2" X ¼" X ¼"
6 sprigs fresh basil, chopped
1 sprig fresh tarragon, chopped
8 ounces or less Johannisberg Riesling

Dust the scallops in flour. Place in hot butter (300 degrees, no more). Turn gently so they won't break. When evenly golden, sprinkle with paprika and salt and pepper. Add cucumbers, basil and tarragon. Stir and simmer for 5 minutes. Add wine slowly, depending on humidity, sometimes not all 8 ounces are needed. Simmer for 1 to 2 minutes and serve. No starch or vegetable is needed for this light but filling dish.

Chicken Breast, "Madam Snow"

Lili Marlene's at Church Street Station

6 chicken breasts, skinned and deboned, 8 ounces each
Flour
4 ounces unsalted butter, melted
6 green onions, chopped end to end
8 ounces fresh mushrooms, quartered
6 to 8 artichoke hearts, quartered
6 fresh marjoram sprigs, chopped
8 ounces white wine (Rhine or Johannisberg Riesling)
Salt and pepper to taste

Dust the chicken breasts in flour. Place in hot butter (300 degrees, no more). Turn until golden on both sides. Add green onions. Stir. Cover for two minutes. Add mushrooms, artichoke hearts, marjoram and wine. Simmer for 5 minutes covered. Salt and pepper to taste. Serve with rice or parsley potatoes on the side. Serves 6.

Shrimp Park Plaza — **Park Plaza Gardens**

28 fresh shrimp, peeled and deveined
Salt to taste
White pepper to taste
Lemon juice to taste
Flour
¾ tablespoon butter
¾ tablespoon shallot butter
½ pound fresh mushrooms, quartered
¼ ounce pimiento, cut in julienne strips
2 tablespoons fresh chives, minced
1 cup sweet Marsala
1½ cups heavy cream or crème fraiche
2 dashes Tabasco sauce
2 dashes Worcestershire sauce
1 tablespoon hollandaise sauce
Rice pilaf*

Season the shrimp with salt, white pepper, lemon juice and flour. Heat a saute' pan until hot. Add butter and shallot butter. Add shrimp and cook until golden brown. Add mushrooms, pimientos and chives. Saute' 3 minutes. Add the Marsala, cream, Tabasco sauce and Worcestershire sauce. Simmer over low heat. Let the sauce reduce. Season with salt, pepper, lemon juice and hollandaise sauce. Serve over rice pilaf. Serves 4.

***Rice Pilaf** — **Park Plaza Gardens**

2 cups white rice
1 ounce butter
1 ounce onion, chopped
1 ounce celery, chopped
3 cups chicken stock
1 small bay leaf
Salt to taste
White pepper to taste
Garnish: fleurons and chives

Melt the butter. Saute' onion and celery until transparent. Add well seasoned chicken stock and bay leaf. Bring to a boil. Add rice. Cook 25 minutes. Season properly when done. Garnish with fleurons and chives.

Snapper Pensacola

Park Plaza Gardens

1 pound red snapper filets
Salt and pepper to taste
4 ounces olive oil
Juice from 1 lime
4 small cloves garlic, chopped
1 teaspoon fresh oregano
1 whole tomato, skinned and sliced
5 ounces Parmesan cheese
Clarified butter

Skin snapper and season lightly with salt and pepper. Coat with olive oil. Then pour the lime juice over the fish filets. Rub the garlic on the fish. Sprinkle with oregano. Place the tomato slices on the fish. Sprinkle with cheese and broil for 4 minutes. Brush with clarified butter and finish in a 350 degree oven. Serves 2.

Veal Corso

Villa Nova

12 (two ounce) scallops of veal, pounded thin
6 ounces Alaskan King crab
Butter
Salt and pepper
1 clove garlic, crushed
8 ounces seafood, chopped (shrimp, scallops, fish)
4 ounces prosciutto ham, sliced
4 ounces Swiss cheese, thinly sliced
Flour
8 to 10 ounces half and half cream
6 ounces veal sauce, made with veal stock and roux (flour and butter)
1 cup wild rice, cooked

Saute' the crab in butter. Season with salt and pepper and a pinch of crushed garlic. Let brown, and then add sherry. Remove from heat and let cool. Strain the stock and save. Repeat the procedure substituting the seafood for the crab. Lay out the veal scallops and top with the prosciutto ham and Swiss cheese. Place the crab and seafood mixture on the veal scallops. Roll up tight. Flour the scallops lightly, place in a buttered pan and brown on one side. Flip over and place in a 375 degree oven to finish. Prepare a sauce with the seafood stock, half and half and veal sauce. Simmer the sauce. Place the veal rolls on wild rice. Top with sauce and serve. Serves 4.

Marinated Scallops

Brazil's Restaurant

1 pound fresh bay scallops
¼ cup honey
2¼ cups red wine vinegar
4 teaspoons tarragon
½ teaspoon marjoram
1 teaspoon whole basil
1 teaspoon fresh garlic, minced
1 teaspoon salt
1 teaspoon pepper
Olive oil

Dissolve honey in vinegar. Add herbs, garlic, salt and pepper. Add scallops. Mix well. Cover with olive oil. Marinate overnight in the refrigerator.

Note: The acidity of the vinegar acts as a "cooking" agent on the scallops. Therefore raw scallops are used.

Shrimp San Francisco

Brazil's Restaurant

12 large shrimp, peeled and deveined
4 ounces soy sauce
¼ teaspoon arrowroot
1 ounce clarified butter
½ clove fresh garlic, minced
1 teaspoon fresh ginger, peeled and finely chopped
2 ounces sherry
1/3 cup green onion, thinly sliced
White pepper to taste

Combine soy sauce and arrowroot. Set aside. Heat the butter in a saute' pan. Add the shrimp to the butter and saute' lightly. Add the garlic and ginger to the shrimp and saute' lightly. Add the sherry and flambe'. Add the green onion and the soy sauce/arrowroot mixture. Simmer until the sauce thickens to a light consistency. Season with white pepper. Serves 2.

Maison & Jardin™

Veal Strasbourg — Maison et Jardin

12 veal cutlets, 3 ounces each
6 ounces pate' de foie gras
Salt and pepper
Flour
Butter
1 quart Morel Sauce*

Pound the veal cutlets thin, but not too thin. Stuff the pate' between two cutlets per serving. Sprinkle with salt and pepper. Dredge in flour. Saute' in butter on both sides for approximately three minutes per side. Place on service plate and ladle Morel Sauce over each portion. Garnish appropriately and serve addtional sauce on the side. Serves 6.

*Morel Sauce:
2 ounces dried morels
Butter
2 tablespoons shallots, chopped
2 ounces Brandy
1 quart heavy cream
1 tablespoon meat glaze
2 tablespoons roux
Salt
White pepper

Soak morels for ½ hour. Drain and repeat with fresh water. Drain well. Cut in half and wash again two more times, insuring that all grit is removed. Drain well. Saute' the morels in butter as hot as possible without burning. Add the shallots and Brandy and flame. Add the cream and reduce for ten minutes. Add the meat glaze and roux and season to taste with salt and white pepper. Cook for 15 minutes until smooth, stirring with a wooden spoon. Makes 1 quart.

Fresh Citrus Soup — Maison et Jardin

3 oranges
3 grapefruit
1 cup sugar
¼ cup water
½ cup currant jelly
2 tablespoons Brandy
Sour cream

Peel the fruit. With a zester make julienne strips from the fruit rinds. Cut the fruit into sections, cutting the grapefruit sections into halves across the width. Reserve all. Cook the sugar, water and jelly for 15 minutes to make a syrup. Cool. Pour the cooled, cooked syrup over the fruit sections. Add the Brandy. Stir and chill. Pour soup in cups and top with sour cream piped from a pastry bag. Garnish with julienne strips.

Mocha Java Pie — Maison et Jardin

9 inch graham cracker crust
Brandy
1 quart coffee Brandy ice cream
½ cup pecan pieces
1½ cups Chocolate Fudge Sauce*
Whipping cream, whipped

Bake the pie crust with a little Brandy sprinkled over it to add flavor. Cool. With a heavy spatula, spread one half of the ice cream on the crust. Sprinkle one half of the pecan pieces over the ice cream. Pour one half of the chocolate sauce over the pecan pieces. Repeat with the rest of the ice cream, pecan pieces and chocolate sauce. Place in the freezer until ready to serve. Cut into serving portions while still frozen. To serve, top with whipped cream and a sprinkle of pecan pieces. Serves 9.

*Chocolate Fudge Sauce:
5 squares Hershey's unsweetened chocolate
½ cup butter
3 cups confectioners' sugar
1¾ cups light cream
1¼ teaspoons vanilla

Melt the chocolate and butter in a large saucepan. Mix in the sugar and cream alternately and bring to a boil over medium heat, stirring constantly. Boil and stir 8 minutes or until thickened and creamy. Stir in the vanilla. Let cool. Serves 6.

Maison & Jardin™

Cafe' Brulot

Maison et Jardin

1 pot of hot coffee
6 sugar cubes
1 teaspoon corriander seeds
6 cinnamon sticks
Brandy

Cointreau
1 orange
1 lemon
12 or more whole cloves

Light the cooking fuel (sterno). Pour one ladle of coffee into a chafing dish and add sugar cubes, corriander seeds and cinnamon sticks which have been broken in half. Using ladle, add 2 parts Brandy and 1 part Cointreau to the mixture and allow to heat over flame. Cut the rind from the orange and lemon in a circular fashion and then insert cloves two inches apart into the rind. Using forks, hold the rinds over the chafing dish and pour the hot alcohol mixture (ignite each ladle from the flame) over the rinds and flambe' several times. After the show, add 4 parts (ladles) coffee to the mixture and serve. Serves 2.

Note: This is an elegant way to end a meal. The second cup tastes even better than the first!

Blinis a la Russe

Maison et Jardin

3 to 4 tablespoons butter
½ cup onion, finely chopped
1 cup sour cream
4 crepes

1 jar caviar
2 hard-boiled eggs, finely chopped
Brandy

In a chafing dish saute' onion in butter. Add crepes, one at a time, putting a spoonful of sour cream and a spoonful of caviar into each and rolling up. When all 4 crepes are ready, pour Brandy over them and flambe'. Maintain medium heat throughout. Top with sour cream and caviar and serve, 2 crepes per plate, with chopped egg and onion on each side. A small glass of Russian vodka will highlight the flavors. Serves 2.

Flaming Spinach Salad
Maison et Jardin

2 handfuls fresh leaf spinach
4 slices bacon
Red wine vinegar
1 tablespoon sugar
1 teaspoon Worcestershire sauce
½ lemon
1 ounce Brandy

Clean the spinach thoroughly several times to insure that all sand has been removed. Remove the stems. In a small saute' pan cook the bacon, retaining the drippings. Cook to just less than crisp. Add just less than an equal amount of red wine vinegar to the bacon drippings. Stir. Add the sugar and Worcestershire sauce. Stir and bring back to a simmer. Squeeze the lemon half over the fresh spinach leaves and gently fold. With wooden tongs pull apart the largest leaves. When the liquid has returned to a boil, pour over the spinach leaves, retaining the bacon pieces in the pan. Mix the spinach and dressing well, insuring that every leaf is thoroughly covered. Dish the spinach onto salad plates, draining the leaves of excess liquid. When the bacon pieces are thoroughly crisp, flame with Brandy. (Heat the pan until it is sizzling, remove from heat and gently add the Brandy. Return to the heat and tilt the pan to the side to bring the Brandy closer to the heat.) Once it ignites, stir the flames well with bacon and spoon over the spinach. Serve immediately. Serves 2.

Chef's Garden

Shrimp and Crab Norfolk
Chef's Garden

½ pound shrimp, cooked and cleaned
6 ounces Alaskan snow crab
6 to 8 shallots, chopped
Butter
1 cup white wine
Roux (flour and butter)
Old Bay seasoning
Thyme
Dash of Tabasco sauce
Mushrooms
1 lemon

Saute' the shallots in butter until golden brown. Add the wine and boil to dissolve the alcohol flavor. Add 2 teaspoons butter. Thicken with the roux to a creamy consistency. Add Old Bay seasoning, thyme and Tabasco sauce. Add shrimp, crab meat and mushrooms. Squeeze lemon juice on top. Serve over wild rice or toasted bread. Serves 2 for dinner.

Veal Richard

La Belle Verriere

1 pound veal, pound thin
Salt
White pepper
½ lemon
Flour
1 egg, beaten
Dry bread crumbs
Margarine

Sauce:
½ shallot, chopped
¼ cup dry white wine
1 small can artichoke hearts with juice
1 tablespoon butter
Pinch of nutmeg
Pinch of thyme
6 fresh asparagus, cooked
½ pound fresh mushrooms, quartered
½ lemon

Cut the veal into 3 ounce pieces. To prepare the veal, sprinkle each slice with salt and pepper. Squeeze lemon juice over; dredge in flour. Dip in egg wash, then coat in dry bread crumbs. Cook the veal in margarine in a hot skillet one minute on each side. Serve with the sauce.

To prepare the sauce, saute' the shallot until brown. Add wine and 2 tablespoons artichoke juice. Simmer one minute. Beat in the butter, nutmeg and thyme. Bring the sauce back to simmer. Add the asparagus, 2 artichoke hearts, mushrooms and lemon juice (to taste). Serve at once when heated through.

House Dressing

La Belle Verriere

½ cup white vinegar
½ cup red wine vinegar
3 egg yolks
3 teaspoons Pommery mustard
1 teaspoon Dijon mustard
2 or 3 shallots, chopped
2 dashes of Worcestershire sauce
Garlic to taste
Salt and pepper to taste
1 quart oil

Heat, but do not boil, vinegar to remove acidity. In a blender or food processor, or by hand, mix together all ingredients except the oil. With the machine still running, pour in the oil slowly while continuing to beat the mixture. When the mixture begins to thicken, oil can be whipped in more rapidly. Process until the dressing is smooth and thick. Put in a covered jar or bowl. Refrigerate. This keeps well. Makes 1½ quarts.

Moo Goo Gai Pan

Jin Ho

½ pound boneless chicken breasts
Oil
½ pound bok choy, sliced
1 clove garlic
2 ounces bamboo shoots, sliced
2 ounces water chestnuts, sliced
2 ounces mushrooms

Marinade:
1 egg white, beaten
1 teaspoon corn starch
½ teaspoon salt
1 teaspoon dry sherry

Sauce:
½ teaspoon salt
½ teaspoon sugar
½ teaspoon dry sherry
1 teaspoon corn starch
¾ cup chicken broth

Mix the marinade ingredients and marinate the chicken for ½ hour. Then deep fry the chicken in oil for ½ minute; drain. Boil the bok choy for 1 minute; drain. Heat 2 tablespoons cooking oil. Add the garlic, bok choy, bamboo shoots, water chestnuts and mushrooms. Stir fry for 1 minute, then add the chicken. Stir fry for another minute. Mix the sauce ingredients together and add them to the chicken mixture. Bring all to a boil. Serve.

JIN HO 金河

Beef with Oyster Sauce

Jin Ho

¾ pound flank steak
2 tablespoons oil
Green onions, diced

Marinade:
1 teaspoon sugar
2 tablespoons soy sauce
1 tablespoon corn starch
2 tablespoons cooking oil
½ teaspoon garlic powder (optional)

Sauce:
2 tablespoons oyster sauce
1 teaspoon sugar
½ teaspoon corn starch
3 tablespoons chicken broth
3 tablespoons water

Cut the steak into thin slices. Mix the marinade ingredients and marinate the steak slices for 30 minutes. Mix the sauce ingredients together. Heat the oil. When it is very hot, add the beef. Stir fry for 2 minutes. Add the sauce and stir well. Serve on a platter or plate topped with diced green onions.

Stuffed Shrimp

Freddie's Steak House

1 pound large shrimp, butterflied

Crab Meat Stuffing:
1 large onion
1 pound frozen premium crab meat
Dash of Tabasco sauce
2 ounces Sauterne wine
1 to 2 teaspoons mustard
Salt and pepper to taste
1 pint heavy cream sauce made according to your favorite recipe
Parmesan cheese

Thaw crab meat; clean and shred. Saute' onion; add crab meat, wine and seasonings. Mix in heavy cream sauce. Simmer until thickened. Stuff shrimp with crab meat stuffing. Top with butter and sprinkling of Parmesan cheese. Bake at 375 degrees for 7 minutes. Makes 4 servings.

Fresh Strawberry Pie

Arnold Palmer's Bay Hill Club

10" baked pie crust
Cream cheese
Sugar
Strawberries
Whipped cream

Glaze:
1 cup water, divided
1 cup strawberries
1 cup sugar
3 tablespoons corn starch

Line bottom of pie crust with a thin layer of cream cheese and sprinkle with sugar. Fill with cleaned strawberries (over flowing) and cover with glaze. Refrigerate for several hours. Serve with fresh whipped cream.

For glaze, cook strawberries with 2/3 cup water for approximately 3 minutes. Mix together sugar, corn starch and 1/3 cup water and add to strawberries. Boil 1 minute or until thickened; cool and pour over pie.

Stuffed Sole

Arnold Palmer's Bay Hill Club

50 fillets of sole
2½ pounds shrimp or crab meat, finely chopped
½ pound butter
1½ pounds onion, finely chopped
1½ pounds green pepper, finely chopped
2½ cups flour
½ gallon milk
1½ pounds fresh bread crumbs
2 tablespoons Worchestersire sauce
½ teaspoon Tabasco sauce
1½ teaspoons dry mustard
1 cup sherry
Garlic salt (pinch)
Salt and pepper to taste

Melt butter and saute' onion and green pepper. Add chopped shrimp and cook for several minutes. Add flour to make a roux. When butter and flour are completely mixed, add milk and bring to a slow boil. Fold in bread crumbs and mix completely; add remaining ingredients. Set aside and refrigerate.

Before serving, spread stuffing on sole and fold in half or roll up. Place in buttered casserole and bake in 350 degree oven for 15 to 20 minutes.

Note: Mixture will also stuff 150 butterflied shrimp.

Marinated Brussels Sprouts **Barney's Steakhouse**

30 ounces frozen Brussels sprouts
2 ounces onion, chopped
¼ ounce fresh garlic, minced
¼ teaspoon thyme
¼ teaspoon oregano
1 teaspoon chives, chopped
2 ounces sugar
½ teaspoon salt
¼ teaspoon garlic powder
½ teaspoon ground black pepper
2 ounces tarragon vinegar
6 ounces cider vinegar
20 ounces salad oil
1 tablespoon dill weed

Blanch the Brussels sprouts briefly in boiling water, no more than 3 minutes, just long enough to thaw the sprouts. Do not let them become soft, they should be very crisp when marinated. Drain thoroughly so water does not dilute the marinade and cool. Put all ingredients for the marinade dressing in a container and mix thoroughly together with a wire whisk. Combine marinade with Brussels sprouts and allow to marinate 24 hours in the refrigerator before serving. Makes 1 quart.

Note: Marinade can be refrigerated up to 2 weeks. Serve as a chilled vegetable or as a salad.

Tamara Salad **Lautrec's**

1 jar fish roe (7 ounces)
3 cups olive oil
2 pounds boiled potato
Juice of 2 lemons

Pound Tamara in mortar. Add boiled potatoes and mix well. Alternately add olive oil and lemon juice, stirring all the while until mixture acquires a uniform consistency. Serve in a crock with crusty bread or crackers.

Note: This has wonderful flavor!

Swiss Cheese Soup

Limey Jim's Hyatt Orlando

2 pounds Swiss cheese, diced
1 cup all-purpose flour
1 quart chicken stock
1 teaspoon cayenne pepper
½ tablespoon granulated (dried) garlic
2 cups Chablis or Sauterne wine
1 pound melted butter
¼ cup Worcestershire sauce

Using double-boiler, melt butter, blend in flour and whip well until smooth. Stir and let cook slowly for 10 minutes; cool for approximately 3 minutes. Add chicken stock; stir until smooth. Cook for 15 minutes on low heat, add diced cheese and stir until all cheese is melted and soup is smooth. Add pepper, wine, garlic and Worcestershire sauce.

Note: Use just a part of the Worcestershire at the beginning, adjust to taste by adding more if needed. Serves 6.

Al E. Gator

Al E. Gator's Alligator

Al E. Gator at Sea World's Florida Festival

4 (5 ounce) fillets of alligator
½ cup minced pecans
1 cup bread crumbs
1 cup flour
1 cup milk
1 egg

Pound alligator with a meat mallet until fillet is ¼ inch thick. Dust with flour. Beat egg into milk making egg wash; dip alligator pieces into mixture. Blend pecans and bread crumbs; bread alligator with this mixture. Saute' in a one-quarter inch deep mixture of equal amounts of butter and vegetable oil about 4 minutes or until browned and tender. Serve with Plantation Sauce.*

*Plantation Sauce
1 fresh mango, diced
1 fresh papaya, diced
3 tablespoons brown sugar
3 tablespoons butter
3 tablespoons chopped pecans
½ ounce rum
1 cup water

Melt butter in pan and saute' pecans. Add sugar. Stir 2 minutes. Add mango and papaya slices and mash together. Add water and bring to boil; add rum. Simmer for 15 minutes. Serve with poultry, game or alligator.

French Apple Pie

House of Beef

Pie crust:
4 cups flour
3 cups shortening
2 tablespoons salt
1 to 1½ cups milk

Cut flour and shortening in by hand until all flour is absorbed into the shortening. Mix salt and milk together and add to flour and shortening. Mix by hand and work into a ball. Divide the dough ball in half. Roll out each half to fit 9 inch pie pan. Refrigerate for 1½ hours.

Filling:
3 tablespoons raisins, well washed
3 pounds apples, peeled, cored and sliced
1¼ cups sugar
2 tablespoons cornstarch
2 tablespoons butter, melted

Mix apples, raisins and sugar together and let stand for 2 hours. Drain juice. In measuring cup, dissolve 2 tablespoons cornstarch in enough juice to dissolve cornstarch. Bring rest of juice to a boil and thicken with cornstarch solution. Add 2 tablespoons melted butter. Mix together and add to juice.

Juice:
1 teaspoon nutmeg
½ teaspoon salt
½ teaspoon lemon juice

Mix apples and raisins into sauce. Put into pie shell; cover with top crust. Bake at 375 degree for 45 minutes or until golden brown.

Glaze:
¼ cup 10x confectioners' sugar
3 tablespoons water
½ teaspoon pure vanilla

Mix at low speed and then heat until glaze thins. Drizzle over baked pie. Makes one 9 inch pie.

Mother's Day Brunch

Orange Champagne Cooler

Elegant Luncheon Crab Quiche

Spinach Stuffed Tomatoes (Cherry Tomatoes)

Day Ahead Layered Salad

Baked Pineapple Casserole

Sour Cream Walnut Coffee Cake *Apricot-Coconut Balls*

Strawberry Festival Brunch

Bacon and Sausage Strata *Baked Cheese Grits*

Fresh Strawberries with Grand Marnier

Tiny Marmalade Biscuits

Key Lime Tarts

Strawberry Tea Punch

Art Festival Luncheon

Strawberry-Banana Daiquiris

The Very Best Chicken Salad

Cold Curried Rice Salad *Sweet Cucumber Pickles*

Asparagus Mold *Tiny Flat Biscuits*

Sherry Cake

Caramel Brownies

Menus

Graduation Luncheon

Holland Rusk Shrimp Salad

Artichoke Fantasy

Lemon Bread

Hawaiian Macadamia Pie

Luncheon Iced Tea

Debutante Luncheon

Mushroom-Sausage Strudel

Best Ever Fruit Salad

Tomatoes Rockefeller

Chocolate Pompadour

Spring Bridge Luncheon

Vichysquash

Pappa's Greek Salad

Milk and Honey Bread

Banana Chocolate Cake

Luncheon Iced Tea

Winter Bridge Luncheon

Lake Virginia Bouillabaise

Frozen Lime-Mint Salad

Sour Cream Onion Bread

Chocolate-Mallow Pie

White Wine *Coffee*

Board Luncheon

Chicken Salad Polynesian

Blueberry Heaven *Asparagus Roll-ups*

Ice Cream Delight

Dutchie's Iced Tea

Citrus Open Cocktail Buffet

Cold Crab Meat Dip with Raw Vegetables

Cheese Asparagus Crisp

Lemon Meat Balls

Chicken Quiche Almondine

Caviar Pie with Melba Rounds

Watermelon Filled with Fresh Fruit

Garlic Cheese Ball with Crackers

5-minute Chocolate Whiskey Truffles

Butter Pecan Turtle Cookies

Menus

Holiday Cocktail Buffet

Manhattan Meatballs

Roquefort Log with Melba Rounds

Stuffed Mushrooms

Dill Dip with Fresh Vegetables

Pineapple Cheese Ball with Crackers

Hot Cheese Squares

Fresh Shrimp with Dip for Shrimp

Penuche Nuts

Chocolate Covered Strawberries

Glazed Bar Chews

Christmas Caroling

Chutney Cheese Spread with Crackers

Sesame Cheese Sticks

Slivered Baked Ham with Jezebel Sauce

Good 'N Easy Biscuits

Boo's Fruit Cake

French Chocolates *Napoleon Creams*

Hot Cranberry Punch

Coffee with Kahlua

Election Party Buffet

Hot Crab Fondue with Bread Chunks

Pecan Spread with Triscuits

Party Mushrooms

Spinach and Apple Salad

Kentucky Chicken Breasts

Rice with Pine Nuts

Carrots a La Down Under

Cheese Bread

Strawberry Torte

Tail Gate Party

Bacon-Horseradish Dip with Vegetables

Barbecued Chicken

Caulibroc Salad

Gourmet Potato Salad

Marvelous Brownies

Fruited Oat Bars

Tangerine Bowl Pre-Game Supper

Spinach Dip with Crackers

Appetizer Deluxe with Saltines

Favorite Casserole

Cleopatra Salad

Butter Sticks

Apricot Ice Cream

Pecan Praline Cake

Menus

Super Bowl Sunday

Broccoli Dip with Fresh Vegetables

Pineapple Cheese Ball with Wheat Thins

Chicken and Sausage Jambalaya

Bean and Pea Salad

Dilly Cheese Bread

Choco-Kahlua Pound Cake *Butterscotch Sticks*

Silver Spurs Rodeo Supper

Sombrero Dip with Doritos

Family Secret Cheese Spread with Melba Toast

Kissimmee Casserole

Surprise Beans

Avocado-Cucumber Mold

Garlic Bread

Napoleon Creams *Apricot Ice Cream*

Seafood Dinner Buffet

Hot Clam and Cheese Spread with Melba Rounds

Crab Pate' with Crackers

Sunsational Caesar Salad

Coquilles St. Jacques

Baked Red Snapper

Mushrooms Florentine *Sweet and Sour Green Beans*

Herb Bread

St. Louis Cake

Gourmet Club Dinner Party

Cheese Clouds *Cold Shrimp Roquefort*

Cream of Broccoli Soup

Shakespeare Salad

Steak Au Poivre

Wild Rice and Spinach Casserole

Dill Bread

Lemon Ribbon Pie

Red Wine *Coffee*

Menus

Entertaining The Office

Cheese Puffs *Marinated Shrimp*

Orange Glazed Chicken Breasts

Spinach Salad (Still Another Way)

Broccoli Puff

Cranberry Bread

Chocolate Swirl Cheesecake

Elegant Entertaining

Egg Caviar Mousse *Bacon Swiss Squares*

Chicken Breasts Wellington

Fabulous Mushroom Casserole

Fresh Broccoli Spears with Lemon Butter

Tomato Aspic on Bibb Lettuce

Marbled Chocolate Rum Pie

Atlantic Ocean Feast

Hot Cheese Squares *Oysters Rockefeller*

Barbecued Shrimp

Summer Salad

Granny's Rolls

Cappucino Parfait

Index

Index

A

B

C

G

H

I

J

P

Q

R

S

T

We would like to thank our members and friends who contributed their recipes for our book, including:

Trudy Anderson
Susie Aspinwall
Maryan Alleman
Sydney Parks Allen
Mary Jo Anderson
Jan Ariko
Amy Armstrong
Sheryl Arnold
Barbie Aufhammer
Alene Baker
Emmy Baker
Lee Baldwin
Margie Ball
Mary Barakat
Betty Barge
Jan Barnes
Nancy Barr
Deborah Battaglia
Jeanne Battaglia
Judy Batterson
Nancy Beasley
Margaret Beery
Barbara Behrens
Ann Bennett
Jane Benzing
Beverly Bidwell
Bernadine Bielby
Corinne Bishop
Trudi Bissinger
Beth Black
Maggie Blackford
Tuni Blackwelder
Julie Blackwell
Jane Blalock
Sandi Bogner
Sally Bondurant
Peggy Bone
Joyce Boone
Ann Boozer
Edward Borsoi
Louise Borsoi
Ann Bostwick
Sally Bower
Jane Bowyer
Marilyn Boynton
Elaine Bradshaw
Sheila Brennan
Rebecca Brown
Ellen Brumback
Frances Brumback
Texann Ivy Buck
Katherine Bunn
Betty Burrows
Joie Cadle
Taffy Carpenter
Ann Carr
Carole Caruso
Virginia Casey
Anna Cash
Lila Cason
Jim Cayce
Nancy Cayce
Carolyn Chase
Linda Chapin
Joanne Clapham
Barbara Clayton
Joan Clayton
Susan Clementson
Donna Colado
Carolyn Coleman
JoAnn Collins
Ellen Cordy
Michele Cottrill
Linda Coughlin
Connie Cox
Louise Creasman
Jean Cumming
Emily Dalsemer
Jean Dasse
Lynnette David
Alice Davis
Ann Davis
Rosie Davis
Wanda Davis
Susie Day
Carolyn Deatrick
Mary deBeaubien
Marilyn DeLong
Edith Dixon
Judy Dowden
Becky Dreisback
Sarah Drummond
Shirley Duncan
Trish Duncan
Judy Duval
Verdene Eggers
Peggy Evans
Edie Fagan
Karen Fant
Patsy Farmer
Carol Fenner
Sandy Fielding
Ginny Finfrock
Cami Flanagan
Nancy Fleming
Candy Fly
Agnes Foote
Jeanne Forrest
Cynthia Forrester
Dinky Foster
Susan Freeland
Sookie Fritz
Happy Gafford
Sarah Galloway
Vicki Gardner
Marcia Garmany
Aline Gay
Dottie Gay
Dinky Gefvert
Robin Geisler
Linda Gill
Dorothy Glad
Susan Gluyas
Donna Grantham
Beverly Greear
Nancy Greenlee
Shannon Gridley
Sally Haddock
Anna Hagle
Cynthia Hall
Nancy Hall
Sandra Hall
Sandy Hall
Jean Halverson
Cheryl Hammond
Ann Hand
Dorothy Hardin
Margaret Hardin
Lynn Harmon
Tinka Harmon
Marion Harris
Mary Harrison
Arrabella Hart
Sandi Hart
Nancy Henley
Saundra Hester
Caren Hewitt
Rosemary Hewitt
Barbara Higgins
Janet Hiland
Ellen Hinkle
Glenda Hood
Dodo Hoover
Cathy Howard
Sara Howard
Sheran Howle
Ann Hughes
Jane Hurst
Betty Jo Hurt
Cindy Huysman
Juanette Imhoof
Ginger Jackson
Carlye Johnson
Colin Johnson
Kathy Johnson
Sandra Jones
Marsha Jordan
Nancy Kann
Mona Karst
Nancy Kasten
Kaye Keaton
Fran Kemp
Elaine Kerr
Sally Kest
Laura Kirkland
Meredith Lacey
Martha Larsen
Patty Laubach
Sandra Laubach
Deborah Lawton
Betsy Leedy
Kaye Don Lewis
Nancy Lewis
Pamela Lichty
Georgette Lightbody
Randy Linton

Gerry Loudermilk
Jane Louttit
Mary Louise Luppert
Rafalar Lynch
Patty MacLeish
Rena Madigan
Suzanne Magee
Jorie Mairs
Deede Mandell
Felicia Manly
Kitty Martinez
Parky Mathers
Michele Mathews
Marilyn Matthews
Judy Maynard
Harriet Meade
Kay Merrill
Kyanne Meyers
Patricia Mica
Betty Miller
Kyle Miller
Frances Millican
Joan Milligan
Diana Morgan
Danielle Morris
Nancy Mouser
Gracia Mudge
Carol Murphy
Allison Muller
Nancy McAllister
Betsy McColskey
Jackie McCoy
Jane McElyea
M.L. McEwan
Joyce McKey
Denise McKinney
Carol McNally
Betty Sue McNiel
Francine Newberg
Winnie Nofsinger
Beth Nolen
Martha Lynne O'Connor
Melinda O'Neill
Jan Owen
Nancy Palmer
Louise Patrick
Jo Patterson
Linda Peacock
Nancy Peed
Willie Peppercorn
Marion Phalin
Mary Alice Phelps
Barbara Phillips
Love Phipps
Rita Pierson
Gail Pinder
Betty Lou Pinel
Susan Pittman
Bethany Pope
Jim Posey
Catherine Posey
Sandra Powers
Karen Plater
Barbara Price
Karen Procter
Lucy Procter
Barbara Ramb
Janice Randall
Angela Ranson
Margaret Ream
Elizabeth Reed
Margaret Reed
William H. Roberts
Ellen Roddy
Donna Ronnick
Marlene Rosenfelt
Susan Rosoff
Georgianna Rozier
Helen Rutland
Dolores Rutledge
Susan Sartin
Gretchen Schapker
Nancy Schmitt
Linda Schofield
Iris Scott
Kitty Scott
Tom Scott
Georgia Seem
Ginny Sharts
Amelia Shearouse
Robin Sheldon
Lee Showalter
Petie Showalter
Sally Simmons
Wendy Simpson
Collyn Slavens
Betty Smeenge
Beverly Smith
Lindsay Smith
Jean Sprimont
Susan Stans
Barbara Stedronsky
Grace Stephenson
Marie Stepter
Rosemary Stokes
Donna Sue Strait
Ann Marie Stuart
Barbara Stuart
Betty Stuart
Ella Swanson
Rosie Tarr
Elizabeth Taylor
Ann Christy Thomas
Kathi Thorsen
Diane Thurbon
Kristen Thurbon
Sarah Tillery
Margie Tippit
Jean Townes
Cindy Traynham
Bonnie Trismen
Be Be Trovillion
Jill Tucker
Alice Urban
Joan Van Akin
Sharon Van Bueren
Bonnie Van Dyke
Billie Varner
Becky Voght
Nancy Wagers
Robbie Walker
Karen Wallace
Chalmers Ward
Paula Ward
Shelley Lorraine Ward
Ann Warren
Jean Warren
Theresa Watkins
Karen Watson
Fi Way
Trish Weaver
Mary Martha Webb
Helen Weeks
Chloe Weisner
Gloria White
Sally White
Rita Wilkes
Shelley Wilkins
Betty Williams
Dee Dee Williams
Jean Williams
Jeanne Williams
Martha Willits
Betty Jane Wilson
Ginny Wilson
Dana Winn
Susan Wood
Marcia Wright
Shirley Yaros
Phyllis Yates
Sally Zarnowiec
Alison Zilioli

and many others without whose help and advice this book would not have been possible.

The Junior League of
Orlando-Winter Park, Florida, Inc.
125 N. Lucerne Circle, East
Orlando, Florida 32801

Name ______________________________

Address ______________________________

City ______________________ State __________ Zip __________

Please send _______ copies of **Sunsational** at $15.00 per copy plus $1.50 per copy to cover postage and handling. Florida residents, add 5% sales tax. Make check payable to "Sunsational."

☐ VISA

☐ MASTER CARD   card no. ☐☐☐☐-☐☐☐☐-☐☐☐☐-☐☐☐☐

INTERBANK NO. __________

Signature ______________________________ Exp. Date __________

The Junior League of
Orlando-Winter Park, Florida, Inc.
125 N. Lucerne Circle, East
Orlando, Florida 32801

Name ______________________________

Address ______________________________

City ______________________ State __________ Zip __________

Please send _______ copies of **Sunsational** at $15.00 per copy plus $1.50 per copy to cover postage and handling. Florida residents, add 5% sales tax. Make check payable to "Sunsational."

☐ VISA

☐ MASTER CARD   card no. ☐☐☐☐-☐☐☐☐-☐☐☐☐-☐☐☐☐

INTERBANK NO. __________

Signature ______________________________ Exp. Date __________

The Junior League of
Orlando-Winter Park, Florida, Inc.
125 N. Lucerne Circle, East
Orlando, Florida 32801

Name ______________________________

Address ______________________________

City ______________________ State __________ Zip __________

Please send _______ copies of **Sunsational** at $15.00 per copy plus $1.50 per copy to cover postage and handling. Florida residents, add 5% sales tax. Make check payable to "Sunsational."

☐ VISA

☐ MASTER CARD   card no. ☐☐☐☐-☐☐☐☐-☐☐☐☐-☐☐☐☐

INTERBANK NO. __________

Signature ______________________________ Exp. Date __________

Please list names and addresses of bookstores or gift shops in your area that may be interested in handling **SUNSATIONAL.**

Please list names and addresses of bookstores or gift shops in your area that may be interested in handling **SUNSATIONAL.**

Please list names and addresses of bookstores or gift shops in your area that may be interested in handling **SUNSATIONAL.**